AND STRENGTH WAS GIVEN

Mr Ian Bell

MR IAN BELL
8 The Orchard Heacham
Norfolk PE31 7HG

AND STRENGTH WAS GIVEN

ISBN 0-95375-750-1

Published in 1999 by
Mr Ian Bell
8 The Orchard, Heacham, Norfolk

First Published in 1989 by
Tyndale + Panda Publishing Ltd
117 High St, Lowestoft, Suffolk

Printed in Great Britain for Mr Ian Bell

AND
STRENGTH
WAS GIVEN

CONTENTS

For Andrée

PRELUDE

The day came when the period of my training for a commission, first at an Officer Training Unit in Cairo and afterwards at the School of Military Engineering (Middle East), was over. I had become a Second Lieutenant in the Royal Engineers, with whom I had already served for two and a half years as a driver and later as an N.C.O. I knew that my previous experience of campaigning in the Western Desert would prove invaluable in my new role. It gave me a heartening confidence, and with youthful eagerness I awaited my posting, hoping it would again be with an Armoured Division, maybe once more with the 'Desert Rats'. I thought longingly of old comrades, especially those of my former Field Squadron, now serving in Syria.

To be captured is ignominious –
to succumb to total domination
by the enemy is a betrayal
of patriotism.

Ian Bell

CHAPTER ONE

It was January 1942, at Ismailia on the Suez Canal. Some six hundred and fifty miles westward in the desert Rommel was massing the *Afrika Korps* for his great drive to capture Egypt. This famous German Army under Rommel — the southern 'claw' of Hitler's great strategic pincer movement which was planned to conquer India — had been specially trained and equipped for its task. Now it was hastening to the aid of the demoralised and severely mauled Italian forces, with only a few weak British units between it and the triumphant accomplishment of its mission.

I filled in the brief period of inactivity before the posting notice arrived with visits to Ismailia, by getting fitted out as an officer and by yachting on the lake in the brilliant Egyptian sunshine. My hopeful speculations of the new posting, and of the coming events, were shared by fellow officers around me who were in a similar situation. On February 10th the notice of the posting arrived, ordering me to report to the 573rd Army Field Company, Royal Engineers, in the Western Desert. The next day, after hurried goodbyes, I entrained at the small and dingy Ismailia main station. As our train pulled out we passed another,loaded with Italian officers, prisoners of war, just arriving from Eritrea. As one or two of them spoke English, I gathered that they had great faith in the invincibility of the Germans and in their capacity to beat the British. I was struck by their jaunty cocksureness, which totally disregarded the crushing defeat we had inflicted on their African Armies twelve months before.

The train gathered speed and for ninety miles we endured the dust, the flies and the appalling humid heat that made every day's existence a torment. At last we rumbled and clanked into Cairo's main station. Here the smells of close masses of humanity and the over-powering heat under the glass roof seemed unbearable. Flies were in their element. There was much coming and going of troops; Tommies stood or sat on kitbags while the Redcaps moved among them in pairs. Disreputable Arabs clamoured incessantly for baksheesh and were continually pestering us to be hired to carry our baggage.

The Mersa Matruh train left about five minutes after my arrival, for which I was grateful. Cairo no longer held the attraction for me which it had in the past. Now I was anxious to arrive at my destination to experience my new life.

The journey to Mersa took about four hours, by-passing Alexandria by way of Amriyah, clattering along through what must surely be the most uninteresting scenery ever viewed from a train window. I dozed fitfully from time to time. Outside, the landscape shimmered and danced in the relentless sunshine. I noted with lazy interest that the number of R.A.F. 'planes at the aerodromes between Fuka and Mersa had increased considerably since I had passed that way ten months earlier. It was evident that something was brewing.

At Mersa, Driver Mallot was waiting. He was a desert veteran in whose skilled hands the pick-up became a Grand Prix racer. After he had introduced himself with much pride, he told me that our Unit was encamped near Buq-Buq. Having quickly piled my kit on to the back of his truck he took the wheel, and as we sped along the bitumen road the tyres sang in a high-pitched key. The easy springing of the vehicle and the freshness of the air after the stifling railway carriage, made that lengthy journey pleasant by contrast. We exchanged snatches of conversation from which I learned that a good hot meal awaited me at the camp — which was welcome news. Once we stopped at a half-way house, which had been taken over by the N.A.A.F.I., where we drank several cups of excellent coffee and I renewed my supply of cigarettes. I gathered useful items of information about my Unit from Driver Mallot. It appeared that No. 1 Section expected the arrival of reinforcements, having lost their Commanding Officer and forty-five men at Benghazi the previous November, No. 2 Section were at Bardia, whilst No. 3 Section were manning the aqueducts at Buq-Buq and supplying water to Sollum at Fig Tree Water point and Halfaya.

From the half-way house I drove the short distance to Buq-Buq. It wasn't long before I saw the faint outline of the tents which I guessed marked the Quartermaster's stores and the workshops. I woke Driver Mallot to inquire whether this was my new camp, and to ask him to direct me to the Officers' Mess, which turned out to be a small sand-bagged dugout set into the side of a large sandhill. This dugout was strongly-built with thick sand-bag walls. In the open side were two small windows and the door was made of a light wooden frame with a very finely perforated zinc sheet nailed to it, to keep out the flies and mosquitoes. Here I met the Commanding Officer who had considerately remained awake at this late hour in order to welcome me. With the introductions over he left me to eat my supper, wishing me a good night's sleep in my new quarters.

The following fortnight was spent in receiving the reinforcements for the very depleted No. 1 Section which had been assigned to me, and in generally preparing for our future work in the forward battle areas. Towards the end of the second week, I received orders from the C.O. to proceed with my section on detachment to Bir Habata. My orders were to collect twenty miles of three-inch water-pipe line and send it up to Tobruk, where it would then be relaid from Bir Butler to Bir Harmet.

The journey was uneventful, except that the last ten miles was a jolting and arduous crawl over boulder-strewn country, which made one wonder how the springs of the vehicles stood up to the punishing conditions. Away in the distance I could see a mound of earth which marked Bir Habata, appearing to rear up to twice its actual height owing to the mirage. In approaching the Bir, we had to cross the Mersa-Capuzzo railhead track which had been laid by the New Zealand Engineers. This familiar sign of civilisation looked very strange there in the desert, miles and miles from anywhere. Over to the right of the Bir was Habata's little station, a tin-shack affair which nevertheless served its purpose. I hunted around for a likely spot to pitch camp and carefully chose a small sandy dip amidst the very stony surroundings. This was to be our 'home' for at least a fortnight. I had been given three weeks to complete the job so we should have to content ourselves with these very basic conditions and contrive to fill in our 'off-duty' spells with our own devices.

Next day I made a reconnaissance of the terrain for the task ahead, then returned to camp to detail the working parties. During my absence, the men had built a creditable cookhouse and had erected their mess tent, having already dug themselves slit trenches with their bivouacs positioned over them. Work began in earnest the following morning and for the remainder of the week the lads were busy unscrewing, then lifting and packing the Victaulic water-pipes. Among my fellows were a number who had just arrived in the Western Desert, but they already displayed remarkable tolerance to the unaccustomed heat and all the tiresome flies.

I asked the men to make a special effort to complete the job in a fortnight, promising to do everything in my power to promote their welfare and comfort under the trying climatic conditions. The days were extremely hot, but at night temperatures fell well below zero. The lads responded nobly, even remaining undaunted by the periodic sandstorms. Thinking of them sweating and toiling in the relentless glare from the sun, I can see now just how conscientious a team they were. After only twelve days our task had been completed, so they were justifiably proud of their achievement. I had arranged to report to my Commanding Officer on the fourteenth day so I devised a simple training programme for the remaining two days. The section was split into groups under the N.C.O.'s. One party performed musketry exercises with fixed bayonets and the Bren gun; another party did demolitions, practising on a nearby wrecked truck; whilst the third group was engaged in camouflage work. The remaining men constructed fieldworks, dug trenches and anti-aircraft pits and the like, suitable for that type of ground. They were all very keen and seemed to welcome the opportunity for this extra training, having had very little before being sent overseas.

The night before we were due to leave, we struck camp — all except the men's 'bivvies' — and so we were prepared for an early start the following morning. Meanwhile Headquarters had moved up to a new location so we re-checked its map reference. Reveille was at 06.00 hours, and after a good breakfast we started on our journey of two hundred and fifty miles across the desert and along the coast road to El Adem and Gazala. After a very difficult trip on which we experienced many mishaps to our vehicles, we finally found Headquarters Section down a Wadi along the El Adem – Gazala escarpment. On arrival I reported to my C.O., who was delighted that we had finished the job so quickly, and immediately gave me orders for the next assignment, which was a more important one. Briefly, I had to proceed at once to a point three miles south-south-east of Bir Harmet, and start work promptly at dawn the following morning. The job was 'most urgent' and 'very important', and I realised that I was being made responsible for the water supply for the coming British offensive. We discussed the military build-up of our forces and the extent to which the Germans were giving trouble. Apparently they were sending over nuisance raiders, which were shooting up vehicles, works, and anything else which would hinder our efforts to prepare for an imminent advance. It was something of a surpise to be told that we were well into the forward areas, and that the Germans were only nine miles west of our present position. Having confirmed my orders, as the hour was very late I took my leave and rejoined my section and we proceeded immediately to Bir Harmet. Arriving at the designated position, we unloaded the trucks and dug ourselves in. When every man again had his bivvie erected over a slit trench and had made himself as comfortable as possible, we had a well-earned meal in the brief twilight before settling down for the night.

The next morning the men were detailed to camouflage our equipment and generally settle in whilst I, with my batman and driver, went on a reconnaissance of the Bir itelf. At the same time I discovered the general layout of other units surrounding mine. I obtained a fair appreciation of the situation and realised that we had a considerable task ahead. We had to reinforce an underground sandstone cavern with concrete to construct a reservoir. The following day every available man in the section was detailed for the task and the supervising sergeants were duly briefed. The Works Sergeant gathered together all the tools and materials which would be required and then proceeded to the site with the working parties, while the Section Sergeant remained behind to supervise the running of the camp and the administration for the section. Again the men toiled hard and persevered for long stretches. Each day I visited the scene of activity I found that by gruelling hard work and the full co-operation of every man we were knocking days from our scheduled programme.

The day came when I could telephone to Bir Butler and request No.3 Section to start pumping. Our quota of water, in all 170,000 gallons, took two days to deliver from the pumping station at

Knightsbridge, further down the line. During that time we were kept extremely busy repairing leaks in the pipe joints and re-marking the vehicle crossings. We always had trouble when vehicles ran over the pipe-line, as they often distorted the joints.

I was down on the site overseeing the final stages for the completion of the pump house when I was summoned to meet the Engineer-in-Chief, (Middle East), who had come along with my Commanding Officer on a tour of inspection. This officer was astonished at the rapid rate of progress our section had made. It was, naturally, pleasant for me to hear his congratulatory remarks to the effect that our efforts had probably advanced the time for the allied attack to be launched. I felt rewarded for all our toil and anxiety, and the men too were considerably cheered by this recognition of their grand efforts.

In the afternoon of 26th May 1942, as I was checking over the progress of the work in the little tent that I had made my office and Mess, I suddenly heard the deep, penetrating roar of a large number of motor transports approaching our camp rapidly from the east. I hurried out to have a look. Stretching from one horizon to the other were thousands of army vehicles of all kinds, from ten-ton supply trucks to officers' pick-ups and wireless trucks, all moving across the desert in formation. Among the vehicles were some of the new secret six-pounder anti-tank guns mounted on portees. The sight was very impressive and one which I will never forget. They came straight through our camp and passed on, out of sight to the west, in a cloud of dust. What a vast difference there was, it seemed to me, between our supply position now and that of Wavell during the 1940 Campaign. In three quarters of an hour all was quiet again and I returned to my office task.

Later in the evening the works party returned and handed me their report on the progress made during the day. All was going well. Everything was now completed except the roof of the pump house. My next job was to send out the mobile patrol, whose task was to do any maintenance work on the pipe-line which was necessary. They would be repairing any damage caused by vehicles crossing over it and tightening up the joints where there appeared to be leaks. Soon the faint murmurs of the fellows in their bivouacs died down as sleep overtook them, and after an inspection of the sentries and the camp area, I too turned in.

The next morning, on leaving my tent I was surprised to see a large number of supply vehicles grouped around our little camp, covering a large expanse of the surrounding desert. Curiously, the noise of their arrival had not disturbed my sleep, nor that of my section. From the sentries I learned that they had heard the faint rumbling of gunfire to the south-east during the night. As there was no indication from the units now in the area that anything special was happening, I came to the conclusion that perhaps the distant rumblings were our own gunners calibrating. However the odd thing was that the noise could still be heard, moreover it seemed to be getting louder. I dismissed the idea that something had gone wrong and carried on with my breakfast. Inwardly I was beginning to feel uneasy as the time drew near to send the working parties to the Bir but, as I had nothing concrete on which to base a change of plan, I sent the men off at 08.30 hours according to plan, telling the Works Sergeant to carry on with the job as usual until I arrived. The party had only been gone half an hour when I noticed that all the surrounding 'transport' vehicles had suddenly changed into brand new tanks of all sizes — 'Grants', 'Crusaders' and 'Honies'.

The lively action of their crews in stripping off all the clever camouflage and the ever-increasing roar of the revving engines was bewildering, delaying my realisation that my 'hunch' that something was amiss was indeed true. Calling my Section Sergeant, I gave him orders to pack all non-essential equipment, including the men's 'bivvies'. I also told my batman to pack my own things and to get my pick-up vehicle ready immediately. Meanwhile I decided to go to the nearest Tank Commander to ask him what all the flap was about, but I was unable to discover any news owing to the speed of their hasty departure. Having abandoned this futile attempt to find out what was happening, I made straight for the Bir. The sky in this direction was completely darkened by a masses of dust-clouds and dense black smoke, through which sounded muffled rumblings like heavy thunder in the air.

The nearer I came to the Bir, the louder grew the noise. It was unmistakably gunfire! The pick-up had never moved as fast as it did that morning. My Sergeant, who was waiting for me, excitedly gave me his report. Meanwhile the sappers continued working, quite unperturbed by the events taking place around them. Using the field telephone, I rang up the Commanding Officer to tell him of the situation. He informed me that the Germans had attacked in the far south of the Gazala line, capturing the Free French Units, and had advanced to within a mile of Bir Hacheim. There they had been met by our armoured forces and a terrific battle was even then in progress to the east-south-east. The C.O advised me that if it should become necessary to evacuate the area the pump house was not to be 'blown', only the injector unit should be removed, so that if we should regain our position we would be able to continue providing water to our forward units.

No sooner had I put the receiver down than shells began exploding around the Bir. The enemy had obviously seen my ten-ton stores truck. At once I gave orders to pack up. The men grabbed their tools while the mechanic removed the vital injector unit. Whilst the men were piling the stores on to the truck I remained on top of the mound behind the tar barrel, keeping the enemy's movements under close observation. It was clear that the Germans were doing their utmost to capture the Bir with its water supply. Soon we were ready to move off and, to my relief, we slipped away without suffering any casualties. As I looked back towards the battle, I shuddered to think of the havoc that was being wrought. The thunderous roar of the guns was terrifying, yet inexplicably intriguing at the same time.

When we reached the base camp we found that everything had been packed in readiness for our return to H.Q. Our departure was somewhat hurried, for Jerry was good at pin-pointing his target. Once again we managed to get away without loss. All around us the other units had been told that the Germans had attacked in the south the previous afternoon and had since made fair progress. We now realised this only too well.

I led the section convoy in the general direction of 'Knightsbridge', but after travelling only half a mile I almost ran on to one of our own minefields which had been laid that very morning by another company of Sappers. That trip to H.Q. turned out to be a nightmare! Vehicles from many units were careering across the desert, apparently quite oblivious of anyone else. All were intent on escaping the trap which seemed to be closing about us. Twice we halted to let large convoys through. Because of our hastily laid, and consequently badly marked, minefields, some of my vehicles came very near to being 'written off'. I made several detours to inform other units of the critical situation, so that they would not be left behind. I advised any units that were still static, not having been notified by Brigade H.Q. that Jerry had attacked, to get mobile immediately. Radio communication between units was chaotic.

Arriving at Company H.Q., which I found packing up at great speed, I immediately reported to my C.O. who was personally supervising operations. He told me that he would immediately pass on my report to the Brigadier. As he left on his mission, I returned to my men. I dispersed my vehicles in an open formation as a precaution against aerial attacks. While we waited for about an hour and a half on the top of the escarpment for the C.O. to return, we could hear the roar of the enemy's aerial activities approaching nearer all the time. It was a great relief to see the C.O. coming back at last, and I congratulated myself on the fact that we could now make a successful get-away without drawing the attention of the enemy. However the C.O. told me that, though it might seem incredibly rash, we were to retire out of the danger-zone by a pre-arranged route, which I knew from experience was now very dangerous. The various 'legs' were, Point 'A' — Bir Bellifa; Point 'B' — El Adem Box; Point 'C' — Bir Zebeda; Point 'D' — Sidi Resegh; the general direction being east-south-east and the distance about sixty-two miles. It seemed that the Brigadier had not received any confirmation of the German attack and refused to believe my report. I wondered why the Brigadier did not trouble to step outside his tent to see for himself the bloody battle which was presently raging on top of the escarpment. So it was with despairing fury that we detailed the sections to leave immediately according to his instructions.

My own Section was to act as guard to H.Q. Section, which was to lead the convoy under the command of the second-in-command. No.2 Section was to follow mine, while No.3 Section would remain behind with the C.O. to finish the 'blowing' of Bir Butler and to act as rear-guard. The C.O. gave us clear instructions. Should we fall into trouble I was to do everything possible to protect H.Q. Section. This was all very well, I thought, but I did not see how a mere handful of men with rifles could fight off enemy tanks. My personal contribution to our armaments was a .38 pistol, only of use in close hand-to-hand fighting, and I wondered bitterly what use it would be against a tank.

Whilst all this was going on, the *Luftwaffe* was continuing to be extremely active. Fortunately we were not seen, otherwise we should have been quickly finished off. It was a ghastly sight to watch the Messerschmidt fighter-planes and the Stuka dive-bombers raining death and terror amongst our tank convoys only a few miles away. The C.O. gave orders to the Second-in-Command to leave immediately. He wished us good luck and a happy re-union — perhaps in Cairo!

I cannot express how very uneasy I felt about everything. Looking east as we drove along nothing could be seen because of a dense black cloud of smoke from the guns and the burning oil and dust, illuminated here and there by the fearful red glare of a burning tank. The noise of heavy gunfire was continuous, and I was sickened to think of the carnage being wrought in that murky, dust-choked hell.

On a signal from the Second-in-Command, we set off in open formation. H.Q. section was a little way ahead and No.2 Section a good distance to the rear. I looked at my watch — it was exactly mid-day. With me were Driver Mallot at the wheel, my splendid batman Driver Fleming and, seated on the roof of the vehicle to keep a look-out, one of my mechanics. Fortunately our departure did not attract the attention of the *Luftwaffe*. Losing no time along the escarpment we soon came across our defence system known as El Adem Box. On the other side of the defences I had to wait half an hour to allow the heavier and older vehicles to catch up after descending a particularly difficult pass. When finally re-formed, we attempted to catch up with H.Q. Section which was about three miles ahead of us.

Throughout the journey I continued to be convinced that we were taking a suicidal route. I felt we should have headed straight for Tobruk and Bardia and concentrated our forces there. Ahead of us and over to our right, the battle seemed to cover an even greater area than when we had started. I was convinced that the menacing black smoke and dust clouds were slowly creeping towards Bardia and the coast road, cutting off our line of retreat.

I had an uncanny premonition of what lay before us and felt an urge to warn the Second-in-Command that we were running into danger. In my mind I could picture the map of this area and I had a clear impression of the position of the battle on it. It seemed plain that as the Germans were short of transport they would try to capture our vehicles. This was a very disturbing thought which I tried to dismiss from my mind. Through my field glasses I could see that the vehicles of H.Q. Section had stopped. This I presumed was to enable me to catch up. Then I noticed that a little further on was a tiny mound of earth protruding above the mirage. Suddenly I noticed a flash almost directly ahead and well beyond the section in front. Groaning inwardly, I felt a sudden sinking of the heart as I saw that my worst fears were realised. The enemy ahead was across our line of retreat. Having no alternative, I approached to within a quarter of a mile of the rear truck of H.Q. Section and I saw that the mound of earth I had previously seen was Bir Zebeda, in other words, Point 'C'. There was a collection of vehicles close up to the mound, but as my field glasses were not powerful enough to discern their types, I paid no further attention to them. I preferred to think that they were our own, belonging to other units which were retreating from the battle area.

My heart was beating rapidly. Just why, I wasn't sure. I suppose my fears were mounting. As I stood up to get a better view, the Second-in-Command standing up in his pick-up beckoned me towards him. Keeping my eye on him the whole time, I moved up slowly, very slowly. All at once I caught sight of a large *Swastika* spread over the bonnet of a large staff car close at hand.

"Germans!" I yelled, immediately signalling to my Section to retreat as fast as they could. Things happened very quickly. As my driver swung round, a shell landed just in front of the car. From behind H.Q.'s vehicles, travelling at high speed, came a light German Volkswagen with three occupants — young Nazis. One of them was training a heavy Spandau machine gun straight at me and yelling, "Halt! Halt!" With only my .38 pistol against the Spandau, I decided that discretion was certainly the better part of valour. One cannot aim to kill with a pistol when both parties are in moving vehicles, especially on such a bumpy escarpment. Once halted, the Volkswagen pulled up alongside and two soldiers snatched my revolver from me. With curt signs and brusque language I was directed towards the Bir.

Our vehicle did not go right up to the Bir, but stopped a little distance away and I glanced back to see if my Section had managed to escape. I was pleased to see the occupants of one truck had managed to drive it a little distance off and had set their vehicle on fire. Unfortunately no other vehicle had the chance to escape capture. I sat on the top of my pick-up and looked around. There were several German columns converging on the Bir, down the escarpment and round the back of El Adem. Meeting with no opposition they were exploiting their success and were endeavouring to encircle the important town of Tobruk, which lay over to our left.

CHAPTER TWO

For a while, I could not gather my senses together. The blatant audacity of the Germans was incredible. Of course I had expected the enemy to come round the back of the tank battle to cut off our line of communication, but it was heartbreaking to think that our gilded Staff had not realised the possibility of such a simple and obvious manoeuvre. Then I could not understand why the Second-in-Command, who was afterwards caught himself, had beckoned me on to join him when he must have spotted the Germans.

The enemy now were consolidating their occupation of the area gained around the Bir. With their usual efficiency they were herding all prisoners together and scrutinising each truck thoroughly to prevent sabotage. Examined vehicles were then rapidly formed up in readiness for further action, but under German control.

I was rudely awakened from my mental paralysis by the yelling of a young Nazi soldier. His gesticulations showed that he meant me to get out of my P.U. He carried a sub-machine gun and a Luger pistol ... I realised I was a prisoner! Stepping down, I was thoroughly searched and stripped of all my webbing, which included my compass. I had to smile when he saw that I had broken my compass. He replied to my smile by saying, "*Gut soldat.*" The breaking of that compass gave me great satisfaction. I was then led over towards the German Commander's staff car.

Men from other units who had been captured were herded together some little distance away from me and, when the Germans had finally rounded up all our personnel from the vehicles, they were lined up in fives and counted. In all around twelve hundred men and six officers had been captured by the enemy. After being counted the men were crowded on to our own trucks with German soldiers occupying the cab. The officers were ordered aboard a German vehicle and the whole force slowly moved off towards El Adem — back the way we had come. We had only travelled about one thousand yards when the whole convoy stopped. The guards on my vehicle ordered us to get out and as I obeyed I took the opportunity to have a good look round to compare the German force with our own. They had a few tanks but the majority of their armoured fighting vehicles consisted of eight-wheeled type armoured cars. There were a good number of 88 mm field guns mounted on half-tracks and two self-propelled 105 mm pieces of artillery. The trucks, which they mostly relied on for hit-and-run tactics, were little Volkswagens with a heavy Spandau machine gun mounted behind the front seats. As I looked around I noticed that the Germans had ordered the rest of the P.O.W.'s to get out of the vehicles. The slowness of our men to obey the orders of their captors seemed to infuriate the arrogant Nazi soldiers.

Glancing towards the edge of the escarpment, I suddenly saw two Tommies racing off as fast as their legs could carry them. They reached the edge of the escarpment without any trouble, then made for the ledge of the next ridge. This ledge was about five hundred yards wide, with a steep drop of several hundred feet leading down to the plain. As they were running towards the second ridge, one of the Volkswagens approached with its usual crew. A young soldier leapt out as the car halted and took very careful aim with his Mauser rifle and fired. He was about a hundred yards short. The two escapers were hampered by the great-coats they were carrying over their arms, and it was easy to see they were tiring already. Regardless of the consequences they were determined to escape. I looked back as the young German took a second shot, but again missed. A very near miss! I could hear myself praying out loud for those two plucky lads to get away safely when suddenly, at the third crack of the rifle, one of them dropped and made no further movement. One of our officers standing beside me spoke, but I was too appalled to say anything. I found myself sweating and then all at once I felt that I would vomit.

Once more I looked towards the spot where the man had dropped and saw that his pal was on the ground beside him. He had turned back when he had noticed the absence of his companion and was desperately trying to lift up his fallen mate. He, too, was utterly exhausted and he collapsed in a heap over his friend's body. I couldn't help becoming emotional at the pathetic scene. Then the sudden sight of the young murderer made my blood boil. I wished that I had a rifle in my hands with which to avenge the murdered man. The German did not attempt to shoot the second escaper, although he could have done so. Instead he just gloated with his comrades and then jumped back on to the car and joined the convoy. We were ordered back onto our vehicles and again proceeded slowly for a further thousand yards.

Suddenly there was a screaming sound over our heads and — Whoosh! — a shell landed close behind us, however it failed to stop any of the German vehicles. Another shell followed immediately ... and then another, and another, until the ground shook and the air was thick with dust and smoke. The shells were finding their targets and it did me good to see the German transport getting a pasting. Our guards ordered us out quickly and moved us away from the trucks as far as possible. They were really in a flap now. Trucks were careering wildly here, there and everywhere. There was no cover for us, so we lay flat on the ground, hoping that if a shell did hit us, it would hit fairly and squarely. It was strangely fascinating to see our shells creating such havoc amongst Jerry's transport. I watched as the Germans brought up their 88 mm field guns. Moving well forward of the transport, these guns were lined up in a row facing El Adem. Then I realised that it was El Adem Box that was shelling us! I had a great feeling of confidence as I realised that our fellows were only a few miles away, but when a shell landed a bit too close for comfort, I began to think differently! My guards must have thought the same as they were just about to move further out of the danger zone when a large staff car came roaring up, its Commander yelling out orders. Just as swiftly he then departed. We were forced by the guards to march right up to their field guns. Soon there were about a hundred P.O.W.'s lying on their faces in groups just behind the 88's, which were blazing away.

All hell was let loose as dozens of our shells, aimed at the German guns, found their mark with deadly accuracy. I won't attempt to describe the horrible slaughter of our men which took place in the next hour. I lay as flat as I could and found myself gripping the sand with all my strength. The rain of death and destruction continued, but fortunately a large number of shells burst harmlessly to our rear. Fear of the sights I might see kept me from looking up. Then came a piercing scream — long and agonising. I looked around in the direction of the sound and saw a khaki-clad figure rolling about in a pool of blood which was spreading rapidly. I dashed over to find that he was an R.E. Sergeant. Seeing a German medical orderly running up, I yelled to him to get me some medical kit. The Sergeant's left leg was torn to shreds from the knee to his hip. After a few minutes the orderly ran back with a large box and dumped it beside me. It was a surgical box and contained scalpels, forceps, bandages and a couple of rows of bottles amongst other medical equipment. There was a small chromium-plated steriliser and other accessories. A quick sniff at the bottles disclosed some morphia, for it was the only one with no smell. Hastily I fitted a syringe with a needle, filling it up with the anaesthetic to the 2.5 cc mark. Jab! It went into the Sergeant's right arm intravenously until the liquid had vanished. Slowly I pulled the needle out. I then picked out a clean-looking scalpel and put it on one side. Several times the German orderly ran off to shelter when the shells landed very close to us, but then his conscience would draw him back to see if he could help. I ripped the remains of the Sergeant's left trouser leg away and then, using bandages, I tried to clean up some of the mess, but the wound bled profusely. All painful convulsions and groaning from the man had now ceased, so I took the clean scalpel and a pair of forceps and cut out the lumps of shrapnel which were embedded in the flesh. I cleaned up the whole wound as best I could and made a splint from bits of wood from a smashed truck. A couple of our own fellows gave me a hand to lift the Sergeant on to the nearest vehicle. After seeing the poor chap comfortably placed at the back, I tried to argue with the German guard to let me stay with him. It was no good. I was curtly ordered back to lie behind the guns with the rest of the prisoners. As I walked back the sight of the dead among the wreckage of the vehicles was numbing. Two of the eight German guns had been silenced and their crews wiped out. By now the sight of the torn bodies no longer sickened me. After that effort with the Sergeant I felt somehow renewed in courage, and found my stomach stronger to withstand the sights of large gaping wounds.

Although I tried hard to convince myself that the shelling would not last much longer, it seemed to be hours before it finally ceased. Surely the barrels of the British 25-pounders must have been red hot. I imagined our gunners throwing buckets of cold water on them! With another scream of shells overhead I fell face downward on the sand. Whack! What was the matter? I couldn't hear a thing. That giddy moment I was instantly back in Piccadilly with all its lights twinkling. Then, like a flash, I was away up on a mountain top and joining me in a chorus were hundreds of voices! Then everything went completely black.

Somewhere a pain stabbed sharply, but I was afraid to open my eyes and look up. Curiosity overcame my fright and raising my head I realised what was causing the pain — I had gripped the sand so tightly that my nails had been partially torn off. Keeping sand on them to help to congeal the blood, I stood up to relax my muscles. Behind me, not fifty yards distant, was a small circle of blackish-grey sand on the perimeter of which were the bloody remains of one of our own fellows and a young N.C.O. One thing consoled me straight away, their deaths had been instantaneous. I tried to fix my eyes on something that would be a relief from the sight of all this horror, but everywhere around there was complete devastation. With tremendous relief I heard the Germans yelling to us to get back on to the transports. Involuntarily I ran towards the first vehicle and was quite happy to know that others were joining me.

When the guards were satisfied that the prisoners were all on board the vehicles, they gave the signal to proceed and the whole convoy moved off due south at a good speed. Apparently they feared the risk of an air attack. It wasn't long before we were all covered with the choking dust raised up by the vehicles in front. There was no water with which to swill out our parched and dust-filled mouths and, to make things worse, we were sitting on petrol tins which gave out the most nauseating fumes.

We had been travelling for about three quarters of an hour when I was suddenly thrown violently from one end of the truck to the other as it made a terrific swerve and hurriedly pulled up. At the same time there was a thunderous roar followed by a crescendo of smashing wood and terrible screams. Almost immediately there came two more deafening crashes. My heart was once again well up in my mouth, and as I noticed that the guards had vanished, I too made a quick retreat from the vehicle. Once out in the open

I could see the Volkswagens and their very excited crews who were forming all the prisoners together. With the exception of the fighting vehicles, the whole convoy had stopped.

We were being shelled by large calibre guns and anti-tank guns. The fire was seemingly as rapid as the bursts from the machine guns. It was obvious what was happening. We had run into a part of our reserve armoured forces and they were replying with a vengeance!

I darted round the back of the truck and on towards the front, hoping to find the cab empty. My idea was to seize the vehicle and attempt to escape. Then I quickly disguised my action when I was suddenly confronted by two tough, but very scared, Germans occupying the two seats. As they were both nursing Schmeisser sub-machine guns, it seemed to be the wrong moment to start an argument. Then I saw the ghastly reason for our violent stop — only a few yards ahead was a burning lorry. It was one of our 3-ton Bedfords and its load had been British prisoners. There were one or two still alive here and there in a heap of debris, but as very near to death as one could be. I ran across to lift the living away from the now rapidly burning wreckage. As I dragged one man clear and scrambled again over the wreckage to reach another, I swore violently and loudly. It was more than I could stand, but my feelings were slight compared to those who lay in agony.

I was laying the second chap down beside the first one, when I felt a strong grip on my arm and was almost swung off my feet. Facing me, as I straightened up, was a German, covering me well and truly with his Schmeisser. Yelling at me at the top of his voice, he pushed me away from the frightful scene and I was forced to join the other prisoners. I explained to the guards as best as I could that the occupants of the truck were not all dead and that there were some who were very badly in need of help. It was hopeless talking to them. However I kept on looking back at the two figures lying beside the smouldering wreckage. Not a soul went to their aid. They were left to die. I thought that this could not possibly be the twentieth century. How could any living creature be so callous about his fellow beings? It surpassed my comprehension and left me with an impotent feeling of rage. I looked at my ugly finger ends where neat nails had been and, wiping away some of the blood, buried my head in my shaking palms.

I felt easier when I joined the other prisoners, but just as I was trying to locate some of my own lads, there was a sudden burst of machine-gun fire and the bullets began whizzing straight over our heads. The prisoners broke away into two separate parties and, in complete frenzy, scattered like frightened rabbits in all directions.

The German guards opened up with their sub-machine guns first firing over our heads, then, when that failed to have any effect, they fired straight into us. I heard someone yelling my name just behind me and on looking round, to my great surprise I saw my Second-in-Command running as fast as his feet could carry him to join us.

The machine-gunning was growing in intensity as I could see now, between the harassed German vehicles, our own forces slowly, but menacingly, drawing nearer.

The cheers from the prisoners were very thrilling. Their wild excitement at the prospect of being released at any moment caused the Germans to continue firing into the crowd of prisoners to stop the attempted mass breaks. It was only natural that this had the desired effect.

One of our tanks, which I could see was leading the attack, was hit fair and square by an 88 mm shell and caught fire immediately. I thought, "Hasn't there been enough bloodshed for one day, without having any more?" Still this was WAR at its worst. The German 88 mm anti-tank guns kept up their salvos unceasingly until finally they compelled our inferior force, first to a halt, then to retreat. Nevertheless, our troops withdrew only to a safe distance and accomplished the task of preventing our captors from reaching their main units which were behind the tank battle. As our forces withdrew, the Germans ordered us back on to the other vehicles and there we remained, closely guarded, for our first night in captivity.

Throughout the night shelling from our gunners was spasmodic but very accurate. All we could do was to hope and pray that a shell would not find its target and blow us to pieces. Fortune was with us for we were all still whole when day broke. Our Armoured Divisions had withdrawn completely to join the battle elsewhere. The total silence from any shelling was unbelievably glorious.

Soon the Germans were on the move again and, much to my astonishment, after only a short journey we arrived at Bir Harmet. It was the usual May day in the desert, extremely hot and without even the faintest zephyr moving the air. As soon as we were permitted to dismount from the truck I took a careful look round. I was astounded to see the strength and order of the German force; their workshops were already busy repairing the damaged tanks, their field hospital was functioning efficiently, their sappers were busy all around the Bir itself and their tanks and artillery were already in position for a ding-dong battle.

My inquisitive gaze was interrupted by the approach of a German Colonel who was bawling out orders to our guards. Then he turned to us,(I had been joined by eight other British Officers) and spoke to us in perfect English. Immediately I asked him whether we were to be given any food and water. He replied by shaking his head and saying that this would be impossible as our sappers had destroyed the water supply at the Bir. As a result, he stated, their own men had to draw all water out by means of a four-gallon petrol can. I could not help feeling happy that it should be so difficult to supply their forces by this laborious method. Apparently he had been so cocksure of capturing the Bir intact that he had failed to carry a field-pumping set in his stores!

The Colonel walked off without saying anything further while we were left to stand around with our guards who were arguing fiercely about the instructions they had just received from the Colonel. Suddenly, just short of the Bir, a shell landed, bursting harmlessly about half a mile away. The untimely shell put the Germans into an immediate panic. First they pushed us over to one place, then loaded us on to the vehicles and finally forced us to dismount again. By this time the shelling had become more intense and more accurate. The Germans began to retaliate using all the artillery at their disposal. All we could do was to go to ground and hope for the best. Most of our shells were bursting amongst the enemy transport to our rear, although a few scattered shells were aimed at some German tanks which were parked just in front of us, and were landing uncomfortably close by.

Blowing a shrill blast on his whistle, a German Gunner Officer called for more ammunition, whereupon four large trucks rolled up, complete with a working party. Soon they had the ammunition unloaded. I knew that this meant it was going to be a long-drawn out artillery duel. During the first lull in the firing the guards rounded up all the prisoners, including the Officers, and herded us into the camouflaged water-filling point, which I recognised as the one I had myself helped to build. It consisted of eight stand pipes for supplying vehicles. Camouflage netting covered the whole area to enable the vehicles to be filled without being spotted from the air. The total space was only fifty yards long by twenty yards wide. This strategic point, of course, was now a prime target for our gunners, along with the Bir itself, which lay exactly a mile away.

As soon as we were inside the Germans moved up two Mark IV tanks and placed them at the openings at each end, thus hemming us in completely. I looked around our men to see how many officers were still with me. To my surprise there was now only one, a wounded man who was lying prostrate, quite oblivious of what was going on. Apparently the other officers had been removed from the group to prevent them inciting the men to escape. I could understand why I was left; when I had been forced off my pick-up truck at Bir Zebeda, I had stripped myself of all badges of rank, including my cap badge. The suede desert boots I was then wearing had been exchanged for regulation black boots, so, in the eyes of my captors, I was now another private. Our men, of course, knew I was an officer but did nothing to disclose my identity to the enemy who were patrolling outside our refuge.

Some of the men had managed to retain their tin hats so I ordered them to dig themselves in as best as they could using these, and their eating utensils, as excavators. Their task was made difficult due to the fact tht the ground was solid rock in places, with just a few inches of sandy rubble on the surface. In some places they could dig round a fairly large boulder, heave it out and use it as an anti-blast wall. They had not long started digging-in when shells from our lines began to arrive. The change in position of the two Mark IV's had no doubt been seen by our observation posts and our gunners were determined to put them out of action.

Stretching in a long line from the water-point to the Bir were the enemy's anti-tank guns, with field artillery in front and A.F.V.'s behind. Every enemy gun opened up and continued to fire throughout each exchange until silenced by the British shells. I ordered the men to keep their heads down and to lie as close to the ground as possible. Some of them tried desperately to dig themselves below ground level using only an ordinary kitchen knife, but it was a hopeless task. What a pathetic sight it was to see these fellows so frantically digging away between the shell-bursts with so little effect. By the end of the first hour they had managed to heap up some stones and rubble to make some head-cover, which at least provided some feeling of protection.

By midday we became ravenously hungry, so during a brief lull I approached a guard and demanded some food. He made no reply, although he understood me, but just pushed me back again with the men. The choking dust cloud kicked up by the shells added greatly to our discomfort and we had no shade from the glaring sun. For the rest of that day and throughout the night we were given neither food nor water. From time to time the shelling would become desultory, which was an added aggravation, for we would doze off hoping to snatch a brief rest, then suddenly a shell would land nearby to startle us out of our wits. That night the men slept exactly where they had lain all day, and I was relieved to wake in the morning to find that we had suffered no further casualties.

As this was the third day since our capture, I went out again to demand something to eat and drink for the men, but again my request was ignored. Returning to the water-point, I caught sight of an officer, a typical Prussian, so I approached to ask him if he could get us some food and water. I told him that we had not been fed since our capture and that the men were in a bad way. He replied that he would send along some food as soon as he could. Hurrying, I rejoined the men to give them the news. It was surprising how their morale rose at the prospect of this relief.

As the sun rose to its zenith the shelling restarted, keeping the men pinned down in their meagre shelter. Words are inadequate to tell of the mental and physical suffering under these conditions. We had to keep our heads well glued to the ground for several hours. Every time a shell landed too close, our body muscles tensed convulsively. Very soon a man feels a complete nervous and physical wreck.

At long last the shelling ceased, but it was quite a while before I could realise the fact, no doubt due to the numbing effect on my mind of the last bombardment. My ears took some time to grow accustomed to the quietness around us. About half an hour after the last of the shelling I heard a vehicle pull up beside one of the Mark IV tanks. Seeing the men rush madly towards it, I pushed my way forward and discovered that some food had actually arrived at last. There was no water however. I took charge of the food, which I could see would be totally inadequate. As I pointed this out to the German officer, he replied that this was all for now, but that more would follow later. Consoling myself with this assurance, I broke open the box and found that it contained Italian two-ounce tins of bully-beef, and only enough of them for one tin to be shared between two men, not very much for our feast. I issued the tins as quickly as I could and every man tucked in quietly but ravenously. Twelve men sharing this ration would have gone short, but I managed to portion out the few tins so that each man had at least a mouthful. For a short while at least the men's faces relaxed, losing the contortions of suffering brought on by three days of starvation and thirst. Smiles began to appear. As morale rose they even joked about the shattering ordeal they had just endured. Always, on such occasions, I felt proud to be British. Never shall I forget their courage. Here was clear evidence of the fine soldiers which are produced by the unmilitaristic British nation.

Throughout our meal comparative quiet reigned. The only sounds were the drone of a Messerchmitt somewhere overhead as the fighter plane bore down on its target, followed by the death-dealing rattle of its machine-guns and the noise of its menacing cannons. While we were eating I took the opportunity of discussing with the men my plans for a mass escape. Just as the discussion was going nicely it was interrupted by a sudden loud noise — WHAM! WHAM! Again shells began arriving in quick succession from the British. There was no need this time to tell the men to keep their heads down. In fact the shelling came so perilously close that they began feverishly to dig deeper. Suddenly a shell landed right on the Mark IV tank at one end of our flimsy shelter, blowing it to smithereens. Unfortunately bits of flying shrapnel and fragments of burning metal landed among us, killing three and seriously wounding four. Amongst those badly injured was Sergeant Cook from my own company. Half his left leg and thigh had been blown away. First I dressed the wounds as best as I could, then we buried the dead immediately outside the water-point, unable to go any further away owing to the heavy barrage. As I rejoined the men, I was called aside to help one of the wounded. His left arm and the ribs on his left side were badly smashed and bleeding profusely. Urgently I took off the ordinary-ranker's shirt which I wore to conceal my officer's one, and ripped it up to use in cleaning and binding up his wounds. It was not enough. About twenty minutes later he died. I buried him in a grave beside the other three and marked the place with a cross.

The shelling continued with unabated fury until eventually some red-hot scraps of flying shrapnel set fire to the camouflage netting. We managed to put out the flames with sand but after this the shelter looked like an enormous colander.

As suddenly as it started, the shelling ceased. I seized the opportunity to seek out some water for the wounded and the others. I dashed off and soon returned with the good news that the Germans had agreed to let us out to get water from the Bir. That German Officer kept to his word and shortly after my return he drove up in his staff car and ordered our guards to escort us to the Bir. On arrival, under strict surveillance, we were each given a mug full of water. How wonderful that water tasted! My mouth was so dry and full of sand the refreshment of that little drink was beyond description.

The air was decidely cooler, the declining sun giving us some respite from the scorching rays.

CHAPTER THREE

It was during the march back to the camouflaged water-point that the artillery duel started again. We just had time to nestle into our hollows when the whole ground seemed to heave under us. I lay as still as I could, so I thought, until on one occasion I opened my eyes and saw my whole body shaking like a leaf in a breeze. As each shell seemed to burst nearer and nearer to us, I could feel my heart beating as if at any moment it would break. Amidst the thunderous roar of the replying German guns and the bursting of our shells I heard the guards yelling to us to get out which we did, and, like a lot of willing automatons, we followed the guards' directions towards the vehicles which they had brought up. We were about half-way between the water-point and the trucks, when great cheers broke out from the men. I looked towards the direction in which some of them were pointing and to my wildest joy I could see our tanks appearing over the high ground. It was a glorious sight to see these iron-clad monsters approach methodically in line, like the knights of old.

As our tanks came nearer the prisoners broke away in all directions. The majority were merely running for cover to escape the murderous rake of the machine gun bullets but the guards became so panicky that they opened up with their sub-machine guns straight into the prisoners, forcing most of them to fall flat on the ground to escape being slaughtered. The British tanks had now approached to within five hundred yards from where I was standing and were still advancing, firing everything they had into the enemy. The German guards, firing their Schmeissers from their hips, forced many prisoners on to the waiting trucks. But many, in sheer desperation for their liberty, faced death with the greatest valour, racing across the desert to meet our tanks. I was hypnotised by their spirit and involuntarily heard myself cheering them on. They reached the most forward tank and climbed up on top until there was no room for any more. Promptly that tank swung round and increasing speed, retired to the rear of the advancing forces. The men who could not get on the first tank ran on towards the next nearest, but just as the tank was turning round to allow the men to climb on, a Volkswagen appeared from behind the German gunners and, ignoring the opposing tank gunners, the Spandau machine gunner fired straight at those plucky lads. It was a ghastly sight to see them drop off the A.F.V., just like flies. What thrilled me most was the sight of those who had been wounded by the machine gunning, still hanging on with grim determination to reach our own lines. I prayed to God at that moment that they would live to make good their liberty.

The Germans brought up more and sent them into action immediately. Under cover of their fire, the guards began urging the prisoners on to the trucks. I hid behind a vehicle hoping to seize an opportunity to escape. All at once I caught sight of my Second-in-Command amongst the frantic mob, so I dashed over to him and began to drag him away, leading him towards one of our captured vehicles nearby. We jumped into the driver's seat, but we were too late. The opposite cab door was flung open and a German sub-machine gun was thrust into our stomachs. That was the end of the that! However, as we were being escorted away to another truck, our guard's attention was diverted to another party trying to escape. Without hesitation he opened up on them with his gun. My Second-in-Command dashed across the 'blue' towards a pick-up which looked like mine, but that was the last time I saw him. I was almost flung off my feet by a Jerry who had approached me from behind just as I had started to run towards his disappearing figure. Then ... whack! ... I did not remember anything else until I woke up inside a truck which was travelling fast towards the south — driven and guarded by the Germans. I must have been knocked on the head with a side arm, for my head ached and whirled. Bouncing at break-neck speed over camel-thorn bushes did not improve matters. However, I managed to get a glimpse of the battle ground and it heartened me to see the destruction the British gunners and "tankies" had caused to German tanks and transports. Great fires were burning and as darkness approached, the exploding of ammunition inside the German tanks presented a pretty picture.

The further south we went, the deathly roar of the battle became fainter and fainter. As I continued watching the glow in the sky from the battle I was overcome by feelings of utter despair in not being able to escape. At one time I thought my guard was asleep so I tried to jump out over the tail board ... his bayonet brought me back. I felt the penetration in my buttocks and yielded to his persuasion!

We seemed to have travelled many miles that night, finally stopping with the usual suddenness. Without hesitation I jumped out after the guard, only too thankful to find a place to rest my buzzing head. It was bitterly cold that night and I had nothing to protect me except the blood spattered clothes which I was wearing.

I was aroused next morning by the feel of a boot in my side. Heaven only knows how hungry I was. To my surprise, my guard gave me half of his coffee ration, but this only disturbed my stomach. With the usual curt orders interchanged between themselves, the Germans were soon on the move again and after travelling for approximately two hours, we finally returned to the scene of the previous night's battle. The destruction which had been wrought was very creditable, for our forces had, beyond measure, created the most glorious havoc. As far as I could see with a quick glance there were six derelict Mark IV's and three knocked-out

88 mm anti-tank guns. It was impossible to count the number of burnt and smashed-up vehicles in so short a time, but I could see that these included some of ours which had been captured as well as the Germans' own.

Our arrival at the Bir was heralded by yet another artillery barrage from our front lines, which succeeded in depriving the Afrika *Korps* of the full use of the water supply. The Germans were forced to replenish their water by means of petrol cans during lulls in the barrage. This sight raised my morale considerably.

We were kept well guarded inside the trucks for quite a long time and, as the drivers had purposely turned the vehicles so that the backs were facing our lines, we could see the shells finding their marks and each time landing nearer to us. We expected that at any minute a shell would land directly on top of us. Looking out over the tailboard of the truck to see what chance there was of making a bolt the ugly grin of my guard met my gaze, leaving no doubt as to what he would do in such an event, so I resumed the crouching position I had taken up on the floor of the vehicle. As I lay tensing my muscles as each shell fell nearer and nearer, I felt that it would be a happy release from this hell to be blown to pieces by one of them. I closed my eyes and resigned myself to the inevitable. My mind wandered back to the days when I was at school, returning home and dashing off to play, with an apple swelling my pocket which I had quickly retrieved from the large fruit bowl on the sideboard in the dining room.

My dreaming was rudely interrupted by the jolting of the truck but as I attempted to rise I was immediately thrown back by a boot in my chest. There were two German guards, well armed with Schmeissers, occupying a seat on either side of the tailboard. One prisoner tried to get up and look out to see where we were going but was hit across the face with the butt of a sub-machine gun. I raised myself up slowly on to my knees and looked out between the two guards. Bir Harmet was slowly vanishing in the distance to the east, but then with the "crowding-in" of all his transports, (a characteristic of the German's movement in the desert) my view became blurred by the clouds of fine sand which the vehicles kicked up. The Germans drove so recklessly and so fast, that it was amazing that they did not hit each other.

When we slowed to a standstill, the whirling choking clouds of sand subsided, enabling us to breathe some purer air and me to get my bearings once again. To my horror I realised we were running on to the minefield which formed part of our defence line from Gazala to just north of Bir Hackeim. A narrow gap, just wide enough to allow a single line of vehicles to pass through, had been cut in the marker fence. Suddenly a shell landed plumb in the centre of the trucks about five hundred yards behind me and I knew then that we were in for a rough time. More shells followed immediately, until the air was alive with a crescendo of whistling, bursting shells and the crack of the replying 88's. It was heartening to see the Germans beginning to realise that they had driven into a trap and getting a first class panic. Whooph! One shell landed and scored a direct hit on an anti-aircraft gun carrier nearby, blowing it to pieces. Our guards jumped out and began yelling to the driver to by-pass the trucks in front by going on to the minefield. Luckily for us the driver refused. The guards, still scared, mounted the running boards. This allowed us to look out over the tailboard and view what was really going on. There were about twenty trucks in front of ours, and literally hundreds behind, all converging towards this one gap, thus offering a wonderful target for the British artillery.

Then, as though the British gunners had intercepted my thoughts, over came the shells. It seemed as if we were never going to move, and more and more vehicles arrived behind us in great whirling clouds of sand. The Germans were in a wonderful flap. They were shouting at each other, at the drivers, and each one was shouting louder than the others to make his order heard. It was, under the circumstances, good entertainment for us.

By now the shelling was heavy and more accurate than I had ever seen. For this to have happened I realised that our forces must have followed the Germans' withdrawal, unrelenting in their pursuit. For one long moment I stood on the edge of the tailboard, hanging on to the canvas roof, staring over the top of the trucks ahead and beyond to the head of the column. I was numbed by the sight that met my gaze. The Germans were using our prisoners of war to clear mines away for them under sheer brutal compulsion. About six trucks ahead and on either side of the track were scattered here and there, bits and pieces of human beings. The poor fellows had been blown to splinters by the booby traps attached to the mines, the mines themselves triggered off by the tripwires. I saw a couple of trucks receive direct hits by the shell-fire — one bursting ino flames and the other just sitting down without its rear wheels or bodywork.

A lump came into my throat and tears filled my eyes as the thought of the mental torture being endured by those plucky Tommies, in addition to the physical strain of lifting those mines, became apparent to me. Clearing mine fields is not a pleasant task under any circumstances. The shelling continued with unbated fury causing an appalling shambles amongst the whole column. Now the Germans were desperate. As I was still standing on the tailboard I saw the front trucks move forward and by-pass the prisoners who were made to remount on to their own trucks by their bullying guards, and they too moved off at a very rapid rate. So, the Germans were finally driven to the choice of having to risk being blown up by mines or blasted by shell fire. The movement was the last straw for the 'Master Race'. Hundreds of vehicles were following behind us and as we were only crawling, they overtook us and dashed ahead for safety. Owing to petrol trouble developing in our truck we could not hurry. I was very relieved for I didn't want to get blown up by a mine at this stage of events. Every now and again the truck would stop and then splutter on for another few yards. The guards were furious at this. Obviously they had fallen out with the driver for they returned and climbed inside the truck where once more they were on guard over us.

One wait delayed us for about a quarter of an hour, but when we set off once more we seemed to move without any further engine trouble, so the driver put his foot down and tried to make up for lost time. Now it was impossible for me to see anything. I was standing up holding onto the roof trying to look out, but the sand was so fine and thick that it filled my eyes. Our driver madly left the safety of the track and overtook other trucks by the score.

Suddenly there was a terrific explosion — and up we went. I was flung against my guard and landed on the splintered, smoking floorboards. The survivors were quickly ordered out and hustled into another vehicle. Our casualties comprised two of our men slightly wounded, the German driver and a guard killed, and another guard, who had been riding on the running-board, seriously wounded.

Another truck behind us hit a mine and blew up with a terrific explosion, bursting into flames. This truck unfortunately also contained prisoners of war and the casualties were very high. As we were now once more on the move it was impossible for me to render assistance. It was sheer mental torture to hear the screams from those who were wounded and trapped in the burning vehicle with nobody showing the slightest interest in them. German trucks gave them a wide margin, their occupants unfeeling and callous. I could not help but stare back at that burning spectacle until it became a mere flicker of light in the mirage. To me the minefield seemed endless. By this time I was quite resigned to my fate. During the whole of this journey the shelling remained deadly accurate. This was apparent from the number of derelict vehicles beside the track. One of the officers with me, from another regiment, shouted excitedly when he sighted the iron pickets which marked the west boundary of the minefield. From that moment, until I saw the pickets well behind us, I held my breath for fear of a last minute disaster. It was only when I realised we were not amongst the burning shells any more that I became aware of the bouncing motion of the truck and that I felt able to relax and make an effort to dry the sweat which streamed from me. My whole body was bathed in perspiration and, to make things more uncomfortable, the clouds of fine sand stuck to my body and hardened in the heat from the canvas roof.

On we travelled, swerving to avoid trucks and tanks, the speed making the trip pure hell. The great clouds of sand that whirled up and covered us with an ever-thickening layer prevented us from seeing anything but the menacing figure of our guard. Suddenly we stopped and, as the engine was cut off, I could hear the excited chatter of the Germans mingled with another strange tongue. As we were ordered out of the truck I saw that we were in a camp which was full of Italians. Actually, as I found out later, I had arrived in the camp of the great General Rommel himself.

After climbing wearily out of the truck I realised how weak in the legs I was and that I was trembling all over. This was the result of the enormous physical and nervous strain which we had endured, especially in passing over that accursed minefield; but I soon found my legs again and proceeded to take in my new surroundings. From the east, the way we had come, more and more vehicles were moving towards us like a stream of gigantic, threatening ants. This had the effect of raising the sand to an altitude of several thousand feet. We were allowed to stand around as spectators under the watchful eye of our guards. Apparently the Germans were waiting for the remainder of their transports to arrive before assembling the surviving prisoners. I had time to make a mental note of the lay-out of Rommel's camp but, owing to the existence of a small rocky hill in the centre, I was unable to estimate its complete size. At the foot of this hill field-hospital tents were laid out in a neat group, with trucks parked beside the larger tents which were fully equipped for surgical operations. Italian transports were moving about everywhere in a disorderly fashion. Heavily armed Volkswagens were very much in evidence but there were few tanks and 88 mm dual purpose guns. A few anti-aircraft half-tracks were coming in with the rest of the column, which consisted mainly of newly captured vehicles.

The small group of prisoners I was with increased rapidly as each truck stopped near-by and discharged its load. The last truck finally vanished amongst the rest of Rommel's equipment massed in the centre of the camp. German officers came up in staff cars and counted all the prisoners who totalled three hundred and twelve. We were herded towards the hill where we were placed under Italian guards. The Italians, with two light armoured cars from the *Ariete* Division, kept their machine guns pointed very menacingly in our direction. Between the cars troops of the *Bersaglieri* regiment patrolled with fixed bayonets. It was a very strong guard indeed.

Menaced by sharp steel and machine guns and being embedded in the midst of Rommel's men and masses of equipment filled us with dismay. Our hearts sank, while the fierce rays of the sun blazed down relentlessly upon our uncovered heads. The majority of us had long since lost any form of head cover. The cruel glare from the brilliant white sand increased the torture to our over-tired eyes. Most of the prisoners dropped wearily down on the hard, rocky ground and mercifully were soon oblivious of their sufferings. My eyes rested on my companions whose ages ranged from eighteen to forty. However, there was one man, well over fifty, an Army Post Office official, who was now sharing the misery and hardships along with the younger men. He kept his chin up and his example of splendid quiet courage was then, and later, a great help in supporting our morale.

I sat down on a small rock trying to discover some weak point that would permit an attempt to escape. The camp perimeter was picketed with anti-tank guns and heavy-field guns whilst German and Italian cars ran to and fro continuously. Far away in the distance I could still hear the deep rumbling of the long drawn-out battle. Everywhere the German gunners were hurriedly bringinging up more ammunition to their gun positions. On the eastern perimeter men, stripped to the waist, were busily digging in 105 mm guns. There seemed no possibility of attempting to escape at all, so I abandoned the idea for the moment and began to look for some of my own men among the prisoners.

We were a mixed crowd. There were Irishmen - two brothers whose father kept a shop behind Piccadilly, in London, some bare footed East Africans who had only been out of their native bush country barely six months, some Indians, a couple of South Africans and the rest were Britishers from a mixture of Regiments. Fellows were wandering around from one little group to another looking for their friends. They would slowly bend down to a body lying very still with its head covered, fearful of discovering a lost chum dead. Pathetically they would apologise for having disturbed some poor wounded devil and go on to the next person.

Walking over into the centre of the groups I called them all to pay attention to what I was going to say. Very willingly they gathered round the Indians and the East Africans. I told them that as we were likely to be here for sometime it would be an advantage to all if they would sort themselves out onto their own Units, as this would help them to over come the strangeness of their changed circumstances and at the same time support their morale. This arrangement would be useful in helping new prisoners to find their friends and would make it easier for me to feed them if, and when, the Germans allowed us food and water. To all this the forlorn, but by no means demoralised, men readily agreed. Though I could not speak the language of the East Africans I soon had the help of an interpreter and found that they too were agreeable to my suggestions. I told them that, as an officer, although I didn't look like one, I would do my utmost to look after them. One man spontaneously told his comrades that if I was to remain in a position to look after them it was necessary not to disclose the fact that I was an officer. These chaps were a grand lot and I could see that, although I was very young and only a 'Two Pipper', I had their confidence and their co-operation

When the men had divided themselves up as suggested I was able to pick out some of my own Section, as well as others from my company. It was heartening to see them again. After swapping experiences of the last few days I persuaded most of them to build some form of protection against the sun for their heads. These shelters were just big enough for one person to get under and were made of four tiny cairns of stone to each corner of which was attached a shirt or jacket or in one case, a pair of underpants! Soon there were little such shelters springing up all around and other Units began doing likewise. As I was walking around, stopping here and there to help the fellows with their little 'tents', I noticed away over to the east a long line of men moving very slowly in our direction. Behind them were two eight-wheeled armoured cars. Even at that distance I recognised them to be more prisoners who were hanging on to bits and pieces of clothing which they managed to save. The fellows around me stopped work and gathered around to give the newcomers a welcome. Desperate as we were, sympathy for those weary men welled up; their exhausted weary gait and air of dejection showed plainly the hardships they had been through.

When they were about one hundred yards away one man, who had been carrying another on his back, suddenly placed the limp figure down and, with a last spurt of energy, raced across the sand towards me. Stumbling and lurching he just fell into my arms, giving a great groan partly of relief and partly of pain. He was my batman. As he looked at me tears filled his eyes and the only remark he made was the strangest one, "Oh sir, I do wish I could wash your shirt!" Seeing the grand fellow in that condition was too much for me. I had to break away, and I went over to pick up the man who had been left lying on the sand. Approaching the pathetic, huddled figure, I suddenly recognised him to be my driver, a lad of nineteen. His condition, with his face distorted by the torture of long starvation, filled me with an intense, murderous rage against the Nazi troops. His colour shocked me. He made no movement. I knelt down beside him and felt his pulse; it was beating only very faintly. I ran across to the nearest German truck and begged the occupants to give me some water saying that it was for a dying man. "If he is dying then let him die," snarled the Germans. Concealing my feelings I hastened over to an Italian armoured car and again pleaded for water. A sergeant gave me his water bottle and speaking English with an American accent he said I could keep it. Gratefully I raced back to my driver, raised his head on to a stone and began to wash his sand-caked lips with a few drops of water. After rubbing his teeth with my fingers, using the water very sparingly, to get the sand clear, I began, just a few drops at a time, to moisten his crusted tongue. Very slowly the youth began to revive and, after a little more, finally regained consciousness.

Then I became aware that others of the newly arrived contingent had gathered around and were begging for water. I had to explain to them that the water bottle held only about a pint of water and that it would have to be reserved only for the most urgent cases. The men pathetically turned away and went to join the other prisoners. Taking the lad in my arms, I carried him to where my batman was sitting. I left them together whilst I went over to talk to the men. I caught sight of a Cavalry major approaching with the last of the prisoners. When he neared, I went over and told him that I was the only officer amongst this group and how grateful I would be for his help in trying to keep the poorer cases alive. I explained what I had done so far regarding segregating the men, and added that we had received neither food nor water. Leaving me in charge of the men he walked off in the direction of the hospital. That was the last time we saw him.

Gathering the men together again, including the new arrivals, I told them of the present chaotic situation and again pointed out that this little hill was likely to be our pen for the time being, and that they should not expect too much in the way of water and food from our captors. I assured them that I would do everything possible to obtain those necessities and that meanwhile they must keep well under some sort of cover in order to conserve their energies, lying down as much as possible.

Counting heads, I found that we numbered five hundred and twenty-two. All had been captured at Bir Zebeda and we were all that remained of the original twelve hundred officers and men. With this thought to appal me, I dismissed the men.

As the hours slipped by we rested ourselves, only stirring to prepare tiny hollows in which to spend the first night. Lying down, my head supported on a stone, I gazed across the vast array of vehicles towards the setting sun. It was a pity, I thought, that it was not possible to conserve some of its warming rays against the cold of the coming night, which we were to spend out in the open without any extra covering.

No sooner had the sun set than we huddled together to keep

each other warm. I slept beside my driver and my batman. The distant rumbling of moving vehicles went on well into the night. Soon we started shivering, first my driver, then Harry, and I. It was impossible to stop shaking and very soon I ached from the involuntary and continuous movement. In order to warm myself I had to get up and walk around, but the little warmth generated by doing that was so short-lived that almost immediately I was shivering again. At every slightest rumble or bang my driver would start up completely nerve-racked, his mind alerted and keyed up to listen, then he would sink back again on to his rocky bed.

We welcomed the rising sun in the morning. Getting up I saw that the men were all looking in a certain direction. Following their gaze I saw a long line of German troops queuing for their breakfast. Each man, as he gazed, bore the look of utter desperation for want of food, especially a hot meal, and only when the last German had been served did the men feel able to turn away to resume their shelter from the heat of the now fully-risen sun. As this was the fifth day since our capture it was only to be expected that the Germans would feed us. As nothing seemed to be forthcoming some of the men approached me and asked if something could be done. I advised them to try and scrounge what they could, and in the meantime I would go along to the German administration office and see what I could do. Groups of men broke away, wandering all over the place, appealing to every crew member of the enemy vehicles for food.

My errand was fruitless, but on the way back I slipped over to the German field kitchen where the cooks filled my water bottle with hot ersatz coffee. Tightening the stopper so as not to lose one single precious drop, I hurried back and gave a small cupful to each of the wounded and those who were so weak as not to know what was going on around them. I was relieved to see small groups sharing a two-gallon tin of water between themselves, smacking their lips as each mouthful was swallowed. The men were lying down carefully guarding their water supply and keeping themselves well under cover, for the sun's rays were now almost beyond endurance.

Suddenly we could hear the faint rumble of gunfire over towards the east, a sound now only too familiar to our ears. Though no shells arrived there was renewed panic among the German troops. The whole of that day the men kept coming up with their mess tins half full of dirty looking water. There were others who never stirred from the position into which they had fallen when they had arrived the previous day. The approach of the night, dreaded so much the night before, was now awaited anxiously for the relief it would bring from the torment of the sun's rays. So another day passed without the group receiving any rations of food or water.

Long into the night I lay shivering and listening to the faint chatter of the Italian guards, wishing I could understand their language. I tried to sleep, but as the cold defeated my efforts I wandered over to some of the men who also found sleep impossible. We chatted about our misfortunes, our regiments, our homes and other subjects. Just about a quarter of an hour before dawn a 'plane passed over, flying very high and circling several times over the camp before it passed away out of hearing. The yelling from the German and Italian guards told us that it must have been one of ours. This gave us a splendid feeling, knowing that at least the position of all this massed equipment of Rommel's was known to our forces.

With the coming of the sixth day the men began to take a turn for the worse. While walking about I noticed a good number of men trying to be sick and looking like death. I spoke to one or two and found the explanation. These bastard Germans who were our captors had bargained gold rings, watches, cigarette cases, indeed anything of value belonging to the men, in exchange for what they had offered as water. The water I had seen the men bringing in yesterday was, in fact, mostly petrol and diesel oil. They had led our chaps to believe that the cans contained fresh water and then, satisfied with their payment, had chased the lads away. The result of this trick caused much suffering, especially when it was drunk on an empty stomach. As the heat became more intense, the victims became crazed with the desire to drink quarts of fresh water, for the foul liquid made them extremely thirsty and at the same time gave them a sickening taste in their mouths. All of them were spitting out the froth that accumulated around their lips. How I cursed the sun that day!

One by one the men dropped down, just mad with the heat. It was pitiful to see them rolling about in sheer agony for want of food and water. They would scream and their whole bodies would writhe in torment until, completely unconscious, they would lie still in a ghastly manner. Yet still no water was brought to us, although the sentries were not blind to what was being endured.

About eleven thirty that morning we heard distant gunfire again, but this time we noted a few shells burst over on the far side of the camp where the majority of the vehicles were massed. The German gunners replied sporadically and this exchange lasted until sunset. Throughout that day the Germans and the Italians continually moved their transports from one side of the camp to the other to escape the shelling. It was only after watching where the shells burst that the men felt fairly safe from destruction. Occasionally, a Messerschmitt would fly over at a fairly high altitude, but, apart from this, there was no aerial activity at all.

That night I slept very little, some of the fellows being in a very bad state. The Indians could not sleep and their chatter disturbed the other light sleepers. The temperature seemed to play havoc with one's nerves too, for it seemed colder than ever. Towards the early hours of the morning we could hear a deep droning overhead, but nothing happened so the men relaxed.

As the sun arose, the whole layout of the camp looked different. The Germans had moved their transports and some of their store dumps. New gun positions had sprung up and, in fact, the whole scene looked very much like the beginning of a big battle. One of the boys pointed to a few specks in the sky fairly high up and, as their engines sounded louder and louder, we found the specks to be our own aircraft. When the 'recce' 'plane had flown over the previous day I had guessed that we were in for some fun and games. The show started about 9.30 a.m., when a 'Kitty-Hawk', an American single engined fighter plane, hedge-hopped over the transports, loosing off its cannons and heavy machine guns and dropping a 250 lb bomb plumb on to a German anti-aircraft gun-carrier, smashing it to bits. No sooner had one 'plane flown around creating havoc than another would appear. All were doing their utmost to destroy the German armour and transports. The bursts from the 'ack-ack' guns were terrific. Every German and Italian used his rifle or sub-machine gun and, with the loud cracking 20 mm quick-firing 'ack-ack' guns popping off just nearby, the noise was frightful and drove some of our poor fellows, already half delirious, into a frenzy.

About mid-day a flock of twelve Stuka 'planes came flying low, straight for the camp. The Germans thought that they were our 'planes and opened up at them with everything they had. The air crews likewise thought that, being attacked from the ground, they must be over enemy territory and so they opened up with their machine guns. Unfortunately we were in direct line of their fire and several of our chaps were hit. Two were killed outright and another died later that day. The 'planes were recognised after they had flown partly over the camp, recognition signals being promptly given.

Little did they realise that our Kitty-Hawks were sitting above them. The 'Kitties' waited until the twelve Stukas were right over the centre of the camp and then dived down for the kill and gave Rommel a real show. In the space of a few seconds twc Stukas were biting the dust and were ending their careers in flames. Most of the boys were sitting up and now cheering away just as they would at a football match back home. The guards threatened to shoot us if we persisted in our demonstrations, but the chaps were far too excited to take any notice. The Kitties were diving in and out of the showers of bullets that were flung at them, for they were very fast and manoeuvrable.

Down went another Stuka! Then the shouts and pointings of the fellows drew my gaze upwards. My heart beat faster as I counted eight Messerschmitt 109's preparing to pounce on to our game little fighter 'planes. They dived down from their great height and blazed away at the Kitties, only to be out-manoeuvred. The ensuing dog-fight was a thrill to watch. The Kitties were determined to shoot down every Stuka without care for themselves, so we saw this battle to the end. The Kitty Hawks forced their attack time and time again until finally the twelve Stukas had been shot down. Then they flew up to settle the score with the 109's.

By this time our throats were sore from shouting. We stood and flung our few remaining tin hats into the air in great jubilation, only to fling ourselves flat on to the ground again to the rake of machine-gun fire from a diving aircraft.

Particularly interesting was one fight between a 109 and a Kitty. The latter was completing a circuit of the camp just after shooting down its fifth Stuka. The pilot suddenly saw he was being chased by the 109. It was incredible to watch the 109 catch up with the Kitty in a matter of seconds, until suddenly our machine climbed almost vertically. The 109 roared past as the skilful Kitty pilot half-rolled at the top of his climb and screamed down upon his victim from out of the sun. The surprise was complete. A burst of fire went straight into the side of the 109, tearing off a wing. After swinging crazily for a second, the enemy plane then crashed to earth.

I tried to cheer but my throat had long since seized up. The Kitty flew once more round the camp, completely ignoring the ack-ack. As he flew over our heads he 'shot us up' and made a victory roll, as if to say, "O.K. chaps, we know you are there."

I did not relax until I saw that 'plane safely out of the area of the ack-ack fire, flying almost at zero altitude and heading back for our lines. I hope the pilot of that fighter was decorated for his magnificent feat of aviation skill, his courage and his splendid tenacity in sticking out until, I suppose, he had no more ammunition and was almost out of fuel. Five Stukas and one 109 was a fine piece of work for one 'plane to achieve in about fifteen minutes.

While this show was proceeding other Kitties and 109's were fighting it out together high above our heads. A further two 109's came crashing down within the perimeter of Rommel's camp. Then, to our great sorrow, we saw one of the Kitties spin down to about one thousand feet. The pilot managed to flatten the machine out but crash-landed at colossal speed, bursting into flames almost immediately. Then the shelling recommenced.

It was hopeless now to expect the Germans to feed us. They were in such a flap after that machine-gunning and were also very bitter about our cheering whenever one of their 'planes was shot down. The heat was our worst enemy, with starvation a close second. Already we were physically weak, and we were rapidly becoming weaker. It was amazing that so many of us survived.

Later the whole horizon seemed to open up from about six to eight miles away. Shells landed, first from one side of the camp and then the other, severely harassing the Germans. Our gunners knew just where the enemy transports lay and were not slow in following up the repositioning. The prisoners in their weak condition were terrified lest they should be hit. It was a hard job for me to convince them that the shells were directed onto the German transports which were a good mile and a half away.

Owing to the continuation of the shelling, the Germans brought up a couple of Italian armoured cars to reinforce our guard. Their crews were a filthy lot. They jeered at the condition of our men and laughed loudly at the delirious ones who were rolling about on the sand. About mid-day these crews received their water ration. Two Italians held a full 'Jerry-can', which contained nearly five gallons of water, up in the air, then one of them held his mug while the other poured fresh water into it. When it was filled he continued to pour so that the water splashed down the sides of the armoured car. The Italians thoroughly enjoyed the wanton waste of the precious water. It was a ghastly sight to watch those poor fellows actually lapping up the moisture from the sand. The Italians spat and jeered as the men fought and they poured more water on to the ground to add to the torment. By this time the whole crowd of prisoners was yelling and screaming for water. Many were too weak to struggle and were trampled beneath the yelling mob.

At first I was glad that the men obtained what water they could, but when I saw that they were eating the sand as well and that a nice little riot was starting, I immediately intervened and eventually succeeded in restoring order. By good fortune a nasty situation with the guards was averted, the tortured men being persuaded to return to their places. Within a few minutes however, I was being besieged by a yelling crowd demanding food and water. Poor chaps, their faces were shrivelled up with the pain of long thirst and starvation. They frothed at the mouth. I appealed to them to lie down and conserve their depleted energy, adding that I would do what I could to satisfy their demands.

Leaving a sergeant-major in charge I set off, taking my water bottle. My destination was Rommel's Headquarters, which was indicated by the number of staff cars parked around some tents. Reaching these tents I took the bull by the horns and went inside to be immediately confronted by a German Major. As luck would have it he could understand a little English. Briefly I described the plight of the prisoners. He listened glumly and told me to wait whilst he made enquiries.

The Germans certainly knew how to make themselves comfortable, even in the desert. The tent was furnished with a long wooden table, very similar to our barrack room tables. On it were "In" trays and "Pending" trays, although these bore none of the markings usually seen inside our offices. The chairs were a splendid collapsible type, of wood and canvas. Hemp mats kept one's feet off the sand. In a corner near a window, was a special typist's desk. My survey of the tent was suddenly interrupted by a German N.C.O. who had come in by one of the three entrances. He offered me a cup of almost boiling hot coffee and then he quickly departed. When the coffee had cooled I sipped it eagerly. Its restorative effect was astonishing.

Presently the Major returned and, on noticing the empty mug, he asked me if I had enjoyed the drink. I nodded emphatically, whereupon he handed me a cigarette and became surprisingly informative. From him I learned that the enemy forces had had to close in under pressure from our attacks and that the enemy columns had been cut off from Rommel's main forces. As a result, Rommel was now extremely short of food and there was practically no water in the camp. They were trying to make contact with a supply column coming from Derna, but so far failed. The Major however, promised to send some food to the prisoners during the afternoon. I left him in no doubt as to the number of men for whom I was responsible Then I departed, devoutly hoping that the promise would be kept.

Though I hurried to convey the good news to the men I was so exhausted myself that I dropped with fatigue several times on the way over. On my arrival the men were somewhat heartened to learn that our forces had now completely surrounded Rommel, but I withheld the news of the German Major's promise. Any disappointment on this vital matter would have been too cruel, not to say quite disastrous, so I merely said that everything possible was being done.

German and Italian vehicles would speed up to us and then, with equal swiftness, drive off. It seemed that their object was to kick up the dust around us which choked our parched throats as a result. Such were the fiends we were fighting .... their tactics caused additional torment to the men because, at first, they thought it was the delivery of the rations and they would get up and frantically dash over, yelling with wild excitement. Only sadistic bullies could be so cruel.

CHAPTER FOUR

The afternoon came and still no rations appeared. How glad I was not to have encouraged false hopes! With things getting desperate and the men becoming weaker, my thoughts turned to the idea of a mass escape with any who were able and willing. Carefully I broached the idea while walking around from one group to another pretending to give some of the boys a water ration. Several times the guards would venture near, suspicious as to what might be taking place, but how stupid they were. It appeared finally that about two hundred men were eager to escape. Then I put forward my plan, going into a huddle to discuss the matter with each small group. It was arranged that the Sergeant-Major and I would each lead a party and if successful, these two groups would make their way independently back to our lines.

Before assembling, the men were able to wander off in small groups, supposedly scrounging for food and water among vehicles and tents. Once through the perimeter and away from German outposts they were to make for the first signs of dawn. As none of us had compasses this was the only bearing I could give them. With this settled, we all conserved our energy meanwhile, as best we could.

Night approached. The distant shelling from our lines opened, and with the continual shifting of transports from place to place, sleep was impossible. Deciding that conditions were more or less favourable, I spread the word, assisting the scheme by moving about as if searching for water. Our small groups assembled, wishing one another, "Goodbye," and "Good luck," in whispers, then wandered off in various directions, gradually bearing round to a point behind the hospital. This was due north from the hillock.

All went well until a sudden burst of machine-gun fire was heard to the rear. A great deal of screaming and moaning followed, the crew yelling in fierce tempo. There was no arguing with that Spandau. We realised that our little scheme had come to nothing. There ensued a few minutes of very anxious waiting as the German guards surrounded us and marched us back to the hillock at the point of the bayonet, so to speak!

Arriving back at the 'graveyard' — so-called because we had to bury our dead there on the hillock — we discovered the cause of our re-capture. The Indians, after watching us wander off, and thinking that we were about to get food and water and that they were not, had followed us. On the way they had begun to quarrel about who would carry the precious supplies if they got any. This row had disturbed the guards who, when they realised the great number missing from the 'pen', had raised the alarm and given chase. These stupid and distrustful Indians had lost five men and had eighteen wounded.

So ended the escape as far as my unforunate group was concerned. Later I had the satisfaction of knowing that the other party had made a successful escape and finally managed to get back to our lines.

That night was a real nightmare to all of us. Because of the trouble earlier on the Indians were having free fights. I did feel sorry for them. They were feeling the lack of food and water far more than we were and, owing to the strain of the past seven days, their nerves were also on edge. The East Africans never gave us any bother, although they too were just as badly off. With the aid of an Indian who could speak English, I calmed them down. The shelling was still going on and although the shells were bursting a mile or two away. trying to rest was a hopeless business. The horror and despair of it all oppressed me. It had been such a long day, starting with that spectacular air battle. My legs were now beginning to feel the strain of the unsuccessful escape attempt and ached dreadfully. "Why," I asked myself, "had men to go through all this unrelieved torment because of one man's greed and stupidity?" I thought of those poor Indians who were now lying in shallow graves scooped out of sand and covered with a cairn of stones. The Germans had murdered them so wantonly. "Oh God," I prayed, "Send me to sleep quickly so I may forget this awful mess!"

Sleep never came that night however. The shelling from our lines gradually intensified, thus creating more changes in the positions of the vehicles. The clatter of the tanks' tracks as they moved about and the yelling of the Indians combined to make sleep impossible.

To crown all, just after midnight, the R.A.F. came over in force and plastered the camp from one end to the other with heavy bombs, causing the most damage amongst the German motor transport. A few bombs landed very near to the hospital which was only five hundred yards from us. Owing to the state we were in, our morale was considerably lowered, rather than raised, by this bombing. The only relief was when the Germans moved their transports right to the other side of the camp. Finally sheer mental and physical fatigue caused me to drop off into a deep sleep. Then one of those horrid nightmares ensued — an aircraft was flying very fast overhead. I could see a small bomb falling from under its port wing and down it screamed coming nearer and nearer. I tried to run but couldn't — the bomb was catching me up. I tried to shout — but had no voice. Two old school chums were watching and laughing at my predicament — HELP! HELP! The bomb will get me, it will ... Then C-R-A-S-H ....

Jerked into consciousness I stood up, scared out of my wits, and shielded my eyes from the brilliant sunlight. Clouds of falling dust some two hundred yards away enveloped the smashed and burning remains of an Italian medium tank which had been the victim of a direct hit. Strange that even in sleep the sub-conscious mind conveys a danger warning.

The Italians and Germans were firing everything they had at our fighter 'planes. The Kitties came in from all angles, flying almost at zero altitude. At the right moment up they would shoot, at the same time releasing a 250 pounder bomb on to an enemy vehicle or tank. The courageous pilots relied on their 'plane's speed and manoeuvrability to avoid the hail of death from the enemy defence weapons. Time after time they miraculously escaped.

Our forces had tightened their grip on Rommel and the shelling was louder and far more accurate and heavy. Shells shrieked over our heads with a frightening menace. Again and again the Kitties, in relays, scored hits with light bombs, at the same time raking everything with their point five inch calibre machine guns. Without any cover whatsoever we were left to take our chance as the Germans refused to move us. Recklessly we stood up and waved frantically as our machines roared over, hoping the pilot would communicate our position to our gunners. This had no effect however, because later in the afternoon the shelling grew to barrage intensity. There was now no fixed target for our gunners as the enemy transports were racing from one side of the camp area to the other and back again.

The sky lost its brilliant blue and took on a ghastly shade of light fawn colour. Dust! That cruel fine dust! This time it was even worse for our noses, ears and mouths were filled almost to the point of being suffocated. The only slight relief from this suffering was when the transports careered over to the far side of the camp. After we had endured this for some time, through a break in the dust clouds I caught a glimpse of a large formation of Kitties fairly high up. As they vanished in the dust clouds I tried to note their course but could not do so.

The shelling from our lines had intensified, to even greater density. Suddenly I caught a glimpse of tanks approaching. They were ours!

"Run," I yelled, "the tanks, our tanks are coming!" Our forces were putting in an attack. "We'll be free yet, chaps. Hang on, they'll soon be here!" The men had no difficulty in hearing me, for I nearly broke my vocal chords with the sudden excitement.

The men were up, moving from group to group, excitedly exchanging comments about our forces' progress. Even those with very little strength left managed to struggle to their feet to see OUR tanks. Suddenly, from nowhere, the roaring of a 'plane engine almost startled us out of our wits. Immediately the most ghastly rake of cannon shells ripped straight through our 'pen' and into a German mobile ack-ack carrier. Skimming low over our heads, a Kitty vanished into the dust clouds. Some of the men, quite dazed, stood motionless.

I yelled to everybody to flatten out and remain still. One young fellow with his back to me remained standing after the others had flattened out. Dashing over to him I saw his face. Suddenly I felt my legs giving way and my throat almost seize up with emotion. The laddie was covered in blood, tears were rolling down his white cheeks. He dropped into a limp form, falling away from me. I caught him in time to break his fall but his weight was a little too heavy and caught me off balance so I went down with him. Luckily his head fell on to my leg, so I laid it on a stone as the only pillow available, and with a little water I moistened his lips. His face was a mass of cuts and blood oozing out from them. He soon rallied after tasting the water and then told me he was all right. He added that only his face 'got it' but he was very hazy as to what had happened. I told him not to worry but to lie still and face away from the sun.

Just as I was getting up, I was grabbed by the arm and led by an hysterical Indian to help his chum. Again I closed my eyes and said a prayer. The Indian would feel no more pain for he was dead.

I could not stand any more of this and decided, in an angry mood, to go down to Rommel's headquarters. As I was talking to an interpreter, General Rommel himself came in!

So this master of cunning and genius of modern warfare was actually facing me now. He bore no distinct emblems of a German general and was wearing a soft peaked cap, faded by long service in the desert. Shorter than I, but stouter, he looked like the man I had always pictured him to be — strong and powerful, both physically and mentally.

The appetite for power was written across his ruddy countenance, which was covered with fine desert sand. His clothes were much worn and also filmed with sand. His boots no longer shone with a high polish. Yet the man himself left a lasting impression on one's mind. I took the opportunity of looking at him straight in the face and observed the cruel determination in his eyes. When he greeted some subordinate officers who had just arrived, he smiled pleasantly. I wondered how sincere that greeting was, for surely no man with such a draconian record behind him could smile so humanely on anyone.

Addressing the interpreter, he inquired what I was doing in the tent. Satisfied with the reply, General Rommel spoke to me in halting English, saying how sorry he was for the situation and that he would personally come along to have a look at our fellows. Then, with a confident air, as though assured that his moves against our forces would be successful, he calmly turned and went into his private tent. Thus ended my interview with the notorious German General. His confident bearing and complete disregard of danger compelled me to admire him. Whatever else he was, at least he was a good soldier.

Later that afternoon Rommel drove up to keep his word. He looked at the men from his lofty perch in his staff car, with complete and callous unconcern. He talked away to his subordinates at an incredible speed, the only answers he seemed to receive being, *"Jawohl, jawohl, Herr Rommel."* He turned to me and curtly said that transport would arrive some time that afternoon to evacuate us, as a gap had been forced through to Timimi. Then his car sped away back to his tent, causing more aggravating dust to float in our direction. The men, now quite beyond saying anything, just stared after the car — but I knew how they felt!

It seemed that we waited hours and hours for the transport to arrive. Eventually it did, just as darkness fell, and we carefully loaded up the wounded and sick. By then it was pitch black, so we could not make out the direction in which we were going. We bumped and banged around in the back of the truck for a long time, seeming to move in a vast circle and being shelled at the same time. Fortunately no trucks were hit. Finally the trucks stopped and to our amazement we found ourselves back again in the 'cemetery'. The rest of that night we were again under severe shell fire and bombardment from the air.

As dawn broke next day, the German transports picked us up and this time they found the gap, forced it, and travelling almost flat out, made for Timimi. We bumped about for hours, going through four minefields which had been gapped. In so doing we ran the gauntlet of our artillery, as our gunners had each gap absolutely pin-pointed. It was cruel, after all we had gone through, to have to watch more trucks, complete with their human load, being smashed to pieces by the shells and mines. When we left the deadly thundering boom of the distant artillery and progressed well behind the scene of destruction, our driver slowed down and for the rest of the journey we took things slowly.

I found out later that our own forces had come to some arrangement to allow Rommel to evacuate his wounded and prisoners but as our Observation Posts had seen knocked-out tanks and smashed 88's on transporters between the ambulances, they had tried to close the gaps to stop the convoy — but it was too late.

When we arrived at Timimi I gathered together the wounded and took them over to the German hospital, with the help of a brother officer who could speak fluent German. He had already been at this transit camp for a few days. We both stayed with two men in the theatre, who were operated on immediately. I stayed because I was curious as to the treatment our fellows would get under anaesthetic. I can only say that the movement of the surgeon's hands merely portrayed his callous mind.

After making sure that these two men were placed fairly comfortably in bed, and that the rest of the wounded had received attention, my German-speaking friend and I went over to the German camp to look into the food situation. As a result we rejoined the men with a truck containing bread, jam and fifty tins of meat between the lot of us. The men ate like savages and I was every bit like a savage myself. Some chaps however could not eat for a long time.

It was bitterly cold that night, for Timimi lies right on the coast, very exposed to the sharp winds that sweep in from the west. The next morning I met the Major who had been with us for only a short time in Rommel's camp. He told me that I now had to stay with the rest of the officers here, and leave the men, as they were going off to Benghazi. Just then, great numbers of vehicles came up and all the men were ordered to mount. I didn't like to see the fellows go. We had been a friendly crowd together. Then there were my own men, including my driver and batman, piling into the truck and imploring me to go with them. Truly they were a grand lot, the majority of them still mere youths. It was then that I knew what a really happy family we had been before our capture. The German guards were shouting, the men were calling to each other, the trucks were moving. I ran alongside, shaking hands with the men. Harry would not let me go — he pleaded for me to go with them. All I could do was to blurt out, "God protect you, lads!" — and then the vehicle became blurred.

Often during our association as No. 1 Section, and during our trials after our capture, there were occasions for sentiment, but for the sake of morale and one's own feeling one had to fight sentiment and fight it hard. These men had become my personal friends through adversity and I admired them for their grit and courage. It was this grit and courage, along with their indomitable sense of humour, their unimpeachable spirit of comradeship, their willingness to work hard when there was a job to do and the thought that not one had ever let me down, that made me feel proud of them, and privileged to have served as their officer.

That afternoon we officers moved off in convoy and arrived at a transit camp just outside Barce. Here I had my first experience of being behind barbed wire, caged like an animal and treated like one. I hadn't the men to talk to or look after — my only consolation was that other officers were feeling the same.

During the night shots could be heard from all over the camp. I could not sleep and passed the time imagining various ways of escape. Perhaps I could creep up on to one of the sentries, the one at the main gate which was so heavily padlocked, overpower him, steal his keys, unlock the gate and, yelling to all the prisoners, run away to liberty? Or hang on to the underside of the bread lorry and ride out to liberty? I knew it would be useless, so I did not try. Those odd shots meant that someone else had tried. No one got away — not even as far as the outside of the wire. Escaping, one soon realised, needed careful planning and co-ordination by the officers in charge of us, to avoid other escapes being jeopardised.

The following day, after the Senior British Officer (the S.B.O. to us) had been in conference with the Italian commandant, he asked us to meet in one of the huts. It happened to be the one furthest away from any guards. He told us that the Italians, having heard that Italian prisoners were not getting food until after they had been interrogated were, in reprisal, going to do the same to us. They refused to interrogate us there and then and in sarcastic tones stated that they did not know how long we would be at Barce. The advice of the S.B.O., we saved our small ration of bread, hoping that a miracle would happen. We spent the whole of the day without any fresh issue of food. I spent the day resting on my bed and conserving what little energy I had left.

About nine o'clock the next day, the S.B.O. informed us that the Italians had made a mistake, misinterpreting a message which had been intercepted. They cancelled the order. Great was our relief at hearing this news and we strolled up and down the tiny compound to see the food lorry arrive. At mid-day, an ancient chain-driven Lancia, steaming at the radiator, jolted noisily into the compound. The row it made was soon drowned by the crowd of excited and hungry officers, all eager to obtain the food as quickly as possible. The issue consisted of a loaf, the size of a small English cob, together with rice and tomato puree mixed. It smelled really wonderful.

That afternoon earlier arrivals were called to the gate in batches. We learned that they were being moved to Benghazi. Those left behind looked on with envy as their comrades clambered into the waiting lorries then cheered them on their way. Next day we were off too. I was more than happy to get away from the filthy place and pitied those who had to remain behind. Even at the gate one could still smell the foul odour from the open latrines behind the buildings. It was obvious that those in charge of the camp had not learned of sanitation.

It was not long before we were bowling along the main Benghazi road, with the diesel fumes making everyone very sleepy. The two guards who accompanied us were sufficiently alert to prevent any escape attempt on our part. Chances of escape were numerous as the road twisted and turned and, because the road contained many hair-pin bends, the drivers were obliged to slacken speed considerably. On one hair-pin bend above our heads, a truck suddenly swerved and stopped precariously on the edge. The guards jumped out and began firing down the road behind them. Then, as we turned with the road and the scene changed, we could only guess the cause of the firing. I wondered whether the escapers got away.

Presently, we entered Benghazi. The Libyans wasted no time in showing their hatred for us. I remembered how that at the close of Wavell's campaign, when Benghazi was first captured in 1941, the Libyans had welcomed us in and how very friendly they had been then. Now that we were vanquished and they were the friends of the Nazis, the situation was very different.

Along winding, narrow streets on the far side of the town we banged and bumped, until we entered a courtyard through very high, substantial gates. Although our chance of escape was now completely gone, I was pleased to be able at last to exercise my cramped legs.

Our 'pen' was a dirty building, one of several which formed a base food supply dump for the enemy. Our forces had at some time given it a taste of bombing. The guards drove us into this building and, locking the door, left us alone. There were only double-decker wooden beds in rows in the room, with one blanket on each side. Ventilation, provided by two small windows looking out into the courtyard, was quite inadequate for our number, consequently there was always a crowd around the door to obtain a breath of comparatively fresh air whenever the guards passed in or out.

That evening we were given a scanty meal of rice puree again.

Through the open window we could see a cheese store immediately opposite to us. This didn't help us physically, but we seemed to derive a sort of satisfaction from our hungry staring. Then our door was slammed shut for the last time that evening. Making sure that it was firmly bolted, our guards posted one of their number outside.

I turned in, sleeping on a bottom bunk. Afterwards I regretted this because the dirty straw from the mattress of the upper bunk kept falling down on me as the occupant tossed and turned. Added to this discomfort was the extremely cold air which rose from the concrete floor of this solid stone building. Efforts to cover my feet with the blanket only pulled it away from my shoulders. I soon gave up this silly game and resigned myself to spending the night shivering until every muscle ached with the cold.

Morning came none too soon. With the day-light I rose and paced rapidly up and down the room to restore my circulation. I was joined by others but although we kept this up for a couple of hours until the sun rose, it was useless to expect the room to warm up until nearly mid-day. At ten o'clock the door was opened and the guards brought in our breakfast. This consisted of a small cup of filthy-smelling coffee — or something that was supposed to be coffee! When we asked if we we were going to have any food with it, our charming hosts replied with a spit on the floor. Only a visit to the latrines under heavy escort allowed one a temporary feeling of liberty. The latrines were open and without any screening. They only catered for two at a time, so the rest had to queue whilst the swarm of flies and mosquitoes tormented them. Attempts to wander from the queue to a safe distance away from the stench were discouraged by our guards' bayonets.

At mid-day a small loaf of bread, the size of a normal dinner cob, was issued to us, along with a ladleful of cabbage water. We were told that the bread was a twenty-four hour ration. I was so hungry that I ate mine in a couple of mouthfuls. Later, I disciplined myself with a great effort, to keep some bread for the next meal by cutting it into three pieces. Often, especially after about eight o'clock at night, I would begin to ache with hunger and a strong temptation to nibble the third piece, reserved for breakfast, would develop. All my new friends had a similar problem and gravely discussed whether they were going to 'bash' the whole lot in one go, or ration themselves. In addition to this severe treatment, the guards would eat bread and gulp coffee all day, right under our noses!

Early that afternoon, the guards were formed up outside our building and after a great deal of confusion they succeeded in forming a barrier of men and bayonets. After this had been accomplished, the officer-in-charge strutted into our room carrying a sheet of paper from which he commenced to read aloud our names, indicating to those who had their names called to form up outside immediately. We all listened eagerly, hoping to hear our own names, but mine was not amongst them. We learned that the lucky ones were destined for Italy but how they were to travel there we didn't know. No-one was allowed outside to see them off so we crowded to the windows to cheer them on their way.

The following day the same pantomine was repeated and, to my great relief, I heard my name read out along with one of the prisoners with whom I'd made friends. He was a young Kitty Hawk pilot who had been shot down and who had also received a nasty head wound. As neither of us had any kit to take along we were soon outside that wretched room and in the fresh air waiting for the others. The guards reported the number of prisoners as correct to their officers, and we climbed into a waiting vehicle, moving off as soon as the last prisoner was aboard. The betting was all in favour of our journey to Italy being by sea, but one or two were of the opinion that we would be sent either by submarine or air. As the vehicle careered madly through the narrow streets, I personally was fully occupied speculating on the future awaiting us in Italy. The driver pressed the horn button almost the whole way, swerving violently and continually to avoid the Libyan natives and their carts, at the same time kicking up a cloud of foul dust, making our trip hellishly uncomfortable.

Those of us who had laid their bets on going by 'plane won. The truck, suddenly bumping around, brought into view some of Mussolini's much misused Air Force. The truck pulled up outside the airfield offices where another reception party of guards waited to take charge of us. We were herded into a small enclosure to await the 'plane. The twenty-five of us who had arrived in our truck were to travel together and soon another truck pulled in and we were joined by a further twenty-five of our friends.

During our wait some of us had opportunity of discussing the possibilities of taking over the'plane when we were well clear of the coast. It was decided not to tell any of the others about our plan until we were actually airborne. The R.A.F. friend of mine was to try to infiltrate himself into the second bunch who were going in one 'plane while I, having a little experience of flying Tiger Moths in my teens, was to endeavour to go in the other 'plane. I realised what this meant to all concerned, but to gain one's liberty one is prepared to do almost anything. I became obsessed with the idea. Chatting with my fighter pilot chum, I refreshed my memory on some of the principles of flying and quickly tried to learn some points about the Italian made "Savoia" bomber as, being a tri-motor 'plane, it was somewhat different to the others. Furthermore, there was a possibility that if we did manage to take over control of the 'planes in the air, we might be able to force the pilots to fly them. So it was decided that we would knock out our guards, seize their arms and then force the pilot to fly us back to our own lines. This action was timed to start exactly one hour after leaving Benghazi in order to escape beyond the extreme range of our fighter patrols. We laughed at the tragedy which might befall us if we were to be shot down by one of our own aircraft on the way back to freedom, after being successful in taking control. No more was said for fear of our plans leaking out and the plotters dispersed so as to allay any suspicion of what was brewing.

Feeling more cheerful now we boarded the 'plane. I could not see the other party. The small windows in the fuselage were well below eye-level and as we crowded in with Italian soldiers going on leave there was no chance for us to peep outside the aircraft. As soon as the last man was in the door was slammed shut, and with a mighty roar we were quickly taxi-ing over the very bumpy ground to the landing strip. A sudden sharp bang caused the crew to bring the aircraft to a hasty stop, then it was confirmed that the tail wheel tyre had burst. The ground staff came out in a 'buggy' and changed the wheel.

At last we were on position for take-off, and as we waited for the signal to go from the control tower, an aching feeling of complete apathy came over me. I fought against that feeling. The fact that the guards were obviously not efficient revived my desire to try an escape at all costs.

To leave Africa was certainly a great event, but I had never contemplated this form of departure. The engines opened up fully with a deafening roar and we quickly became airborne. I had flown before many times and was used to take-offs but the uncertainty of what lay ahead almost caused nausea. Benghazi was immediately below. The block-like houses stood out very clearly, their white walls reflecting the brilliant sunshine. A convoy of vehicles was leaving the town going towards Derna on the black tarmac road. The view one received of the dock area was extremely heartening. Naval and merchant shipping had suffered very severely from our bombing. Wrecked vessels were lying on their sides or alongside the wharves, burnt out. They looked hideous with their shattered and twisted superstructures. "Our heavy bombers raided Benghazi last night for the fourth night in succession," was a frequent announcement on our radio. It did not seem to mean much to us when we were well up in the forward areas, but now we fully comprehended its significance.

As if hypnotised by the sight of leaving Benghazi and the desert for good, I stared long and steadily at the port and the long tragic coastline stretching for miles towards Derna. Quickly it receded and became smaller. Suddenly I felt that I did not want to leave the desert, which had been the scene of so many adventures and where so many friends remained, but I knew I was looking at Africa for the last time.

CHAPTER FIVE

As we were still within range of our long-distance fighter sweeps, the gunner busied himself between the mid-gun turret and the two waist guns. The weapons were point five inch heavy Bredas. Very, very faintly in the distance, beneath our tailplane, I could still see the African coastline. Inside the 'plane it was very hot and smelly. The heat, the gentle rise and fall of the aircraft and the penetrating drone from the three engines, were a powerful soporific. As the time drew nearer I began to think of our plan to escape. My excitement grew and my nerves became tense. Every thought was concentrated on the effort being successful. I watched the two pilots intently to see how they controlled the 'plane and no movement of the crew escaped me. The guards were sleeping with sagging heads. The soldiers at our feet had been asleep for quite some time. One of the guards was close to me, but fortunately I was the prisoner furthest away from the pilot's cabin.

Waiting until the gunner had walked once more to the gun-turret, I whispered my plan of action to the officer next to me who passed it on to the rest. Eagerly I looked along the two rows of officers facing each other and studied each face carefully for its reaction to my scheme. Would they co-operate? They must not let this chance slip by. Evidently there were two schools of thought. At first it seemed as if all were going to agree, then came the depressing decision — "No!"

I couldn't believe it. Why had they decided not to attempt the execution of this plan? It seemed so easy if everyone co-operated. I pleaded with them to reconsider, telling them I was confident of my ability to fly the 'plane if necessary, but feeling sure that we could force the pilots to fly us to our lines or Malta even. It was all to no avail.

The gunner fumbled his way between the legs of the sleeping soldiers in order to pull in the two waist guns and in so doing wakened up many of them. Then they began to chatter and excitedly peer out of the window. Through the window nearest me, I could see very clearly the rapidly approaching coastline of the heel of Italy. I remained watching until a lighthouse on the very tip of the coast seemed within touching distance of the 'plane as we flew steadily over it. Looking back, the colour of the sea appeared to merge with the colour of the sky and lose its beautiful blue. Below, the topography of the ground looked very attractive, with here and there tiny white villages nestling between the mountains. Many of these villages were built right on the tops of some of the mountains, with the village church being the highest building. Just a little white winding thread of a line marked the road which connected each village to the plains and the larger towns.

I felt the 'plane bank to the left, my ears went numb and then the pilot throttled back the engines and levelled out for the landing. We bumped down and came to a halt. We were greeted by a fairly strong guard who ordered us out of the aircraft. After counting us they ushered us on to waiting trucks which drove swiftly into what turned out to be the town of Lecce. As the trucks were open the inhabitants were not slow to recognise us as prisoners of war, and our welcome was far from friendly.

We travelled through the town and continued on for about four kilometres, finally passing under the archway of a fairly modern building where we came to a stop. The reception party guided us to a large room upstairs where we were to spend our first night on Italian soil. The building had been a cigarette factory and was quite substantial in its proportions.

We each selected a bed and having been issued with one blanket per man, we were getting ready to turn in when an orderly accompanied by a guard, came in with two large dixies of foul-smelling meat stew. Our unanimous opinion was that, judging from the smell, it could be none other than rotten horse meat. However it was very hot and was very welcome. After this we were left alone to settle down to a good night's sleep.

Next day, we were each issued with two cobs of bread and a two ounce size tin of horse meat and were then hustled on to waiting vehicles. We were counted and then the convoy moved off in a northerly direction. We were soon covered with the much-hated dust from the filthy unmetalled streets. There was no talk on that journey as everyone was feeling depressed. The country looked very beautiful. Fruit trees were in full blossom and showed to advantage against the green leaves and fields. A large town came into view and in a short while we found ourselves travelling through the streets, among the other vehicles. Arriving at a railway station, we discovered we were in Brindisi. It seemed a long time since I had seen a civilised town, but I was struck by the fact that the streets were untidy and could have done with a good cleaning up. The houses appeared bedraggled and needed repainting. The population, or a great part of it, stood about in groups, probably discussing the news of the recent successes of the *Afrika Korps* in Africa. I thought at the time that the Fascist system might have been given the credit for Italy's progressive empire overseas, but it certainly had forgotten to develop the villages and towns in this region. When our presence became known, hundreds of people from all corners of the square came to the front of the station, where we waited in the trucks. We were duly inspected by the converged crowds, which gave us some amusement. A few of them tried to take advantage of our position by coming right up to us to humiliate us with dirty misbehaviour, much to the amusement of our guards and some of the crowd.

Then, all at once, an Italian officer gave an order. The guards moved the crowd back and ordered us to dismount, whereupon they marched us inside the station. Three-quarters of an hour later, the same Italian officer reappeared and, much to our surprise, we were marched out of the station again. The streets were now thronged with masses of people, leaving only a narrow passage down the centre. For a moment we thought that this had been organised so as to give the civilians an opportunity to gloat over us. Surprisingly however, the guards kept moving us further towards the throng. Suddenly the crowd started to cheer and clap with tremendous jubilation. Immediately we were ordered to halt and to stand to attention. Above the heads of the people I saw a procession of cars appear, whereupon the crowd became almost hysterical. The first car passed slowly, then the second car appeared with several persons standing up in it. Arms shot out in salute for the car contained Italy's pugnacious dictator — Mussolini! We all got a good view of him because we were far taller than the average Italian.

He was dressed like the leading man in a comic opera, and was sticking his arms out in response to the thousands of cheers yelled by these misguided people. I was glad to have had the opportunity of seeing this wretched little man. During General Wavell's campaign I had found a poster of the face of Mussolini; he was ugly enough then, but here in person he was revolting.

The large car pulled closer towards me. He held his head upright and his jaw stuck out as though permanently dislocated. The chest of his light beige coat was almost completely covered in medal ribbons. Round his waist was a cheap Sam Browne belt.

Although the cars passed out of sight his unique figure had left a clear, but distasteful, impression. I was not sorry when the procession had passed and we resumed our march. The *Carabinieri,* who lined the route, held the crowds in check as we plodded across the town to another railway station. We were very relieved to get there and to be on our way further north. For the greater part of our journey we travelled along the coast, through field after field of almond groves. One of the officers drew our attention to a large town ahead which we gathered was Bari.

As the train pulled into the station we braced ourselves for the coming ordeal of being marched through the streets. As soon as we alighted on to the platform, some hooligans out of the large crowd began to shake their fists at us and some even lowered themselves to spitting in our faces. Hurriedly we were guided out of the *melée* beyond the station and on to a road which led us out to a transit camp which consisted of two very small compounds and two long wooden huts capable of holding fifty officers each. We were halted at the main gate and then, one by one, were taken before the commandant and his staff.

After being subjected to a thorough search and having our particulars noted, we passed into a small hut for a welcome shower bath. Here also our clothes went through the de-lousing process. After this, we were allowed to join our compatriots who had been in the camp some time before us. The welcome was simply wonderful. They surged forward to grasp our hands, pouring out questions at a great rate. Singly, we were escorted into the bungalow and shown to a bed. These beds were of a double-decker type far from comfortable but, after a long day of travelling and many hours without a substantial meal, they were welcome enough.

For my night attire I slept only in my shirt, for which I was sorry, because when I awakened in the morning, I was a mass of flea bites! It was rather funny, yet pathetic, as we helped each other to hunt fleas. As time went on this became a regular habit on each awakening. There was always jubilation when an inmate claimed to have caught the most number of the pestering insects!

Two officers had been detailed to collect the coffee ration and at seven o'clock in the morning. We each received a small cupful of coffee. At first the taste was repulsive but I persevered as it was warm and refreshing. The fellow who slept in the bottom bunk below me told me not to worry too much about this as the coffee was the staple drink for the prisoners; it was made, he said, from sunflower seeds.

I was glad to get out of that 'bug house' and stroll about in the compound. In the centre was an Italian tent which housed some of the most wretched specimens of humanity that I had ever seen. For a long time I puzzled as to their nationality and to satisfy my curiosity, I strolled over and began chatting to them. They were dressed in old, ragged garments, some were half naked and all were bare-footed. This, I subsequently found out, was in order to save their boots. To my surprise two of them had on a battle-dress type of jacket and I recognised them as R.A.F. sergeants. Although imprisoned in this dump for many a month they showed a true spirit of discipline and courtesy when I spoke to them. It was a very touching episode. They had not seen any British officers or men for a very long time and their joy was plainly visible. With a thrilling desire to hear fresh news they relished every single item of topical interest. They even excused themselves for being so poorly dressed. It was ironic to think that my filthy and sand-stained shirt, shorts and a pair of desert boots should seem to be sartorial elegance.

A great consolation were the hot rays of the sun which kept our skins fairly healthy. Two of us went in search of the ablution facilities and found, at the bottom of the compound, a stone trough with two taps at either end. I don't think I ever remember drinking any water that tasted so refreshing or so cold. Although it felt like ice compared to the outside temperature, my friend and I splashed in the trough to cleanse our begrimed skins. Our shouts drew others also and soon there was hardly a space for any man to wash. We were all youngsters again, as one or two of the brighter elements began to drench one another. Strange how human happiness lies often just below the surface. The sudden change from filth to cleanliness made us feel wholly rejuvenated and boosted our self-respect.

After this we brought our blankets out into the compound and sunbathed until lunch. This, when it arrived, consisted of a handful of cherries, one thin slice of cheese and the daily issue of one cob of bread per man. The meal over we returned to our blankets and lazed again in the sun. Our evening meal consisted of vegetable soup with a couple of pieces of macaroni floating on top. To work off the effects of this large banquet we strolled round and round the tiny compound until we became almost dizzy. While strolling, we talked of the future when we should arrive home once more. At sunset we turned in and, lying on our beds, carried on talking until the flies and mosquitoes forced us under the blankets with the fleas for company.

Badgered by the flies and the mosquitoes almost beyond endurance, and with a stifling atmosphere in the room, sleep was impossible. Morning found us tired, weak and consequently dizzy. For days we received just coffee in the morning and weak soup for our main meal. After five days on these starvation rations the majority could only stand on their feet for a short while. I became so weak that one of the new arrivals did me the kindness of bringing my meals to me in bed. To illustrate the sorry state we were in, one day a senior officer thought he had received smaller rations than a junior officer, who had been served before him. The latter had received a ladle of soup with eight pieces of macaroni, whereas the senior officer received only five! Though the younger officer was not to blame in the matter, the older man, his nerves frayed to an edge by his sufferings, vented his anger most unjustly on the subaltern. Scenes like this occurred frequently. The strains and stress under which we lived were a testing ground where a weak character could not survive.

We were two whole weeks in this condition with no variation in the food, and, to make things worse, we heard rumours that eight thousand officers, mostly South Africans, were arriving any day. The Italians told us that Tobruk had fallen and that the whole garrison of forty thousand men had been captured. We laughed at them and said that it was preposterous but inwardly we felt that some disaster had befallen our army and that it was actually quite possible, although we believed the number of prisoners claimed had been greatly exaggerated.

The next two days were spent in moving from the bug-ridden bungalows to a new set of brick buildings just below our compound. These were built in blocks and at one end of each block was a tiny compound, capable of holding about a hundred officers.

About ten o'clock, on the second day, hordes of South African officers arrived. From our hut we could see right up the road to the main gate so we watched them all arriving. We estimated that they totalled over two thousand. All appeared very cheery and glad to have reached their first transit camp. We were locked in our compound and were not allowed to mix with our compatriots. All we were able to do was to shake hands with them through the wire fence as they were herded past for their interrogation in the top compound. After the interrogation the South Africans were crowded in with us, with the result that there was hardly room to walk about.

We pumped the South Africans for news. What a pathetic story they had to tell. Many of them had been captured within the perimetre of Tobruk, having been completely unaware that the Germans had occupied the key points in the town. It seemed that orders had been received from the Officer Commanding to cease fire and surrender. We sympathised with men who had to obey that surrender order without a fight. The majority of the South

Africans, although appearing to be very cheery, could not help giving us the impression that they felt shame at having to surrender en masse. No-one knew who was to blame, yet it was evident at that time that someone had blundered.

No sooner had the new arrivals settled down than the call was received to line up. We queued up outside near the gate to receive our meagre rations. Little did we know that the food we had been eating previously was regarded as a fairly good meal. I received half a mess tin full of watery soup which contained precisely five pieces of macaroni together with several blades of grass and the top of some herb. With my small cob of bread I went back and sat on my bed, hoping this was not going to be the last meal for that day.

In the afternoon, as the compound was far too crowded to take even a couple of paces, I lay on my bed and talked to some of the new arrivals. Throughout that evening every man was expecting the call for "Grub up," but we waited in vain. The ditch water was our last meal of the day.

On July 5th 1942, an Italian officer interpreter came into the compound and read out the names of the officers who were to be sent to a permanent camp. One part was despatched to a camp in the north of Italy. Half an hour later a second party, including myself, were told that we were being sent to Padula, south of Salerno. Extremely hungry and somewhat excited, I collected together my belongings. Soon we found ourselves marching to the station where we had a long wait. During this time an Italian officer came up to me and, to my utter astonishment, spoke to me in a broad American accent. He told me that he had come to Italy on a holiday before the Abyssinian war. On applying for his papers to return to America he was politely told that he would have to join the Italian army, and his papers had been confiscated. He was very sympathetic and bought us some books from the bookstall. Then, wishing us good luck, he vanished amongst the crowd. At long last the train came in and we were hustled aboard. We had a first-class compartment and settling ourselves down for a long journey we gazed out the window at the Italians.

Speculating upon the kind of reception we would receive at our new camp, one officer ironically painted a picture of our being conducted to our quarters by a courteous reception committee. There would even be a Red Cross parcel for each man! After being shown to our lovely, comfortable beds, we would be escorted to the mess for a very big dinner, where a band would be playing our favourite music throughout the meal. Next would come a hot shower so we could be in a fit state to receive the many gifts that would be showered upon us. We all laughed uproariously!

Through glorious country we travelled on. Parts were mountainous with the railway running through deep ravines. Only an artist could have done justice to the beauty of the flowers and fruit blossoms clothing the hillsides. In the open country near Naples were fields upon fields of different cereals, and in a suburb outside the city I saw a small amount of tobacco being grown.

We arrived in Naples about dusk and so did not see much of the town. The environs of railway stations are notoriously depressing the world over and Naples was no exception. Several factories were visible, going full blast on war production. Soon we were off again, and the slow movement of the train sent me off to sleep. In the early hours of the morning I awoke and learned that we had passed Salerno a couple of hours earlier, and that soon we would be at Padula.

We finally pulled into a tiny station, and reading the name on a hoarding as big as the station itself, we saw that we had arrived at Padula. To shouts of "*Veniti-veniti,*" we then scrambled out of the train on to the platform, to be counted once again. This check completed, off we marched up a long lane towards a little village perched on the side of the mountain. Below this village we could see a large, long, grey stone building surrounded by massive high walls. It had been an Italian monastery and was now our new prisoner-of-war camp. How we cursed the sun and the sun-baked earth. Clouds of thick white dust were flung up into our faces by the marching feet in front. We had been a long time without a drink and our throats soon became parched. By the time we reached the main gates of the monastery we were quite tired.

The sentries at the gate were regular *Carabinieri* wearing a peculiar type of tricorn hat. Inside the gate was a cobbled court-yard, surrounded by stone buildings which were the guards' quarters. At the far end, opposite the main gate, a massive flight of steps led up through a large archway into a stone flagged cloister. Presently, through huge iron-studded doors, the Commandant and his staff came out. One by one we were taken into the office, searched, interrogated and then handed over to the guards who escorted us to our own part of the camp.

Before passing through the solid wooden doors, I glanced back through the arch-way to the main gate and for a painful moment I felt that never again would I see the outside world, nor my home and friends. It made me utterly miserable. So absorbed was I by the pleasant sight of freedom beyond the main gate that I was deaf to the orders from my guards. A firm grasp on my arm and a push brought me sharply out of my day-dream and I found myself behind closed doors. The shock of realising that I was imprisoned made me feel physically sick and deprived me of any initiative.

CHAPTER SIX

Suddenly I heard a clear voice say, "Can I help?" It was a young lieutenant and with him was a young R.A.F. pilot officer. They took us into their Red Cross parcel store, where, to our bewilderment, we gazed at hundreds of the famous and greatly prized parcels. There were tears in my eyes as I saw those wonderful packages and realised what they contained. Decent food at last! An Italian orderly opened a parcel and with the spike of a jack-knife prodded each tin, then handed the parcel over to me. I grasped it with the feverish excitement of a poor child receiving its first Christmas present and hurried out of the room. What a thrill I had inspecting the mysteries of this great gift! I remember saying to my newly-acquired friends that I would 'bash' the lot in one sitting as everything appeared so delicious. As long as I live I shall never forget the moment I first saw that parcel. Carrying it under my arm and gazing at the contents every few minutes to see that I had not dropped any tin or packet, I was escorted up into the rooms above the cloisters where the prisoners slept. Down a corridor at the side of a long row of beds, officers were busy playing cards and making strange things out of pieces of tin. They stopped their work and each said, "Welcome. Glad to see you." Finally they found me a bed and left me to settle in. But the parcel held so many little plain packages that my curiousity got the better of me and I had to open every one. There was a bar of chocolate, a small packet of sweets, a tablet of soap, a tin of cheese, a tin of sugar, a large tin of apple pudding, a tin of condensed milk, a tin of margarine, a tin of bacon, a tin of meat and vegetables, a tin of salmon, a packet of tea and a tin of jam. So as to be able to gaze at them I arranged all these delectable treasures on the top of the cupboard which was beside my bed.

A bugle sounded just below my window, making me jump almost out of my wits. The fellows around me said that it was the call for "Grub up." Along came my two new-found friends to show me the way down to the Mess. Before following them I carefully placed my treasures inside the cupboard. I was led into the old refectory along with the other chaps who came from Bari. Our astonishment knew no bounds when, on entering, we were greeted by music played by the camp band! I could not believe my ears, nor my eyes, for they were all dressed in a costume of white and navy blue slacks, with a large red sash around their waists.

I looked round the hall. Tables were sticking out from the side walls, leaving a corridor down the centre of the Mess. Each table was covered with a different coloured check cloth. The blues, reds and greens certainly brightened the place up. Each man's place was laid out with cheap, but nevertheless correct cutlery, and on every table stood a vase of flowers. Orderlies were standing beside each table waiting to serve up as soon as we were seated. No sooner had I sat down than a plate of soup was placed in front of me. With this we were given a cob of bread, the equivalent of the normal size we used to eat at home. Later I was to learn that this small cob was our twenty-four hour ration of bread. The second course was cottage-pie, cabbage, potatoes and gravy. I was hungry and ate mine far too quickly, for when I had finished I wanted to start all over again. It was really tasty, and far beyond the dreams that I had had in the desert as to what a good meal should be. My empty plate was whipped away and the sweet was put in its place. It was a good solid apple dumpling with custard. By jove, it was good! — but all too soon my plate was empty again.

With the dance band still playing familiar music we sat back drinking our Italian coffee and smoking one of the Red Cross issue Capstan cigarettes. Thus we stayed for a further quarter of an hour.

when we were led off to prepare for a hot shower! By this time we were all quite bewildered, for it seemed that our dreams and hopes were now becoming reality.

While I was preparing for my shower my two friends explained the system which allowed the camp to have meals such as the one we had just enjoyed. Parcel day was every week but on alternate weeks, we would hand in all meat tins, fish and puddings to the Mess caterer. Judging from the meal we had just eaten, such a scheme fully justified its institution. As soon as I was ready, I was shown downstairs to the showers. An officer was controlling the temperature of the hot and cold flow. He gave me and the other new arrivals the signal to get under. Wow! It was hot! How long I remained under the showers I do not know, but I revelled in the hot water and felt the longer I remained there the lighter I became! It was a wonder really that the drains did not block up, for the amount of dirt on us was considerable.

The shower over, we were taken on a tour of the camp. The monastery had belonged to the Carthusian Order and dated back to the fifteenth century; the cloisters were reputed to be the longest in the world and the enclosed square was capable of holding seventy thousand people. Opening off the cloisters were what had been the private rooms of the monks. These were now occupied by our senior officers. The larger rooms held up to ten. Above the cloisters a continuous gallery ran right round the four sides of the square. We divided this gallery into wings, numbered one to four, and for documentation purposes those in each wing were thus identified. At the north-west corner of the buildings was a very fine double spiral staircase built in marble which led out into a field at the back. This was our recreation ground.

The actual compound was approximately one hundred and fifty yards long and fifty yards wide. Round the perimeter ran a barbed wire fence with a machine-gun post at each corner. Outside this was a further space, approximately twenty five yards wide, bounded by a high stone wall in some places thirty feet high. At the top end of the compound were a few olive trees. My fellow prisoners had already marked out a soccer pitch and, judging by the look of the grass, it had been well used.

Coming back to the living quarters, I noticed the beds were in pairs, placed parallel right up each wing. Between each pair of beds was a cupboard to serve two. There were no partitions at the ends of the wings, so smoke drifted from all parts of the galleries, which reminded me of a London Underground station on a busy night.

As I toured each wing I was intrigued to see many officers engaged in hammering small pieces of tin while some were cutting up empty tin cans and others were playing bridge. The less energetic were lounging on their beds reading. Here and there, amidst all the hammering, chatter and smoke, individuals were trying to play some instrument. Bitterly I realised that sooner or later I would have to settle down to the hubbub and confinement and forget my longing for freedom. Only those who have been deprived of liberty can truly appreciate the feelings of a prisoner-of-war.

That evening, as I admired the sunset and the view of the valley from the top step of the massive spiral staircase, I wondered how long I would remain here. The shouting of the guards to the prisoners in the compound that it was now time to turn in, brought me abruptly back to reality. I went to my bed in number one wing at the south end of the compound and tried to cheer myself up by opening my cupboard to stare once again at the contents of the wonderful Red Cross parcel. One by one I took the tins out and gazed at them, not from the lack of something to eat, for the meal earlier that night had been like a banquet, but to dwell on that great spirit back home, the careful packing and the generous subscriptions that our people had made in support of this fine cause. Making certain that there were no tins left out, I replaced them, locked the cupboard and turned in.

During the night heavy footsteps approached the corridor. Without warning the bedclothes were suddenly whisked off my bed! The guards wished to be certain that a prisoner and not a dummy, occupied the bed. Cursing them silently for chilling me, I realised that they were up to some of our tricks of deception — that they were alerted against our attempts to escape from captivity.

The following morning I became better acquainted with my fellow prisoners and the general routine of prison camp life. I spent the remainder of the day in finding out how the officers made the ingenious contraptions which they called *stuffas.* This word was Italian for stove. First one collected some empty biscuit tins, then the lids and bases were cut to shape with a pair of nail scissors or a penknife, and then next the sides were flattened out. Several sheets were then joined together to form the body of the stove, while from another sheet small and large circles were cut out to form the top. By scrounging around the camp men had found a few tiles from which to make a base, and these were bedded in cement stolen from an Italian working party. This made the firebox, and half a dozen or so cocoa tins joined together made a chimney. The holes in the top of the stove, which seemed a strange shape at first, were designed to take the Italian mess tin. Then came the problem of fuel. The Italians refused to issue any, but the problem was solved by using pieces of timber from the roof of the Monastery. Having learned the method of construction I quickly went on the scrounge and, aided by my own tins, was soon able to build myself a *stuffa.* It was great fun, but before I drafted my plans I studied the better type of *stuffas.* Within a week I had built a little *stuffa* with an oven attached. It worked very well, although I soon found that it burned more fuel than I was able to scrounge.

Tuesday was the day when our wing collected its parcels so on this day every week I became as excited as a small boy and I could hardly wait in the queue to collect mine. When I had received it I wasted no time in rummaging about among the tins to see what wonderful surprises were there. Some of the older lags would immediately commence bargaining with one another for different articles and large-scale swappings took place. Back in the wings officers would appear from all parts of the camp hawking items they wanted to exchange. This, at first, was very amusing for they were evidently past masters at the art of bartering!

One or two officers had managed to buy, through the Italians, some fencing irons, and as I was very keen on this sport I too placed an order and joined the class. It was not long before my irons arrived — a foil and a sabre. We were taught by a former British champion, and for a couple of hours a day for several months I learnt the art of fencing.

Being also keen on soccer and rugger I was able to join the wing teams and, as inter-wing competitions had been arranged, I was lucky enough to play often. On Saturday afternoons we usually played in, or watched, a match between the Army versus the Navy and Air Force, or England versus Scotland, or inter-regimental matches. Even watching was always interesting, and the excitement of the spectators and the sporting atmosphere brought one's home background somehow closer, and took one completely out of the life of a prisoner-of-war. Oranges could be obtained from the Italians and we provided the teams with refreshments at half-time which all helped to create the right setting. I don't think there was a single match played without Brigadiers Martin and Sneddon and Commander Scarlet R.N., our leading spectators, being present. Brigadier Martin, Indian Army, was the Senior British Officer at the camp.

Being in southern Italy at that time of year we enjoyed beautiful weather, and as a sun-lover I was able to take full advantage of the sunbathing and being out of doors as much as possible. It was at this camp that I took up painting. The glorious countryside was fascinating and picturesque and encouraged this pastime. I was able to buy my water-colours through the Italian canteen.

First roll-call was at nine o'clock each morning. After dismissal I would tidy up around my bed and wash my dirty clothes. Then I would spend a couple of hours at my favourite sport, fencing. A bugle-call announced lunch, when we ate the usual meal of risotto (rice with sauce). After lunch I would take my blanket into the field and would pass the time painting or reading a book, whilst sun-bathing, until half-an-hour before dinner. Again, at a bugle-call we would all collect and enter the Mess to sit at our usual places. Dinner was a more elaborate meal. We would have part of the Italian issue of vegetables made into soup, and the rest served with our second course. Along with the vegetables for the second course we would have some kind of meat or a tin of stew from the Red Cross parcels. The sweet, on the few occasions we had one, consisted of small tins of various kinds of puddings, also taken from the Red Cross parcels. One tin would be shared by three officers. On many a Saturday we had music from the band playing for us during the first and second sittings of dinner. On Sunday mornings, church services were held in the Mess. It was a grand sight to see the Navy, Army and Air Force officers who were lucky enough to have their service dress uniforms with them, entering the church together. After the service the officers would walk round and round the cloisters until lunch-time. Usually on Sunday afternoons we would hold the big soccer matches, drawing practically the whole camp as spectators. Although there were only about six hundred officers in the camp, I am sure the cheering from the touch lines equalled that of the big matches at home. During the hot summer evenings the majority of officers used the compound to have a quiet stroll or sit out until sent back in by the guards.

The *nominale* or roll-call was held in the mornings at nine o'clock and at approximately five-thirty in the evenings. Each wing formed up in lines, which were separated by two guards with fixed bayonets. Often we had to wait quite some time for the Italian orderly officer and the Interpreter with his orderly N.C.O. to come along and count our numbers. The soldiers of the Italian garrison were mostly much smaller in size than the average British Officer, and so on many occasions when the guards stood between us we would play tricks on them. One day we saved our oranges issue and hid them in our pockets when we went on parade. Then, when the guards had taken up their positions and settled themselves for a long wait, we stealthily stuck our oranges on the ends of their bayonets! Throughout the whole ceremony the guards were unaware of what had happened. It was only when the orderly sergeant organised his men to fall in that they realised what we had done. Then the fun started. Bitter protests were made to our senior officers but this had no effect on us — we were hysterical with laughter.

Escapes were continually being attempted and it was always amazing to me how the escaper managed to keep his endeavours unknown to the majority of the camp. Tunnels and escape equipment were being made practically every day, but only a mere handful knew this. When such attempts had been frustrated by the Italians the bugle would immediately sound for roll-call. Every soldier in the garrison would be mobilised, those who were not guarding us were sent into our wings to carry out a search and to take possession of the escaper's property for thorough scrutiny. As a reprisal, all *stuffas* in the wing concerned in the escape were destroyed. Standing below in the cloisters, we would look up to see our *stuffas* suddenly come flying out of a window to break into pieces on the ground; parts that were still not broken were trampled underfoot. As each *stuffa* descended we would cheer for all we were worth. On these occasions we were kept on parade anything from one to three hours at a time.

Another occasion I remember well was the day we were ordered out into the courtyard, in order of wings and in single file we had to pass a table where the Commandant and his staff were searching for, and confiscating, articles of value, such as rings, cigarette cases, silver pencils and any small articles made of gold or silver. The word went down the line as to the nature of this parade, whereupon those waiting their turn to be searched frantically removed rings and so forth, and hid them in odd corners of the courtyard. After passing the table each man was ordered to the far side of the compound, and only when the whole camp had been dealt with were we allowed to return to our quarters. The Officers who had had articles of value confiscated were assured that these items would be kept for them and deposited in the Bank of Italy under the auspices of the State Maggiore. Needless to say, their haul was very unrewarding!

We had only one large-scale escape when one night, after tunnelling underneath the outer wall from one of the downstairs rooms, thirteen officers made their exit only two feet away from a sentry-box, and right in the corner of a maize field. Luckily for them the sentry was sound asleep so they made their get-away comfortably. The escape was discovered the following day and in consequence our kit and *stuffas* received the usual treatment. We were always delighted when some chaps made an escape and we all cheerfully tolerated the consequences.

We were very sorry to see the summer come to an end and, as the Italian rations were diminishing week by week, we had grim visions of the coming winter. At four thousand feet up in the mountains we anticipated plenty of snow and a great deal of rain. Presently the winter season did set in and about the end of October we had the first fall of snow. The majority of us possessed only the khaki drill apparel in which we had been captured in the desert, and still our next-of-kin parcels had not arrived. Each day, when the officer in charge of mail posted up a list of those who had received either letters or parcels, the whole camp would scramble down to the mailing office and badger him. Week after week we were disappointed, and so throughout the winter of 1942 we passed our time lying on our beds wrapped in every available piece of clothing and huddled in our blankets. Whenever we went for a stroll around the cloisters, we wrapped our blankets round our waists like skirts, in order to keep our bare legs warm. The desert knew how to be cold but never had I been as cold as I was during that winter.

We had very little sport during those winter months. It seemed too that we were kept out on roll-calls for longer than was necessary. It was a hard struggle to stand for a couple of hours in the bitter weather and with an empty stomach.

For Christmas we had saved some odd tins from our Red Cross parcels and these, together with the last issue of parcels to arrive before Christmas, were handed over to the Mess to provide our Christmas fare. Since the summer and throughout the beginning of the winter some enterprising officers had kept a couple of pigs in a downstairs room and had been fattening them up on the swill from the Mess.

Just before Christmas, when the pigs were ready for slaughter, the guards seized them with the excuse that an order had been received from the State Maggiore that all animals belonging to prisoners-of-war had to be confiscated. We, of course, would not listen to this nonsense and there was quite a fight between the Commandant and his staff and our own orderly room personnel. So that we should not be robbed of our Christmas fare, one of our officers who was in charge of the Mess broke into the room where the pigs were kept and retrieved the beasts. It was decided to slaughter them and hide the carcases in our kitchen. When the guards found out what we had done they were extremely angry and confiscated the fat!

On Christmas Day we sang a song depicting the life and death of the much-discussed pigs to the tune of *The Three Little Fishes who Swam and Swam all over the Dam*. The kitchen staff filed in, dressed for the occasion, bearing the roasted heads and carcases of the pigs on huge platters. The whole effort caused much excitement and much cheering from the officers. How the Mess caterer had managed to create such a huge, delectable meal as we had that day was quite beyond my comprehension. Throughout the feast the band played under an ornate canopy. The entire Mess was beautifully decorated and the tables displayed vases of imitation flowers. For the evening's celebration after the meal, the prisoners who had saved up their wine issues proceeded to make merry and in no time the whole camp was a riot of fun. An arrangement had been made between the Italian Commandant and our S.B.O. that we would be allowed an armistice for Christmas Day and that all prisoners-of-war would be placed on parole. Lights out was extended from the usual time of 10.30 a.m. until midnight and throughout the day not a single guard entered our compound.

I was sorry when Christmas was over for we could only look ahead to the grim months of still colder periods before the spring. When we went round the wings to play bridge with our friends, we would take with us a Red Cross cardboard box with paper shavings in the bottom to use as a foot muff. This was quite effective but far from satisfactory. For months we dreaded the nights, even though we wanted to sleep to forget the monotony and dreariness of prison life. Only on rare occasions did I pass a night without shivering continuously from the time I went to bed until the time I awoke. Long icicles greeted us each morning as we looked out of the window hoping for better weather. As the weeks rolled by, this hope became a fervent prayer.

At last, after an interminable absence through the long winter the sun came out and as the days passed the snow diminished. What a wonderful reaction there was to the sun's rays. We became lighter of spirit and began once more to take an interest in life. Soccer games took precedence over any other sport.

Flowers began to appear in the valley and the mountain-sides changed from deep brown to light shades of green. It was a pleasure now to stand on the massive staircase and watch the quickening of nature. I remembered how often I had stood on these steps during the winter looking out across the valley on the rain and snow-sodden field, watching the villagers going slowly about their daily tasks. At that time I had felt that life had completely gone from our surroundings, and had been morbidly tempted to end it all. Now I was glad that those horrible thoughts had been conquered for the spring gave me a greater incentive to battle on and to withstand what was yet to come. My limbs had lost their numbness and now ached for exercise so during the spring of 1943 I played as many games of rugger and soccer as possible. Walking around the compound it was heartening to see the officers with smiling faces.

One day a rumour leaked out that a large party of officers was to be repatriated; this turned out to be correct, the lucky ones being Naval personnel. They had been captured in the Red Sea, on the Mediterranean and were being exchanged for Italian prisoners-of-war. When the day came for them to go, the whole camp crowded round the main gate that led into the Italian compound and gave them a great send-off. Many carried messages from the rest of us to loved ones at home. Not long after this another rumour leaked out and, thanks to our efficient news agency, we soon learnt which officers were concerned and where they were going. This time it was not a case of repatriation but a transfer to another camp.

Following these two occasions a further list of names appeared on the orderly-room notice-board and, to my surprise, I found my name amongst them. Twenty-three of us were to be moved to *Campo Concentrimento,* P.G. 49, Fontanellato, in the north of Italy. No-one had the slightest idea of where that was, nor of the type of camp, but any sort of change was welcome and lightened our spirits.

The following day we departed, amid a noisy send-off, like the others. We shook hands with the two Brigadiers and in answer to the *Bon Voyage* greetings from our chums we wished them God-speed home and good luck.

CHAPTER SEVEN

It was a great thrill to be outside that main gate and although we were surrounded by numerous guards the feeling of being free from the encompassing wall was glorious. Slinging our belongings on our shoulders we marched off down the dusty track to the station in great style. Although we had just endured a grim winter and were hampered by our kit, we paced along so fast that for almost the whole of the four kilometres, the guards had to run from time to time to keep up. As we were few, there was no special train, but several first-class compartments had been reserved for us on a civilian train and we quickly settled in. Almost immediately we steamed out of the station. Unfortunately the train travelled too quickly for us to make any attempt to escape. Apart from this there were two guards at each door, two sitting beside the window opposite each other and two more at the other end of each seat, all with fixed bayonets. We travelled like this for three solid days, in an atmosphere charged with garlic.

Italian soldiers coming and going on leave were travelling on the same train. Some of them did not conduct themselves very well, stopping at our door and, after babbling to us in Italian, spitting vulgarly in to our compartments before proceeding on their way. Our protests only brought laughter from the guards.

We did not see much of Naples as we were shunted on to sidings behind the town, where we remained for several hours. Between Naples and Rome the country was beautiful and a mass of colour. Our appreciation was sadly impaired by the fact that we were suffering from cramp and drowsiness from the foul air.

Rome was reached very late at night and all we could see of the city was the brilliantly illuminated station. Here we waited for several hours, until we were shunted on to a siding about four miles from the city, where we remained for half a day. In the afternoon we moved off again, bound for Pisa. During this trip I fell asleep and awakened with some surprise to find that we were just entering the town. It was early morning on the second day of the journey. We stayed there for a further half-day and from the train we had an excellent view of the famous Leaning Tower

The country from Pisa onwards, through the Apennine Mountains, was simply magnificent. The massive mountains in all their ruggedness swept gracefully down to the valleys which were full of vineyards and apple groves. The peasant houses differed from further south for these were larger, had more highly-decorated balconies and were cleaner in appearance. Many of these houses had bunches of red tomatoes hanging from their balconies, ripening in the sun. Their brilliant colour added to the general picturequeness. With some effort I could just see the tops of some of the steep mountains covered in fir trees. It seemed to me quite extraordinary that trees perched in such precarious positions could find sufficient water and soil to live.

We came out of these beautiful valleys on to the vast expanse of the Lombardy Plain. The railway ran through small villages and took us straight through to Bologna. It was not possible to see much of the town as we were taken round the outskirts to join the main railway line just outside the centre of the city.

Here some of our officers were ordered on to the platform and were formed up in fives. They were going to a camp near the city while the remainder, including myself, were going to the much-talked of Fontanellato. We were not allowed to leave our seats so we waved to them and wished them good luck from inside the compartments. A few minutes later the train pulled away.

We travelled on for a further three quarters of an hour and finally halted at a small country station — our destination. To the accompaniment of much excitement from our guards, we all scrambled out of the train and collected on the platform. Strangely enough the Italians failed to count us, but just said "*Avanti.*" Suddenly, after the train had jerked into motion, we heard a voice yelling from one of the windows! It was one of our fellows who had been left on the train. Apparently he could not find his odd bits of luggage and was too occupied to notice that we had already left the train. To our amusement, the Italians tried to run after the train, leaving us completely alone except for the station master who was too bewildered to appreciate the situation. Neither the engine driver nor the guard of the train knew what was happening and the train carried on gaining speed rapidly. Finally our guards gave up the chase and arriving back completely exhausted they began remonstrating with us as if we had organised the affair. We laughed as loud as we could to embarrass the Italians and sat down on our kit greatly enjoyed the ensuing argument between the guards and the station master.

Marching down a long, narrow road for about six kilometres, we finally reached a small village with a very modern stone building on our right which was surrounded by a double barbed wire fence, partially completed. Passing the sentries posted on either side of the main gate we entered the courtyard which faced the road where we were immediately greeted by fellow prisoners who themselves had only been in the camp for a couple of days.

Feeling like lost sheep and showing the effects of our long and tiring journey we were made to wait in the compound for some considerable time before we were marched into the building. Some of the officers with me had already recognised friends they had not seen for several months, or even years.

Once we were inside, the Italian guards left us alone to find our own accommodation. This was made easier by the willingness of the inmates to show us to our rooms, which were spread over different parts of the 'E' shaped building. The welcome was very cordial and in no time we made many good friends.

The room on the ground floor to which I went had a very pleasant view of the front compound of the camp and the main gate leading into a field. When settled, I was shown to the quartermaster's stores and there I drew two blankets. To my great relief these blankets were larger and very much warmer than any issued in previous camps. I was also issued with an Italian dixie, and an odd pair of underpants and a vest from clothing sent to us by the Red Cross. It was reassuring to know that this brand new camp was already known to the Red Cross authorities at Geneva. The Q.M. assured us that those who were badly equipped with clothing would receive an issue from the first supplies that came through.

Later we were taken on a tour of the building which had been built as a Roman Catholic Girls' Orphanage School with money from the convent next door. It had however, never been used for this purpose. We each had a spring bed, a cupboard and a mattress. The whole building had tiled floors and very modern lighting equipment. After the filth of Padula it was a joy to be in a place like this. The building was designed with a large hall in the centre, for use as a church, with a balcony running down both sides. At the opposite end from the altar this balcony led off both sides of the hall into two wings, each with a further two wings set at right angles on either side, forming a huge letter 'E'. Near the stairs leading into the hall from both wings were two ornate double doors. Opposite was the much larger front entrance to the whole building. Immediately above the front door, on the first floor on part of the balcony, the prisoners had made a long bar where we could draw our daily issue of red wine, Chianti, Vermouth or Marsala. Obviously this was a great improvement on the ordinary red wine dispensed by the authorities at Padula. The ground floor of the building was about four feet above ground level and underneath, in the basements, were shower baths, a food store, the kitchen and three dining rooms. The dining rooms were furnished with large tables covered with white table clothes and set with excellent cutlery with a glass tumbler beside each place. Everywhere looked spotlessly clean and seemed too good to be true.

As I was being shown around an Italian officer strolled in smoking a pipe and, to my surprise, he spoke perfect English. He told me that his name was Camino, that he had an English wife and that he had lived for twenty-five years in England before the war, working as manager in an Italian bank in London. He showed every willingness to meet our administrative staff's requirements and I was told that all the pleasant things there, such as the decent dining-rooms and the sleeping amenities, were the result of his splendid work.

At the back of the camp was a courtyard paved with large pebbles similar to those on the beaches back home. It was surrounded by a double barbed wire fence with a sentry path between them. This courtyard was roughly twenty yards wide and a hundred yards long. In the centre of the double barbed wire fence were two gates leading out into a field which was being prepared as an added compound. Eagerly we watched day by day the completion of our sports field.

After a few weeks I became used to the routine in this camp. The roll calls were the same as at Padula, and after that we were left to our own devices for amusement. The Italians co-operated in finding us the articles we required for sale in our canteen, and through this I was able to buy some oil paints and drawing materials. Red Cross supplies arrived fairly regularly and we were never short of those great food parcels. Dental equipment had been provided and our own dentist had a room to himself for a surgery. There was also a first class Medical Inspection room, partly built up with our own Red Cross equipment and partly with Italian; added to this we had our own hospital.

All told, it was reputed to be the best camp in Italy and I, for one, did not doubt this. It was a great relief to find that we no longer had to scrounge around the camp for fuel for our *stuffas*. All that messy and laborious work in cooking our food under trying conditions was now over. Not once during my stay here did I see any officers use or make *stuffas*.

For meals the camp was divided into two sittings and as we were organised into battalion compound — with three companies — each company had its own dining hall. The food was more than satisfactory, for the contents of the Red Cross parcels were supplemented by the Italian rations. All our parcels were handed into the Mess for communal feeding except the chocolate and sweets, which each man kept. This was a good arrangement, for it allowed everyone to have a greater variety of food.

Although we were in new surroundings and clean quarters, prison life was just the same as we had been used to, but there was one consolation. The weather had become very hot now, making it possible for us to remain out of doors the whole day. After months of sunbathing I was as brown as a berry and feeling very fit.

By the end of the first month the Italians had completed the wire fencing round the sports field and the day when the double gates were opened we all rushed into the field like a lot of youngsters. We began at once to make our own soccer pitch and provide further facilities for basket ball.

True to the traditions of P.O.W. life, the 'Cloak and Dagger' section was constantly thinking out methods of escape, and with the co-operation of the camp in general, preparations were put in motion for a first-class escape. Day after day, officers who were used to taking their blankets out into the field to lie on for sunbathing were asked to hide in their roll of blanket a small bag of soil from the tunnel which was being dug under the basement. Although there were guards patrolling around the grounds during the day, not once did they have any suspicion that large quantities of soil were being brought out of the building and dumped into the field.

Besides this, an alternative plan was being matured. A group of officers were making a basket-ball pitch, levelling it out and extending it towards the building, filling in the dips in the undulating part of the field. While this was going on, the actual party concerned in the proposed escape attempt brought out many lengths of thin planking each being one yard long. These were placed across a high part of the ground and covered with soil to a depth of between nine inches to a foot. Before the boards were put into place, by first removing some of the soil, enough space was made to permit three officers to lie in safety underneath them. All this preparation went on completely unnoticed by either the patrolling sentries or by those who were on guard in the machine gun posts at the four corners of the compound.

As those operations progressed, we camouflaged our activites by organising games of basketball, soccer and a team of P.T. enthusiasts to play with a medicine ball; as well as this a group of officers arranged to sit in a circle with their camp chairs positioned at the mouth of this trench to cover the movements of the escapers who were testing it. Once or twice we thought the Italians had discovered our activities. After we had left the compound as usual at six o'clock, we would nervously look out of the windows at the guards searching the compound for lost shovels or picks, and prodding for any likely tunnels! We soon knew that they had no suspicions whatever, but on many occasions they came very near to prodding through the soil on to the wooden roof of the trench.

Then came the night for this memorable escape. The officers

who were detailed to keep up their activities of sport and those who usually sat around the entrance to the trench, took up their customary positions after lunch and strove hard to provide entertainment for the sentries. This was not hard to do as they usually showed great interest in our sport.

At the peak hour of the entertainment, we pulled away the roof in front of the trench and slipped the three escapers under the planks, wishing them, "Good luck and God speed home." The entrance was again covered with soil. Each of the three had been provided with a length of rubber tubing to be pushed through to the surface for breathing purposes. These were almost invisible at close range and were sufficient to allow each man enough air. We chatted to them until it was time to vacate the field.

Zero hour for their emergence into open space was planned for midnight and the escape had been timed to take place during the darkest night of that month.

The following morning when we were allowed to enter the field again, those of us who knew of the escape, inspected the trench casually, so as not to attract attention, to see if everything had gone according to plan. Apparently it had. All the escapers, after covering up their hole, had crawled to the wire fence, and had managed to cut their way out, although searchlights were continually flashed along the perimeter wire. Then they had repaired the gap before making a successful get-away. Had I not known exactly where they were going to penetrate the fence, I would have sworn that it had never been cut.

During the morning and evening roll-calls for the next two days we managed to make up the three absentees' places by arranging for a couple of men, who were supposed to be sick, to occupy the beds of the escapers in turn. When the N.C.O. interpreter made his inspection of the building whilst we were standing on roll-call outside, one of these 'sick' men would slip over to the other wing when the Italian N.C.O. was downstairs. Then, when the N.C.O. came to the first floor of the unchecked wing, he would see a man in bed, so being satisfied that the numbers tallied he was able to report 'all present and correct' to his superior officer. It was amusing how this simple ruse worked for so long, but in order to enable us to use the same trick again, the officers who had organised the escape decided to inform the Italians of the escape.

On the third day however, our attention was attracted towards the main gate when, to our surprise, in marched our three unlucky comrades under heavy escort. They were taken into the commandant's office. For several hours we waited for them to come out, and when they eventually emerged into the open one officer was clad only in a blanket. As soon as they were inside our building we gave them a hearty welcome. They were immediately sent before the Senior British Officer to whom they told their story. Apparently one had caught his clothing on the outer barbed wire fence and in getting away had ripped it to pieces. As a result of this mishap he had missed contact with his two companions at the first rendezvous point so he made straight for the second which was the booking office at Piacena railway station. Noticing that his chums were not there to meet him, he tried to buy a ticket. His limited use of Italian and his tattered appearance caused the booking clerk to inspect his papers, which were at once spotted as being forged and this led to his arrest. The booking clerk immediately informed the station master that earlier two other people had booked for the same destination. A message was sent to have that particular train searched. The search party, who had a description of the officers, soon arrested them without any warning.

This episode was a setback but did not discourage future attempts. In fact the 'Cloak and Dagger' section were even more determined to make every effort to shorten the long list of intended escapers.

As time went on the camp organised football and many other games, in which practically everyone joined. One enterprising officer raised a football pool and in no time aroused great interest in our enthusiastic six-a-side tournaments. Most afternoons matches were being played to an ever increasing roar from the touch lines. All this culminated in a Grand Sports Day. Everybody trained for the short and long distance races, the obstacle, sack, and egg and spoon races, throwing the hammer and other novelty events. The same football pool officer ran a sweepstake on the favourites for the short and long distance running events.

At last the great day arrived and in true British sportsman style the competitors and spectators turned out in whites or their best khaki, cleaned and pressed. Side bets were made and the cheering was comparable to a Wembley Cup Final. Even the Italian garrison turned out in force to witness the prisoners enjoying themselves.

That day and many others were crossed off the calendar. Red Cross parcels arrived regularly and we were fit through having enough food and plenty of sun and exercise. Morale was high for each man had found an occupation, and with encouraging news of allied successes, we settled ourselves down with high hopes of a quick liberation.

CHAPTER EIGHT

It was September 8th, 1943. The outside world was in a carnival mood, for in Fontanellato the villagers were celebrating a yearly Fiesta known as the *Festa di Santa Maria Immaculata.* On the village green behind the convent, a country fair was in progress. The weather was extremely hot, and it seemed that the world and his wife were out of doors. Hundreds of people were coming in from outlying districts on their bicycles and parking them in ready-made cycle parks opposite the camp. Our garrison were on short leave except for the main guards and the patrols. The soldiers, on meeting their girl friends, would saunter up and down the road opposite the camp, showing them the British P.O.W.'s. As the crowd grew it was difficult to say which was the bigger attraction — the fair or ourselves! Only here and there did we receive a wave from a sympathetic soul.

Inside the camp, the main hall was packed with officers playing bridge. Others were banging away making final preparations to the stage and scenery for Julian Hall's production of *Czarina.* The remainder of the camp, myself included, were sitting on the window sills of almost every window which had a view on to the main road. Suddenly, I gripped my friend's arm and drew his attention to the spontaneous retreat of all the Italians.

Excitement among the crowd was growing every second until in a few minutes everybody seemed to be in a panic. Those who lived outside the village were frantically striving to reach their bicycles. Others were blocking the road by gathering into small groups, jabbering about what had caused this hysteria.

Suddenly we noticed that the guards were returning, throwing their caps into the air and turning cart-wheels. Above the noise of all that hubbub, we heard the cry of *"Pace! Pace! Pace!"* Groups of Italians would swarm around the crier and besiege him with questions. The soldiers who came into the compound were calling up to us *"Pace! Pace!"* We looked down towards the side gate and saw an Italian soldier trying to unlock the gate from the outside. One of my friends could speak Italian and quickly he spread the word around the camp that there was "Peace!" We then dashed around to tell the news to the others. It was thrilling to hear that word "peace." After all that time of monotony, now there was peace. I wondered if it really was peace or just some trick.

We rushed downstairs into the main hall to spread the word but as usual the news had travelled fast through the camp. People were already talking about this great event. At one table there was a bridge party still playing and I just managed to hear a call of, "Three spades!" through all the chatter. Work had stopped on the stage. Behind me was a group trying to get some sense out of the complete chaos that appeared to be brewing. We heard that only yesterday someone had seen a company of Hitler's crack infantry march through the village with complete mountain warfare equipment.

By this time, the Senior British Officer who had been playing bridge, had gone out to get some official 'gen' from one of the Italian officers. Meanwhile the whole camp assembled in the main hall. It was a little time before the S.B.O. returned, but when he did, we were more than impatient to hear the result. He told us that an Armistice with our forces had been signed by Badoglio. This news was received with a terrific cheer. When the cheering died down he went on to tell us that the Commandant had warned him that the Germans were pouring troops into the north of Italy as fast as they could, but that he, the Commandant, had assured the S.B.O. that he would take steps to ensure that we did not fall into the hands of the Germans. He went on to say that we must remain calm and watchful to all outward events. The S.B.O. then advised us to go quietly back to our rooms to gather our kit and then to have ready a small package with shaving tackle, water bottle and a spare pair of socks etc., in case of a hurried departure. The remainder of our kit we were to leave packed up on our beds. He stressed the point about not antagonising the Italian garrison and asked us to refrain from crowding at the front windows. Finally he advised everyone to have an early night. The dismissal was quiet but each officer was unquestionably restless.

That night, as one can imagine, passed with little or no sleep. The majority of the fellows were up early to finish packing, and taking a lively interest in what was going on outside. Breakfast was eaten to a hum of conversation about our predicament. One question was still left to be answered, namely, what steps would the Commandant take to ensure our safety? Breakfast over, we were told by the adjutant that the roll call would not be held, instead there would be a parade headed by the S.B.O. at 09.00 hours, for all the officers and other ranks. He said that he wished us all to show that we were British and that in a time such as this we could maintain a sense of decorum. He mentioned once again the pledge that the Italian Commandant had made for our safety and then gave an order for all ranks to be dressed in battledress, as far as possible and to be prepared to move at any moment. Should the Germans be seen approaching the camp the bugle would sound the alarm and all officers would form up on the playing field in their respective companies without delay. Then he said, "Let me make this clear to all. I order no one to break away. You will remain together until I give the order for individual dispersal."

The parade was dismissed and we returned to our rooms for a final check of what we would leave or take with us. We watched the Italian garrison inspecting their arms and ammunition and other kinds of equipment. Soldiers rode in and out on bicycles. Later we learned that these were the Commandant's 'scouts'.

A working party came into the compound and right at the bottom of the sports field, they cut a large gap in the wire fence. Then we saw Colonel Mainwaring with Prevadini, the Italian interpreter, coming along the outside of the compound towards the building. He had been out before breakfast on reconnaissance for a hide-out for the whole camp. A small rivulet about four kilometres away had been found, well covered by trees and bushes and banked by a high Dutch-type embankment. This line of cover stretched for approximately one and a half miles.

Mid-day soon passed and we were all feeling very hungry. Rumours had been flying around camp all morning to the effect that three thousand paratroopers had landed on Parma, only twelve miles away and that our forces had made a successful landing at La Spezia. However up to that moment no Germans had been seen.

Suddenly, without warning, the bugle sounded the alarm. We dashed off to our rooms, grabbed our packs and made our way into the crush of officers heading down the stairs. The officers who were in front, on reaching the door that led into the compound, immediately drew back, for looking out and up over the fields beyond they saw a Junkers 52 Troop Carrier heading straight for the camp, flying almost at zero altitude. We all withdrew into the building to avoid being spotted. As soon as the 'plane had flown over, we formed up on the playing field under our company commanders and the S.B.O. The Italian Commandant was raised higher in our esteem by giving Ronnie Noble, our own correspondent his camera back. This enabled him to record this memorable event. Ronnie placed himself at the other side of the gap in the fence and took snap after snap of us as we marched out to evacuate the camp completely.

When we reached the small road that lay parallel to the camp, a few peasants who had already had news of our escape, were waiting to give us words of encouragement. Although outwardly happy, one could detect an inner nervous tension among them. As we made our way quickly along the ditches, more and more of the peasants came running out to greet us. Having seen their soldiers changing into civilian clothes and escaping into the country, they were becoming more and more alarmed as to their destiny under the dreadful Germans.

After a tiring zig-zag course through vineyards and maize fields, we finally arrived at our hide-out. Each company was told to lie down quietly under the nearby vines and to remain there until further notice. It was most refreshing to eat the glorious black grapes, for the day was extremely hot. The spot where I was hiding afforded good cover and enabled me to keep close watch on a nearby farmhouse. Liaison with the two Italian interpreters was extremely good and worthy of particular remembrance. Captain Camino told us that the Germans arrived at the camp only twenty-five minutes after we had left. They made a systematic search of the place, but finding nobody, began to wreck the building. They found the Italian garrison's wine store and proceeded to get drunk. Not content with this they then began to terrorise the village. Unfortunately the Italian Commandant, being the Military Governor of the district, was held responsible for our escape and was taken prisoner immediately. Two girls who refused to give any information about us were shot. Camino, being in civilian clothing and knowing the village well, kept coming with news of the German intentions. His latest report was that the Germans were massing for a complete comb-out of the area for us. The same Junkers 52 was flying low over the fields, apparently joining in the search.

For hours we lay in our hide-out, only moving to quench our thirst. By sunset most of us were becoming restless for want of exercise. Then I heard a soft warning. In the silence that followed we could hear the noise of an engine. We waited with bated breath as the vehicle came closer and closer until, between the leaves, I saw it halt abruptly outside the nearby farmhouse. All the family were brought out in front of the house and were carefully questioned. The Germans seemed to spend more time on the children. Although the voices were clear I had difficulty in understanding what was going on.

By their actions and facial expressions we gathered that the Germans were unable to find what they were looking for. Without searching the farm, they jumped on to their truck and headed back the way they had come, smashing down the family's maize and other crops in the process.

After breathing with great relief, we passed the message back to the S.B.O. that the Germans had gone. A return message ordered all officers to withdraw under cover of the 'bund'. 'Leopard crawling' to safety behind the embankment we located our respective company commanders and found a well hidden spot to bed down for the night. Mosquito-bitten and fly-pestered, we lay under the bushes talking to each other about the situation. By the time I had made my bed of bracken leaves and moss I was quite ready for some sleep.

The still, cold night air was splintered by a call to, "Come and get it!" This startled me into new activity. Slipping on the wet bank and finding several patches of nettles on my way, I finally came across a grassy clearing which was being used as Battalion H.Q. Here the senior officers were dealing out food. I had expected to be offered bully beef, but instead there was bread, cheese, salami and home cured meat of all descriptions. With my hands full of food I cautiously made my way back to my bed, where I fell upon it and guzzled like a hungry wolf. Never before had dry bread, garlic and cold meat tasted so very delicious as at that moment.

With a full stomach I felt contented enough to crawl back into bed, but my mind continued to go over all that had happened, causing me to speculate on the future. These thoughts kept me from sleeping. Back in camp the Italian guards had never been friendly, yet the Contadini had not previously shown any animosity. They were now being extremely cooperative in giving no clue to the Germans as to our whereabouts and bringing food to us at great risk to their own lives. What a mad world it was. One moment we were prisoners of the Italians, now we were being fed and shown every kindness by them. Finally with thoughts such as these rambling through my confused brain, I fell asleep.

The following day we spent talking about home and how to get there, about food and drink, about women, and everything a woman does, and doesn't, do. The Italians kept up their wonderful missions by cycling out with baskets of more food and, to our amazement, Red Cross tinned food as well. Apparently they had salvaged the tins from right under the noses of the Germans who were now occupying the camp. Tins of condensed milk were brought along, together with cocoa, sugar, bully beef etc., which they could have kept for their own under-nourished children. Even the children came out with their pockets and bags full of cigarettes and tobacco from our once well-stocked store. I had a strange feeling of deep gratitude for the tiniest article given to me. In planning escapes one is taught never to rely upon any person outside the camp for help in the way of food and lodgings. Now, we witnessed loyalty such as this! "Barmy, ain't it?" I heard a soldier say.

Later on towards evening, there was so much food coming in, we had to organise a distribution point amongst the bushes as there had been a continuous stream of peasants coming and going all day with parcels of food. Then, to help us further, they collected amongst themselves clothing of all descriptions. When night-fall came, word was passed to all ranks to collect a pair of trousers, a jacket and anything else necessary to hide one's identity. Military clothing was to be concealed under the thickest bushes. I found some trousers made of sacking, a jacket and a thin cotton shirt. All were too small for me, but they were better than nothing. Underneath all this I wore a thin pair of 'Celanese' underpants and vest, which my parents had sent to me. I kept my army boots and socks. I decided not to shave for a while, in order to look more like an Italian peasant.

After I had drawn my clothing, Major Carver, R.E., my Company Commander, was called away to a conference with the S.B.O. We lay on the bank for quite a while waiting for him to come back and trying to guess the reason for the conference. On his return, he told us that the S.B.O. had decided to let any officers who wanted to go off alone, to do so. Others who wished to stay with their groups could do so at their own risk. Those who wanted to leave were to be fixed up temporarily in farm houses by Camino and had to arrange themselves into groups of four. Everybody was advised to carry some form of ex-prisoner identification. The S.B.O. sent a personal wish to all officers of "Good luck and God-speed home." Captain Jack Gatford, R.E., Lieutenant John Alexander, R.E., and myself planned to go straight away. So saying goodbye to our friends, Lieutenant David Williams, R.T.C., Lieutenant Kenneth Bligh, R.E., and to Major Carver, we went to meet Camino at the rendezvous. There we checked each others' outfits, to see whether we would pass as peasants. Camino cautioned us to follow him at intervals of twenty yards, and to walk only on the grass verge at the side of the road. There was no talking. Camino beckoned us to follow him. I brought up the rear. I wondered how many of us would be able to get back to our forces. I must admit that I was scared; I expected to run into the Germans with every step we made. The sight of the others in front, however, sustained my courage and I cursed myself for thinking that our adventure was bound to end badly, instead of a gloriously happy ending across our own lines somewhere.

Camino took us along a narrow road, which turned and twisted around small groups of houses, until it finally reached a secondary road. Before the junction, we turned off into a large farmyard where we were met by some very inquisitive folk. Camino greeted them, and it was obvious that he had their consent to let us pass through and on into their fields at the back. It was no easy job picking one's way along the winding path, sometimes ducking one wire, then climbing over another. Now and again, I could hear faint curses coming from my friends ahead as they bumped into obstacles in their path. If I had not heard their warning I would have gone slap into the wall of a small shed. Fumbling my way around I saw Camino framed in the light coming from a doorway, talking to a peasant woman. As soon as the four of us reached the door we were ushered straight into the house. Two steps from the door was their living room. The scene was cheery, but their poverty was obvious. The room, lit by an oil lamp, had a large open brick fireplace where a cauldron was hanging. A large wooden table, set for a meal for six, was in the centre of the room. The meal consisted of two small cheeses, six bread cobs, two small decanters of red wine, a large plate of sliced salami and a massive bowl of macaroni and cheese. On the far side of the room was a cupboard, the top of which was well scrubbed and opposite to this was a tall glass cabinet, filled with the family's much treasured wine glasses and heirlooms that had presumably been handed down from generation to generation. The floor was of well-worn red tiles, unadorned by any form of covering and apart from eight rickety chairs, there was no other furniture.

The owner of the house was a man in his fifties, stout and poorly dressed. He was in his shirt sleeves and his chin was covered with four days' growth of beard. With a deep gruff voice, he bade us a hearty welcome and shook each of us by the hand. After a few words with him and a quick glass of wine, Camino departed to carry on his good work. After the outside door closed, we three turned to the fourth member of the party and learned that he was Lieutenant-Colonel B. Peddie of the Cameron Highlanders. We had seen him take his daily walk around the camp, along with another colonel, but none of us ever had the opportunity to speak with him before. With the introductions over, the old farmer made us sit down and share his 'humble meal' as he called it. He chatted away in Italian all the time. John was the only one who could cope with the language, although he found the going very difficult since our host spoke in a strange dialect. I felt awkward at not being able to speak the language, for the two old dears were doing everything to make us feel at home.

Our plates were piled with the wonderful looking macaroni dish and no sooner were our glasses empty than they were filled again. When we were actually feeling the effects of the wine and the warmth of the room, John tactfully asked the farmer where he had arranged for us to sleep. The reply of the old farmer was to invite us to pull up our chairs to the fire. All the time John was being taxed to the utmost to answer the many questions that were put to him. John had to translate the conversation to us in the brief spells in between the questions. Feeling worn out with trying to understand the farmer and from the effects of the quick acting wine, we finally persuaded the old man to show us the way to our new quarters. Carrying a primitive oil lamp to light the way, our host's stocky frame filled the door as he asked us to follow him. John thanked the farmer's wife on our behalf, for the splendid meal which she had so kindly given us. Signor Mari, for that was the farmer's name, led us to a large double door, but as he opened it the smell of cattle and sour hay which met us made my stomach turn and I had to turn away to breathe some fresh air. Along the wall the hay was heaped up and was obviously prepared for our beds. There was an old man sitting on a stool, leaning against a pillar in the centre of the stable, under a much-battered oil lamp. He had a slightly hunched back, his hair looked as if it had never seen a comb and it had been allowed to grow well over his ears. He badly needed a shave and though we were very badly dressed, his clothes were far worse than ours. He was reading a book aloud — presumably to his cows — and seemed quite oblivious of our presence. It was only when I walked over to stroke one of the cows that the old man looked up and took notice of us.

Whilst we were becoming acquainted with the old fellow, Signor Mari had gone out and he now returned with an old double blanket and a large black cloak, which he handed to us. Calling to his farm-hand to leave, he bade us goodnight and left us to sleep. We could hear his dog outside, so we knew if there should be any Germans or strangers about, the dog would give us plenty of warning. Our sleep was very much disturbed that night, for whenever we heard the dog bark, we dashed out the back way to the nearby maize field, where we would remain until Mari found us to assure us that it was safe to return to the barn.

At five o'clock the following morning we were awakened by Mari's eccentric old character, whom we christened 'Happy'. As soon as the cows realised he was present they stamped, rattled their chains and made an unholy noise with their cow-bells tied round their necks! They were fed and later, about six o'clock, were milked. By this time, finding the noises unbearable, (apart from the smell), we got up and washed outside in the stone trough. We had only one mirror between us and when I saw the state of my hair I was quite horrified by my grizzled appearance. I decided immediately to change my mind about letting my beard grow and, borrowing a razor from John, I shaved myself, resolving never to grow a beard again. As I was finishing the old lady called us in for breakfast. At half-past six we sat down in the kitchen and enjoyed a large bowl of bread and milk. Apparently this was the usual peasant breakfast. After this she produced a jug of coffee. She poured it into the same bowls as we had used for our bread and milk and I noticed it had a peculiar colour and smelt differently from ordinary coffee, so I asked John to find out what kind of coffee it was. It was made from sun-flower seeds, roasted, then ground. The taste, to say the least, was interesting and, after a while, very pleasant.

The first morning the farmer led us across the open yard, through the vines alongside his maize field, across a ditch, down a small, well-concealed path and through more thickly growing maize. Here we made ourselves as comfortable as possible for the day. Signor Mari told us he would bring out lunch and tea, and if the Germans were searching, he would inform us immediately. He left us, adding that we could eat as many grapes as we liked. It was not yet seven o'clock. As the atmosphere was still damp, the mosquitoes were very troublesome, but we dared not move for fear of attracting attention. We could hear the German transport travelling up and down the road. Being tired on account of our disturbed night, we slept the whole morning under our coats to protect us from the pestering flies and mosquitoes.

I was awakened by Jack tugging at my feet and saying, "There's someone coming." I lay flat on the ground and held my breath until I saw that it was the old farmer who was creeping slowly through the maize towards us. The old chap had kept his word and brought us some bread and vegetable soup. John asked him for the latest news. We learned that the British were supposed to have landed at Spezia, Genoa and Leghorn, and that three thousand paratroopers had taken Parma. The Germans were supposed to be clearing out of Italy altogether. All this of course, we found difficult to believe.

After Mari had left us we discussed the situation. The Colonel suggested that we should remain where we were until we had a true and clear picture of what was happening. John and Jack wanted to risk making a break for it, but I thought it would be better to follow the Colonel's advice. We laid low the whole day and talked about the Germans, our troops, and about how wonderful each of our localities were back home. Now and again, the sound of a passing car would put us on alert, for fear it would stop at the farmhouse. We talked until the sun set low over the tops of the maize fields. The mosquitoes came round again and, along with the persistent flies, made that hour and a half before dark a complete misery. When Mari finally came for us, I don't think he had ever had four men follow him so willingly!

That night, for dinner, the usual wine was on the table, in the centre of which was a large frying-pan holding the most complicated mess of fried chicken and onions. All of the chicken seemed to be there, as I saw its head resting among its chopped remains. The same suet-like food lay cut up on an oval dish beside the frying-pan. Throughout the meal, more questions were fired at us. "Are you married?" "Have you a fiancée?" "Where do you live?" "Have you got any photographs?" "How old are you?" When we told them our ages, they seemed surprised that we were so young. They both showed great interest in our families and in what we were doing in civilian life before the war. Just as we were finishing our meal four old peasant women trooped in and from the moment they entered the room, they gabbled away at a tremendous pace, giggling the whole time. I admit that perhaps we did look strange in our rags, and to them we must have looked like scarecrows. They spoke in a strange dialect which was extremely difficult to follow. All I could do was to pretend to understand them and give them a big smile of appreciation. Still giggling, they finally departed. "Thank God, they've gone and I hope they don't come back," said John. Afterwards, with great relief, we returned to our bed of hay and fell asleep immediately.

The next day there was a repeat performance. We could not walk beyond a twenty yard stretch which was well hidden by tall maize, for fear of being spotted. Four days went by in this manner. I spent the time studying Italian. I had picked up some words here and there and John had given me a few important verbs to learn.

I was stretched out under a low hanging vine pursuing my study of language, the Colonel pacing up and down, when Jack and John approached us from the barn, to tell the Colonel that they had decided to leave that night after dark. They discussed their plans with the Colonel and for the rest of the day prepared themselves for their journey. As darkness fell, we went with them to the end of the path behind the maize, and wished them good luck at their departure.

The Colonel did not say much, but I knew what was in his thoughts. We went to the cow-shed and dropped down on to the hay. The Colonel produced an Italian school map, which Mari had given to him and which he studied carefully and attentively. He looked very worn and his expression was far from being a happy one. He was in his late forties and it was plain to see that he had never 'roughed it' in his life. I could see that he was very worried about some matter. I thought to myself that if he was a married man, he had every right to worry whether he would ever get back home safely. I attempted to cheer him up, by telling him that we would stick together and have a celebration in Piccadilly when we got through. That night we bedded down early, but neither of us slept well. I do not know what upset the cows that night, but their bells clanged louder than ever, the smell was worse than ever before and so was the heat.

A couple of days later as I was studying my Italian vocabulary under my favourite vine, I saw the Colonel approaching, looking extremely worried. He came and sat down beside me and I knew we were about to have a conference. He told me that he believed that the news we had heard about the landings of our troops was false and that they were still south of Naples. He suggested that we should leave and make for our own lines after we had endeavoured to find out exactly what was going on by listening in to the latest news broadcast. I agreed and said that I would try and make sense of their news. We strolled up and down the vineyard discussing our future plans.

After the evening meal was over, I asked Mari if he would take me to where I could hear a radio. Mari was only too keen and, fetching a cycle lamp, he led the way into the night and with me fumbling my way a few paces behind him and tripping over everything I encountered, we crossed a ditch, passed another of his maize fields, climbed over a rickety fence, and plop — I landed right in a ditch! Mari must have had eyes like a cat, for he found his way perfectly. We walked across more fields, down a small lane, over another fence, then by some vines and arrived suddenly right in front of a large farmhouse. Mari whispered to me that the house belonged to his friend Zilliotti, who manufactured cheese. Mari added that he was very wealthy, owning a radio, a large house and a car! In reply to a soft knock, the door was opened by a young girl who calmly ushered us into the living room, which was well furnished.

After being introduced with great excitement by Mari, I had difficulty getting down to business. I could not get a word in edgeways, for the same questions were asked as before in Mari's house. They were charming people, of Swiss origin I found out later. Zilliotti was well thought of by his neighbours, who treated him more or less as their counsellor. I was then further interrogated by the whole family before being led into another room. This was obviously their 'best' room, for it had the appearance of only being used on very special occasions.

I tried unsuccessfully for some time to find the right station on the radio as Signor Zilliotti withdrew from the room. London was eventually contacted and, as I could hear dance music being transmitted, I was tempted to listen, for I had not heard music from home since the desert days. However, I resisted the temptation and instead I tuned into Rome and heard the announcer deliver the German controlled version of the latest news. He rattled it off far more quickly than I had expected, but I managed to get the gist of what was being said. Not being quite satisfied I tried other stations and I managed to contact Tunis, which was an American station, giving the news out in English. It was extremely depressing. It was clear that we must never again pay attention to rumours.

Switching off, I joined Mari and my host. I remained for a short while, trying to relate in Italian what I had heard from Tunis, but as my Italian was very limited, I was quite worn out by the time I had finished. Swallowing another drink, Mari and I left, after Zilliotti had checked that the coast was clear. On the way home, the words of the American announcer kept returning to me ... "Our troops, finding opposition stiff, were fighting a bitter battle along the whole front from Benevento, Salverno to Foggia." I could not figure out how the Germans had managed to get their reinforcements down there so quickly.

It had been raining whilst we were at Zilliotti's and without a doubt I fell in to every ditch there was on our way back. How we managed to backtrack I do not know, but when I saw myself in the light of Mari's kitchen, I found I was covered with mud. There was a lovely fire going, which the dear old soul had prepared for us, so I was able to relate the news to the Colonel seated beside the crackling wood. It was late by the time I was dry, so with reluctance, we left the fire and turned in to bed.

CHAPTER NINE

After breakfast the following morning, we went out to our usual place in the maize and continued our discussions of the previous night. Suddenly, we heard the tall maize stalks rustle violently and Signor Mari, who was in a complete state of panic, appeared gasping, "*Tedeschi e Fascisti!*" He went on to say they were carrying out a house-to-house search not five hundred yards down the road, and that they had already recaptured ten of our officers in the comb-out. As our house was right on the road, we made a hasty retreat to about a quarter of a mile behind the house and lay low in another of Mari's fields. I could see a pair of boots creeping closer and closer to our prone positions and I knew it was not Mari. The intruder failed to spot us and slowly went away. We waited impatiently for Mari to come to tell us that the 'raid' was all over. When he finally arrived he told us that he had arranged for us to go over to his neighbour's farther back from the road. We would be safer there.

Following him we quickly reached his friend's house, where we were introduced to our host, Signor Ferrari. At once we were taken into their living-room. Mari left immediately, telling us that he would come over to see us now and again. We thanked him for all he had done and wished him well. Ferrari and his family were totally different from Mari and his wife, Ferrari being younger and much better educated. His wife was in her thirties and had a vivid personality. Both were always cheerful and full of optimism. They were poor, very poor, but never once did either of them say anything to give the impression that they were not happy.

The following afternoon Ferrari's young brother arrived, after trekking from Brindisi. He was a sailor and had escaped from the Germans when they had taken over the port and had commandeered the Italian fleet there. He seemed to be well above average in intelligence and gave us a clear and concise story of what was going on in the south. Like many others who shared his views, he lamented the fact that Fascism had forced Italy into the war. Now he felt free, and was ready to help us in any way that he could. When he learned that we had only a very inadequate school map, he cycled into Parma and brought back a better one. It showed the main line railways, the trunk roads and more villages. It was far from being detailed but it was good enough for our purpose and we were glad to have it. He also brought us some cigarettes and a few razor blades. Nothing was too much trouble for Signor and Signora Ferrari to do for us and they were always finding something to give us to make us more comfortable. They were even willing to turn out of their own bed so that we would have a few nights of comfort.

Between discussions of our plans, we would help the Ferraris by peeling and stripping the maize husks which were used, after being ground to flour, for making bread and cakes. One afternoon, when we were busy helping, Ferrari flew up the stairs and told us that there were two suspicious-looking men coming up the path towards the house. We dashed downstairs and out of the back door to a haystack, where we dug ourselves in thoroughly. Usually when the Colonel came close to any hay, he would approach carefully, listening for rats or other animals. This was the only time that I ever saw him forget about rats or any such things. If I had wanted to talk to him I couldn't, for my mouth was full of hay and feathers. By the time Ferrari came to tell us that the coast was clear we were nearly dead from the heat. He told us that the men had been sent by the local German Commander to arrest British fugitives. Ferrari was quite unperturbed by the whole business.

That night we decided to clear out and before bedding down we lay on top of the hay and discussed the best way to tell the

Ferraris of our intention. Knowing how very hard the family had tried to persuade us to stay with them throughout the winter, we knew that they would not like to see us leave. Suddenly, I gripped the Colonel's arm and bade him quiet. Three men, whether Germans or Italian Fascists I knew not, were walking around the house, prying into the cowshed and the other small shed at the back of our haystack. Luckily we were on top of the hay. If we had been in the house they would certainly have heard our voices. Whoever they were, they had a good idea that we were somewhere near this house. After an anxious few minutes all became quiet and the only sound was the cooing of the pigeons on the roof of the barn. After whacking the hay with a stick to chase away any would-be-venturesome rats, we settled ourselves down into the hay and fell asleep.

The following morning, we broke the news to the family that we had decided to leave that night in order to gain our lines before the winter set in. They pleaded with us to remain with them until winter was over. After much discussion they finally realised that we were right and so prepared food for our journey. Mari came over in the afternoon to wish us goodbye and to bring a cake made for us by Signora Mari along with her good wishes. With the whole Ferrari family and Mari crowding around the table, the Colonel and I pointed out to them the route we planned to take. Signora Ferrari suddenly told us to be quiet and went to the window. She pointed out a peculiar figure who was strolling up and down the vines pretending to pick them. Every now and again he would look up at the house from underneath the umbrella he was carrying. We watched him for some time before he strolled away. Signora Ferrari went to see whether there was anybody else around. Coming quickly back into the room she told us that more people were coming towards the house. We fled to our hideout and, digging furiously deep down into the hay, we covered ourselves over and lay still. We remained there for at least an hour.

We were almost stifled by the time Signor Ferrari came to give us the 'all clear'. We had only been back in the house for five minutes when Signora Ferrari called us to their wine store, where, out of the little side window, she showed us two spies creeping along the ditch at the side of the path. I went to the other window which overlooked the fields and to my surprise I counted a further three men taking up positions amongst the crops. Then Ferrari came through to tell us that there was a spy in the centre of the maize field in front of the house and another close to the vines towards the right of the house. We had some difficulty in keeping them in sight for they continually changed their positions. I was thankful that it was raining hard, for I knew that they would not stay around long in the rain. I was right, for after about half an hour they left us in peace.

That evening the meal Signora Ferrari had prepared for us was the best that she had so far produced and some special bottles of wine were brought out. Signor Ferrari presented us with a real Red Cross parcel. We could not find words adequate enough to thank him. He realised that the tins of food would be very useful to us and he had begged these from a friend of his, whose son had somehow salvaged them from the camp. The biscuits, bully beef, tea and chocolate we kept for ourselves, but we gave the remainder of the contents to them.

We took a last look at the map and Ferrari indicated to us the route which would afford the best cover from his house. We checked over our things and in doing so we felt a sense of relief that at last we were ready to move on. With a final "*Buone notte,*" we climbed up on our haystack for the last time. Before we fell off to sleep we lay talking about what we were going to do when we got home and what we should give the Ferraris as a present in return for their extreme kindness. When the conversation flagged

I thought again of the time of horror in the desert and those wretched days at Bari transit camp until, hearing the Colonel's snore, I turned over and went to sleep.

The next thing I knew was someone tugging at my feet and I could hear Ferrari telling us to wake up. I awoke the Colonel and flung on my jacket and laced up my boots. The Colonel was quickly dressed and, sliding down the haystack for the last time, we joined the Ferraris in the kitchen where we ate a bowl of hot bread and milk beside a warm stove. As we were gathering up our sacks I could see that the parting was not going to be an easy one. There were tears in Signora Ferrari's eyes. As I grasped their hands I thanked them for all they had done for us and, with a final word of thanks, we left the house.

It had been raining for an hour and the ground was soaking wet but the stars began to appear between the slowly passing clouds, making our way a little easier. The freshness of the night was glorious after the smoky atmosphere of the kitchen. Strips of sacking served as puttees around our ankles, as a protection from the wet ground. We came to the end of the path and started to walk across a field. Suddenly, with a mighty splash, I found myself up to my waist in a very watery ditch. I could hear the Colonel calling to me and I pulled myself out in the direction of his voice. He heard me coming, for the amount of water I carried in my boots was enough to irrigate the whole plain of Lombardy! Approaching a tall wire-mesh fence which bounded the field we had to make a detour so, giving the farmhouse nearby a wide berth, we found a gate which led on to the road clearly marked on our map. As I walked I could feel my socks moving around inside my boots, so we halted while I removed my boots and wrung out the socks. I discarded the puttees, their being of no use at all. When I tried to get my socks back on, my heel went straight through the sock on one foot. The other sock was not much better and the boots felt cold as I drew them back on to my feet. This was a fine start to our journey.

No sooner had we started walking on the metalled road, than ! was aware of an uneasy feeling that we were being followed. I observed that the Colonel was also becoming nervous. We both stopped to listen for tell-tale footsteps, but there was not a soul anywhere. The same strange feeling haunted us until we hit the 'bund' exactly at the spot where I had gone to collect the rations when we had all been together. I had no need to use my map, for I was already well acquainted with that area. We followed the 'bund' until we came to a little wooden bridge and, crossing it, followed the stream under cover of the thick bushes and trees. Again, I had to halt, for the squelch, squelch, squelch of the water inside my boots was beginning to make my feet ache, as well as making a good deal of noise. When I took my socks off I was astonished to see that there was no foot left in one sock and the other was looking very pathetic. Still I wrung them out and, much disconcerted, drew them back on my feet as well as I could. We carried on, taking first this path and then that, dodging trees which, in many cases, turned out to be mere shadows. There was no doubt about the multitude of ditches! The next few miles proved to be disastrous for the Colonel, for the wet grass had loosened his ankle sacking and the moisture had seeped into his boots.

Looking across the countryside everything seemed very hostile. The trees looked black and menacing, their bold outlines silhouetted against the steel-grey sky. The mountains looked formidable and secretive, daring one to venture into their depths. The hedges seemed great embattlements, insurmountable to even the strongest. The grass, however, was our greatest enemy, for as each foot pressed the ground it would sound as though a lemon was being squeezed. Over to the east the dawn was stealthily creeping over the cold, grey sky, but we were keeping well up to our schedule.

For the first seven miles we made good progress, but from then onwards we encountered many small groups of farm houses whose fields were bounded by high wire fencing which forced us to make frequent detours.

At last we managed to get out of that maze. Suddenly, I heard a noise of escaping steam, then a blast from a whistle told us that we had reached a railway. Skirting a signal-box we crossed the line and headed down a small lane to the main road. Dawn was now fully upon us so we moved more cautiously than ever, gaining the road just as a car full of Germans came speeding towards Parma. We dodged into cover and, as soon as the road was clear, walked across the road and down a lane opposite. The Colonel found a small gap in the hedge which enabled us to have our breakfast in safety. By the time we had finished the sun was well up into a glorious blue sky.

Breakfast over, we walked on towards the mountains. The scenery was wonderful. The hillsides were covered with row upon row of vines. Dotted here and there among the green were small white peasant homes, each having window-boxes full of deep red flowers, a type of geranium. Some of the walls of the houses were covered with a beautiful flowering creeper. Looking up the valley we could see ahead the mountains that we would have to climb, an ever present reminder that our journey had only just begun.

We walked on and on, keeping away from farms as far as possible. That evening just before dark, we knocked on the door of a small farmhouse and asked the farmer if he would let us sleep in his barn for the night. He seemed somewhat ill-at-ease, but went inside and, bringing out a lamp, showed us to his barn. The Colonel, who disliked rats intensely, was worried by these pests nearly all night. He must have actually hit one of them with his stick, for its squeal startled me out of my sleep. At the crack of dawn we set off on another long day's trek.

For days we walked and walked, over one range then another. We shaved little, for we had long since finished our soap and razor blades. For several nights we found ourselves in an area where people went in fear of roaming Fascist spies, so we had to sleep out under the vines or bushes. Those nights were cold! It was a blessing that the days were so hot, for it enabled us to thaw out. Often the Colonel would want to follow cart tracks in the wooded slopes of the mountains, thinking that it would be much easier and quicker to follow these to the top. On these occasions I went my own way and as a result would have to wait a long time before the Colonel's puffing figure could be seen emerging out of the woods. It took a long time for the Colonel to appreciate that those tracks were made by carts coming into the woods for wood collection and as a result they were only leading round and round in circles.

Our diet was becoming monotonous with having to live off the land and, coupled with this, we had long since run out of tobacco. The Colonel was an inveterate pipe smoker, so it was very hard on him. The whole journey was a strain, about fifteen to twenty miles per day we walked, and on very little food. The food that we did get was not sufficient to replace the energy used up the previous day.

One day we were on the top of a mountain, nearly forty miles from Florence and overlooking a small hamlet. Leaving the Colonel resting after our strenuous climb, I went down to try to listen to a radio. For all I knew the Americans might have made a landing on the Italian Riviera or the British might have already opened an officers' leave centre outside Bologna!

I found a good local contact straight away and he led me to the local padre, who invited me, in perfect English, to enter his dwelling. He asked me if I was alone, to which I replied that a friend of mine was waiting for me just above the village. A local bright-faced youngster was sent forthwith to fetch the Colonel. I asked the padre whether he considered the hamlet safe for us. "You need not be afraid here, for all in my parish are very much against the evils of the Fascists and the Germans," he replied. It was a great treat to be able to speak to someone again, for my friend and I had not conversed with anyone since we left the Lombardy Plain three weeks ago. I found it especially delightful to speak with someone who could understand English, for the padre had been to Cambridge and had lived in London for over four years.

Eventually the Colonel arrived with the boy and was welcomed by the padre, who sent the boy out to his housekeeper with an order for three cups of tea. He showed us his radio and told us that in twenty minutes there would be the latest news from London. Those twenty minutes seemed like twenty hours. The padre had already tuned in, all he did was to switch on — and there was the B.B.C.! We heard Stuart Hibbard's voice reading the news. It was grand to hear his voice again. We listened right through to the end, then the padre turned the radio off. In the brief silence that followed, the news repeated itself in my head.

"Bitter fighting is taking place along the whole front. Our troops are holding on to the positions gained in yesterday's fighting around Benevento, but find that the opposition has stiffened considerably. According to yesterday's German communique — the enemy are reinforcing their troops in that sector. On the Yugoslav front, the Germans are meeting with stiff opposition and have had to bring up reserves of tanks, men and equipment." The rest of the news was about the Russian front and home events.

Having drunk as much tea as we could, the Colonel and I thanked the padre for his hospitality and set off along the ridge of the mountain. As we were walking along it occurred to me that we could do better by changing our direction. We sat down on top of a large rock at the end of the mountain ridge, which overlooked a beautiful valley running towards Florence, and discussed my idea, which was to make for the Riviera where the Germans would be unlikely to have troops based, as the coastline was unsuitable for sea-borne landings. While we sat there, admiring the view and smoking the Italian cigarettes that the padre had given us, we continued to discuss plans. I was in favour of making for the coast to try to steal a boat in order to get to Corsica, which I believed would soon be in Allied hands. I had some experience of handling a boat because I had done some sailing with my tather and brother before the War. There was also the possibility of finding a fisherman who would sail us over to the island. The Colonel was of the opinion that the coast was too far away, but a study of our map proved that it was nearer than the front line.

So we made ourselves at home where we were for the night, intending to set off first thing in the morning. My mind was content. I lay back, gazing at the glorious scenery in front of me. Away over on the far side of the valley I could hear a barking dog and a peasant shouting to his oxen. It was not easy to see him, due to the vast distances across those valleys. I noticed that the Colonel had fallen asleep, and no wonder, for the soft moss and grassy bank where we lay served as a most comfortable bed. We were also being warmed by the bright sun. The faint noises and the peasants at their work were soft music in peaceful rhythm, enough to send anyone off to sleep!

When we awakened the sun was just slipping behind the mountains and a few yards away from me, I could see a little boy sitting on the very rock where the Colonel and I had discussed our plans. He was a good-looking youngster with black, wavy hair, bright eyes and a very rosy complexion. His physique was good and he was well proportioned. He had a stick in one hand, the other resting on his knee. He was looking down at us with great interest. When

I spoke to him he became very excited to learn that we were English and he invited us to come and meet his father, who, he said had lived in England for a long time. I sensed the youth was not just an ordinary peasant boy. He led us towards the little village where I had listened to the radio. Calling his animals as he walked along beside me, every now and again he would glance up into the face of the Colonel and then into mine. He said that the *Fascisti* did not come near this village because they were scared of his father and his friends.

Returning to the village we were delighted to find that our friend the padre was 'the father' the boy referred to. Arriving once more at his dwelling, we were invited in. After the boy had gone to stable the cattle, the padre told us that there were other boys in his care and that he intended to send them to England for their schooling. The present war, among other factors, had prevented this happening, so he had educated them himself. He told us we could use his radio and stay with him as long as we liked. That evening we talked to the padre and his family and listened to his radio. Corsica was liberated and there was improved progress on the Benevento front. The two young lads kept us amused by their attempts to speak English. Guiseppe had the best knowledge of English, but this was on account of his eagerness to keep it up. I shall never forget that evening.

The following morning we said our farewells to the padre, and being escorted by the two boys to the boundary of their village, we headed north-west in the general direction of the great chain of Apennines. Taking the mountain paths helped us to cover the ground in far better time than going along the valleys. Along one of these paths we came to a stretch which was covered with bushes on either side. I suddenly saw a head pop up from behind one of the bushes and I grabbed the Colonel's arm. It was too late to retreat so we decided to proceed as if we had not seen anything and not to say a word if anyone spoke to us. We held our sticks at the ready and pretended to be what we appeared to be — just peasants.

"Buon giorno! Dove andate?" I knew immediately that they were not Italians, but at the same time I was puzzled in deciding exactly who they were. The Colonel remained quiet and closed up beside me when I went up to the bush. Out popped another head and I was relieved to see that he was no taller than his partner and that they both were a good deal shorter than the Colonel and myself! Now I could feel more relaxed in speaking to them.

"Buon giorno," I said, "Where do you come from?" There was a slight hesitation in answering this question. They offered us Italian cigarettes, which we accepted. Now I was fully prepared for their story of bluff, for the Italian they spoke was far from correct. They said they were German deserters, against the Nazis and the stupid Fascists and that two days ago they had jumped off the train that was taking them to La Spezia, where they were trying to reach our forces in order to give themselves up. Now I was fully on my guard, for if they really intended to do what they said they should not have been in this area, as we were far to the north-west of the main railway to La Spezia. I nudged the Colonel to start moving and with a cold, "Cheerio," we left them quickly. When we were well out of sight i heaved a deep sigh of relief.

Fearing that they might attempt to follow us, we almost slid down the side of the mountain, through the dense wood and undergrowth and made our way to the next ridge. There was no sign of the two Germans, so we were once more able to enjoy one another's companionship. Further and further west we trudged, sleeping in barns or under hedges. Only once did we experience the comfort of a bed, and due to the strangeness, neither of us slept that night! We therefore resolved to sleep only in barns until our trip was over. Now and again we came to areas that were held in the grip of Fascist terror for no one would volunteer information and as a result we were unable to obtain either food or water from them. We could trust no one, for if we were only seen we would be jeopardising our chances of freedom. Even those who might have been loyal to us given the chance, were not to be trusted, for their greatest fear was of those cruel, treacherous, vindictive, fanatical Fascists.

CHAPTER TEN

It was now three weeks since we had left the Ferrari farmhouse and it had been raining hard for the last two days. We had to keep going on account of the unfriendly areas and we were hungry, cold and soaking wet. Sleep that night was impossible, in wet clothes in an open barn. The following morning we had to be on our way before anybody was around to see us. It was about five-thirty and still pouring with rain. Nobody heard or saw us depart, for it was just first light. We climbed more mountains and penetrated dense woods, where the rain-drenched leaves further saturated our very thin clothing.

As we came to the top of the mountain, the ridge came to an abrupt end, dropping down very steeply to a small valley below. Half-a-mile away there was a small road leading into a village which lay on either side of a fast-flowing wide river. The greater part of the village lay on the farther side of the river, between it and another river flowing down from the north which joined the river facing us to our right and when we studied our map, we could see that the river coming from the left was free of bridges for a good fifteen miles. So there were no bridges to the left or to the right, except the one in front of us. We decided to cross that bridge and make for a house on the opposite mountain, where we planned to stay until we were dry and comfortable again. I suggested to the Colonel that we must be careful not to stop, or to talk and that we should walk in a slovenly way rather than march in step. He agreed that these precautions were important, so that he would not betray ourselves.

We slid down the steep slope and finally bumped on to the muddy road. There were few people to be seen on this side of the bridge and those few were too busy with their own affairs to pay attention to us. We were soon clear of the bridge and, turning with the road, we came upon a small market square, filled with carts and farm implements, sacks of farm produce and, of course, the entire population of the surrounding country. I swore under my breath. To think that of all the days we should pick market day to be here. I urged the Colonel to keep his eyes in front of him and to slouch along. My heart was in my mouth, for as we ventured deeper into the throng all eyes seemed to turn towards us.

Just as we were getting through the mass of people we smelt a wonderful aroma of coffee drifting from one of the shops. We had been without food for three days, just eating a few blackberries here and there and the strain of climbing had left us weak and very cold. The smell of coffee being prepared is a great attraction at the best of times, but under these conditions the temptation was overwhelming. I was the first to enter the shop. Luckily there was nobody inside drinking, so we sat down at a small table and waited to see who would come to take our order. Looking round, I could see a woman's face peering from behind a beaded curtain, covering a doorway. I called to her and she slowly came up to the table. I ordered two coffees. In a few minutes she came back in what was a rather peculiar manner, gingerly placing the two cups in front of us. I paid her out of our meagre resources, being left with only six lire from the amount which the padre had kindly given us. The coffee was too hot to gulp down quickly, so we had to wait for a few moments. I felt that our own identity had been given away. Two youths sauntered in and carefully looked the place over, then they came over to us.

"Germans?" one of them asked me.

"No," I replied. There was a brief silence, then again he asked, "Germans?" I said we were Italians, but this time the speaker shook his head and glanced at his companion, then at us.

"No, you are Germans," he affirmed. Meanwhile we had finished our coffee, so kicking the Colonel on the shins as a signal to leave, we got up and made our way out of the cafe, and out of the village, as fast as we could go.

I kept looking behind to see if we were being followed but I could not see anyone. We crossed over a small rivulet flowing down from the direction of the farmhouse we had previously seen from the opposite mountain. Darting from one boulder to another, we climbed up. Every now and again I looked back, but neither of us could see anyone watching us. Several times we crouched behind a boulder to keep watch. Upwards and upwards we climbed, zig-zagging from one side of the stream to the other as we went. Finally we reached the farmhouse, about fifteen hundred feet up from the village. I knocked at the door. A red-faced, stocky man opened it and I asked if he would kindly allow us to dry our clothes and if he could let us have some food. He asked us to come in, and I was surprised to see the house was full of people.

When we were inside the house, he asked us who we were and where we had come from. Before I replied, I asked him who were these people in the room. Straightaway he introduced them to us.

"This is my son," he said, "who has just arrived home from France. He escaped from the Germans there, as they were trying to force our Italian army to do all the dirty work. This is my wife, these are my two daughters and my son-in-law. My son-in-law was in the army but he too ran away, so you see you need not be afraid, *Signori.*"

He spoke in a strange Italian dialect, but I managed to understand. I thanked him, telling him it was nice to feel safe, and that we were British officers. My Italian was not very good, but the farmer understood me very well. He seemed pleased and invited us to come nearer the fire, telling his wife to bring some food. When I heard this I was all too aware of pangs of real hunger. We put our coats, books and socks near the fire and warmed ourselves as the clothes dried. We took off our shirts, but when the farmer's wife saw us in our undervests she told us to take them off as well. The heat in the room was now beginning to make me feel uncomfortable, for the wet trousers and underpants were becoming very sticky and very irritating. I was beginning to wish that I was the only occupant in the room! The *Signora* gave us a large chunk of cheese each and two 'doorstep' slices of bread. Whilst eating and chatting to the family, we kept close watch on our clothes.

Suddenly there was a sharp knock on the door. We grabbed our things together and fled into the back of the house. There was no escape that way, so we stood still and listened to see what would happen next. We heard the farmer open the door, then we heard the callers ask where the Englishmen were. We heard the reply that there were no Englishmen in the house. We could hear heavy footsteps inside the room and an excitable chatter develop between the visitors and the farmer and his family.

"Povera noi, povera noi! Mama mia! Mama mia!" These were the only clear words I could hear and they were spoken by the farmer's wife, alarmed by the danger.

All at once she came into the kitchen where we were. She asked us to come out, for the *Carabinieri* had come to arrest us. She said she hoped they might be talked into letting us go, as they were friends of theirs. I could see the tears in her eyes and the fear in her face. The *Carabinieri* knew where we were, so there was no alternative but to show ourselves and to try and talk them into letting us go. When we confronted them, I could see that they were armed and had their pistols drawn.

"Are you British?" one asked me.

"Yes," I said.

"Where have you come from?"

"We have come from the prison camp outside Parma."

"Have you any identity?"

With that, I showed him proof of our stay in our last camp.

"Listen," I said to them, "It won't do any good to arrest us, for our troops will be here soon and it will not be to your advantage to prevent us from leaving."

The police officer said, "*Signor,* why did you have to come this way? This village is full of Fascists. Two of them were those who spoke to you in the cafe. One of them watched how you came here, whilst the other came to us and forced us to come after you. Now, *Signori,*" he continued, "If we do not take you, the Fascists will only tell the Germans, then we ourselves will be arrested and shot for helping you. I have a large family and I am a poor man. If I let you go, what will happen to me?"

I was in no mood to argue with him, my only thoughts were set on getting away. The *Carabinieri* then turned to the farmer and started to wail at having been sent to arrest us! I tried to make a bolt for the door, but a pistol in my stomach stopped me.

"Don't try to get away, *Signor.* Come, we will have to go, for the *Brigadiere* is waiting for us. *Signori,* do not try to escape for it will be foolish. We are armed and you are not!"

I could follow the reasoning behind this, but I told the Colonel to make a dash for it if he got the chance. We dressed in our still fairly damp clothes, then we were told to walk in front of the *Carabinieri.* It was still teeming with rain, and as it was drawing towards evening the cold air coming up from the valley was penetrating right through to our bones. I felt so miserable, especially at the thought of having to meet the Germans after all our efforts to evade them.

I had bitter thoughts of the past journey, of the days sweating over the high mountains and nights sleeping like animals. I thought how we had been living off the land like wild beasts, starving for days and having to walk and walk till we were nearly dropping with fatigue, when to be seen meant that we could be picked up. I turned to the guards behind.

"Bah!" I said, "I shall never go to Germany!" My fury was unbounded every time I looked at these two guards. I attempted to bribe them. I tried being passive and meek. I tried to escape again, but their warning was in earnest and there was no cover behind which to hide from their bullets.

As we approached the village I was pleased to see that it was deserted. We crossed the bridge, which we had crossed only a few hours previously as free men. What an ugly thought, now that we were under guard! The door of the Police Station was flung open and we were thrust into the office of the *Brigadiere*. In Italy, where there are only small police stations, Police Sergeants are in charge who usually have command over six to twelve constables. The Sergeant asked us for our ranks and names, and when the Colonel gave his rank the *Brigadiere* jumped up and offered him a seat. He expostulated about his feelings regarding our capture, saying that when he was informed that we were in the village, by the Fascists, he had no alternative but to send his men out to get us. The whole time of the arrest his men were being watched by the Fascists to see that they did arrest us.

With the formalities over, we were allowed to destroy all photographs, maps and anything which would provide the Germans with information. Then we were shown up to the *Carabinieri's* common room. We had our clothes taken away to be dried and in their place, we were provided with two blankets which we wound round our waists like skirts. Then we were given a good meal. I shall never forget that meal, although it was consumed under the roof of a hostile building. We ate until we were fit to burst! The police gave us some of their cigarettes, then we sat round a fire and answered all their inquisitive questions. The same questions asked before by the peasants were now being asked again.

The police entertained us further by tuning the radio to an English broadcasting station. We heard the news, of course. Our troops were still down in the south. I was in no mood to listen to the dance music and the more I heard the voices from home, the more keenly I became aware that it would be a long time before I would see England again.

I suggested to the Colonel that we should turn in early and he agreed. By this time our own clothes were returned, well dried, and we asked our hosts to show us the way to our new quarters. A heavy door was unlocked and we walked into a cell. This was the first cell I had been into and I was grateful for the lack of any previous experience! With a sickening thud the door closed behind us. We were alone. There was a window high up in the wall. I drew the wooden-plank bed underneath it. The Colonel stood on the bed whilst I climbed on to his shoulders. I found the bars to be well embedded into the wall, so we had to abandon that notion. We then tried the door, but that was solid. I had then another idea, which I explained to the Colonel.

"When we get into bed we will have all our clothes on. I will complain of the cold to the guard and perhaps he will bring another blanket for us if I ask for one. When he comes back, you fling a blanket over his head and then we will lock him up in here while we make a rapid escape." Everything was fixed. Knocking on the door, I yelled to the guard that we were cold and needed another blanket. They agreed to bring one and so I warned the Colonel to be ready. I stood by the door ready to spring. The footsteps came nearer and nearer, until the key turned in the lock, and — two men stood in the doorway with automatics in their hands. The *Carabiniere* with the blanket was in the rear.

"I thought you would try some sort of trick before the night was out, *Signor*. I wouldn't if I were you, for you are wasting time and precious sleep. Here is the blanket you asked for. "*Buona notte,*

Sketch of prisoners coming in from the minefield to Rommel's camp at Bir Hamet.

(Previous page)
Portrait of Bell taken in March 1942 to celebrate his Commission.

29 May 1942. Caption reads, "The Bosch and British forces were forced to dig in, whilst the Allied forces were preparing to retake the vital water supply. The Bosch held 500 British P.O.W. inside the camouflaged water-filling point. The shelling and aerial bombardment caused heavy casualties amongst the P.O.W."

Contemporary photograph of Sergeant-Major Fernando Maroni and Sergeant Vigilo Martinelli from the Italian partisans.

(Opposite, top)
The *Gestapo* H.Q. at the Citadel in Parma. During the German occupation a huge *Swastika* flag was draped above the door.

(Opposite, bottom)
Inside the Citadel. The window of Bell's cell is on the second floor next to the doorway. The interrogation room was on the left of the doorway on the ground floor.

The section leaders from the partisans photographed at the end of the War.

(Opposite page)
Throughout the War Bell was able to keep his *Wartime Log for British Prisoners*, provided by the Y.M.C.A. Page 107 shows how he spent Christmas Day 1944 at *Oflag 79* at Brunswick.

(Following page)
The liberation of *Oflag 79* dramatically photographed by Frank Sharpley, 27 April 1945.

XMAS DAY. I got up at 7 o'clock and brewed up a strong cup of tea for my room. I gave it to them in bed with a cigarette each at 8 o'clock. There was an Armistice for the day so there were no Roll Calls.

9. A.M. BREAKFAST. Biscuit Porridge; Cream; 4 slices of bread with plenty of butter and marmalade. The Coffee was excellent too. Cigarette to finish.

The whole morning up to lunch I went around the camp visiting and wherever I went I was given a brew and some little snack.

12.30 p.m. LUNCH. GERMAN ration pea soup. Bread and cheese to follow. Tea. Senior Service cigarette.

3. P.m. TEA. Sandwiches; biscuit with nestles milk spread; XMAS CAKE. Tea. Cigarette.

6.15 p.m. DINNER. GERMAN stew, which I curried; Chocolate pudding with chocolate sauce. Coffee and cigarette to follow.

I intended to eat my trifle for tea, but I could not eat it so I thought I would tackle it for supper, when supper time came round I could only eat half, for even then I felt so full with the stew.

THE INGREDIENTS FOR CAKE PUDDING AND TRIFLE P.T.O.

Signori!" The door slammed shut once more.

I was more determined than ever that they were not going to get the better of me. However, there was nothing else to do now but to turn in, though I was too awake to sleep as I kept turning over ideas of ecape in my mind. I knew we should be taken by the local bus, under escort to Piacenza. It was some distance away and the road passed through some hilly country. I thought of another wild scheme of seizing the opportunity, as we travelled through a lonely stretch of road, to overcome our guards, halt the bus, and make the driver let the air out of his tyres, to give us a chance to ecape into the hills. I told the Colonel of my plan and he agreed that it might be tried as long as we did not endanger the lives of the others who might be on the bus. So, with our minds made up, we settled ourselves down to sleep. Unfortunately as the Colonel turned over he took all the blankets away from me! The whole night long I lay awake, shivering and becoming more and more sore from lying on the bare boards. When morning finally came, I was so stiff and ached so much that I could hardly move.

We left the next morning without any breakfast. As we came out of prison, we were watched from the bus by many pairs of eyes, as if we were extra-terrestrials. We boarded the bus with the guards close behind us. Then came the worst part. All the occupants gazed at us with open mouths as we walked towards the rear of the bus. "How young!" I heard them say to one another. That was all right, but then my blood really began to boil when I heard someone say aloud, "Young yes, but bad." I swung round and caught the eye of the man who had spoken and said, "Mind what you are saying." This had a very good effect, for presently he reverted to minding his own business. He was as surprised as the rest to find that I could speak their language. The guards came and sat down beside us as the bus moved off. Now and then a head would strain round in our direction, but with an answering stare from me, the head would return to its former position! Luckily, none of the guards could speak English, so the Colonel and I were able to talk to each other without being afraid. We noticed that there was an emergency door in the bus, and also that we were coming to a wilder part of the country. It seemed that the guards noticed this, because we saw them draw out their automatics. I swore softly.

Soon we pulled up outside a police post near a small village, where a non-commissioned officer called a *Maresciallo* waited. The *Carabiniere* next to the Colonel got up and reaching in front of us, opened a window and carried on a conversation with the *Maresciallo.* Being next to the window I was able to hear the whole conversation. It really was laughable, listening to the guard as he spun a long yarn about the many times we had tried to escape. He said he thought we should be handcuffed. He also thought we were desperate enough to wipe out the whole bus in order to attempt to escape before we got to Piacenza. I laughed so much that I could not contain my laughter. I rose and said, "*Maresciallo,* we are English, not German!" With that, the *Maresciallo* ordered the driver to proceed.

We soon pulled into a fairly large village and drew up at a railway station. On a large board, almost the size of the station itself, was written 'Bettola'. We were ushered on to the platform and into a large crowd of peasants who were going to Piacenze. The *Carabiniere* stayed very close. Suddenly I felt something being pushed under my arm. Without attracting attention I grabbed it and slowly looked round. There was a peasant beside me who whispered, "A little food, *Signor.* Courage." I thanked the man warmly and edged away from him, so that the guard would not know who had given it to me. I opened the parcel and inside were two large salami sandwiches. The Colonel and I both tucked in. I only became aware that there was an overdose of garlic in the meat when I drew closer to the Colonel! As the crowd increased I tried to sidle off towards the gate, hoping that the guards would not spot me, but I was soon pulled back and then the people realised that I was a prisoner. That was another chance lost.

The train arrived and we were told to climb in. It was a corridor train and we were made to sit on the window side while the guards sat near the door. We were again subjected to curious stares. I must say our appearance did not commend us, for by this time we were looking really grubby. After all we had not shaved for days and our clothes were worse than the poorest wore.

We had been travelling for about a quarter of an hour when we pulled into another village, a little larger than Bettola. This was Ponte d. Olio. At this point some Germans boarded the train. Some *Luftwaffe* personnel came into our compartment along with one or two soldiers. Now I gave up all hopes of escape and spent the remainder of the journey blankly looking out of the window. Occasionally I glanced at the Colonel but he was doing the same. Neither of us spoke for we did not want the Germans to know who we were.

Piacenza was reached and following the crowd with our escort behind us, we left the train and went out of the station by the side exit. One *Carabiniere* went in front and the other walked behind. We crossed the square in front of the station and passed along a road running opposite. We turned and twisted down many streets until finally we walked through large double gates straight into a courtyard in front of a massive building. Here were the headquarters of the German police force. The Nazi flag looked sinister hanging from the top of the centre block and I saw the Germans in black uniforms with gold insignia and I knew that these were the notorious *Schutzstaffeln* or 'SS'. I noticed that some policemen wore dark green uniforms, with a plate attached to a chain draped across their chest. The words on the plates were covered with luminous paint. They also wore a flash-lamp attached to their belts. I presumed these men to be some sort of security police.

We were ushered into the guardroom, whereupon the *Carabiniere* left us to be guarded by several SS men. They did not pay much attention to us. I suppose they realised we would not attempt to escape because to do so would have been suicide. They had good reason to so think for at the main gate stood two sentries armed with Mauser rifles while inside the guardroom, along with us, were four burly and ugly looking types who were off duty, and who would have revelled in a spot of target practice.

For about an hour the Colonel and I waited anxiously to see what was going to happen to us. SS personnel came and went. An SS Sergeant known as a *Feldwebel* came into the room and eyed us excitedly, while discussing us with the guards. Every time a new face appeared, I cringed in my boots, holding back my inward fear. I dreaded the moment when someone would eventually come for us, to dispose of us as they saw fit. Just at that moment the *Feldwebel* strutted through the open door and gruffly yelled, "*Rauskommen!*" He escorted us on to the back of a waiting lorry where the SS men were already in their places as our guards. As soon as we were on board the lorry pulled out on to the road and then the driver put his foot hard down on the accelerator. He drove with such speed and recklessness that I wondered which scared me most — the SS or being driven by a maniac! At least I thought, if we were to crash, we might stand a chance to escape. After swinging furiously round one bend after another, we finally joined a main road. I had some idea that we were travelling along the main road from Piacenza to Parma and it was after we had been driving for about half an hour that I saw the spot where the Colonel and I had crossed it a little earlier.

We arrived at Parma after a very nerve-racking three-quarters of an hour. Dodging overcrowded trams and causing people to jump for their lives on to the sidewalk, we turned off from the main road into a small back street which wound its way behind the centre of the town. With a shriek of skidding tyres, we pulled up outside a large modern building. Across the street from this building, stretching to a house on the other side, was a huge banner which displayed the words *HAUPT KOMMENDATUR SS*.

We decided not to mention where we had intended going. We were led inside and up two flights of stairs, and brought to a halt outside the door of the *Haupt des Sicherheits Polizei.* German officers and N.C.O.s in all manner of uniforms were pouncing through first one door then another, creating a highly nervous tension amongst our guards. No sooner was one Nazi salute and stupid heel-clicking performance over than another would start. At least it did provide us with a little amusement while we waited. The door in front of us opened and a young orderly called the Colonel to follow. I was unable to hear any talking going on which made me more nervous than ever. All sorts of fears were going through my head. The most frightening of these was that we were certainly going to be shot as spies. I could not get that out of my head, although I still had the evidence that I had been a prisoner-of-war. I was greatly relieved when the door opened and the Colonel came out looking a little more relaxed. "I did not tell them anything," he said out the corner of his mouth. I was quickly led in by the same young orderly.

"Come and sit down here." A suave, tall, neatly dressed civilian was standing behind his large desk.

"You speak very good English," I said.

"Yes, I know England well. I furthered my education at Oxford and learned a great deal about England and the English language. You see, I knew that one day I would return to England with our occupation forces and so my command of English would be very useful." What a cocky little upstart I thought to myself!

"You are a lieutenant?"

"Yes," I said.

"Of course, you need not answer all my questions. Where have you escaped from?"

"Camp 49 at Fontanellato."

"Where is that?"

"I think it's near Parma." At that he got up and examined the huge map that hung on the wall beside him.

"Ah, let's see. Yes, there it is. Where were you caught?"

"Ferriere."

"Where were you going to?"

"Nowhere in particular," I retorted.

"Did you want to reach enemy lines?"

"Not knowing where they were, we could hardly head for one particular spot!"

"Have you any documents or maps?"

"I have only this piece of paper which was our camp money issued to us by the Italians as part of our pay." What a treasure that dirty piece of paper was then!

"Have you any photographs?"

"No, I left them all behind in my trunk."

"And you say that you were not heading for any particular part of the coast?"

"No," I replied, "the coast was miles and miles away from us at the point we were picked up, just in which direction I was not sure." Again he took a look at his map and turning back to his table he pressed a button with his finger.

"Would you like a cigarette? Or perhaps you would like some of these chocolates from Holland?"

"No thank you, I would prefer to have a solid meal right now."

"Just as you wish." A neatly dressed SS guard came in and giving the Nazi salute stood rigidly to attention.

"That is all, thank you. You will be going to a good transit camp, where there will be ample meals and accommodation, while you wait transfer to Germany. "

I was led outside to where the Colonel was waiting and he immediately asked how I fared. I told him that I had been interrogated as to where we were going and where we had been recaptured. He asked me whether I had shown the camp money.

"Yes," I replied, "and thank God that I had it too!"

In the courtyard below was a vehicle waiting for us. No sooner were we aboard than we were driven off at the same German style of speed as previously. Presently we bumped over an old wooden bridge spanning a wide moat and passed through two huge solid double doors and under an arch.

As the vehicle stopped, out jumped the guards, yelling at us in German to get out as well. The Colonel was made to follow the guard into a small room and after a few seconds I followed him. I had to sign my name in a book and I could see the Colonel's name was there too. After that we were made to follow the guard through the arch into a courtyard and past the guard-room, up a flight of stairs and along a stone-flagged corridor with cells either side. Taking a large bunch of keys out of his pocket, the guard fumbled one of them into a rusty-looking lock. With a loud screech the door was unlocked and flung open. Suddenly I heard a familiar voice say, "Heavens! Fancy seeing you here!" It was Spencer who was a young officer who dined at my table in Fontanellato. There was another young officer with him.

For half an hour we talked about the escape back at the camp and how each had fared before being recaptured. During that time we had forgotten about the grim realities of a cell. Spencer's friend, whom I had not known very well in the camp, joined in. It seemed that they had preceded us here by two days and were still waiting for something to eat.

"I suppose you both saw the same chap we saw at the *Kommendatur* — the civilian?" I said.

"Yes, we saw him all right." There was a good deal of anger in Spencer's voice when he uttered that remark.

"I suppose you have tried all possibilities for escape, Spencer?" asked the Colonel.

Spencer told him to put all thought of escape out of his mind as one would have to get across the moat. One poor Italian had tried it and had not lived very long after. He thought it better to wait until we got out of the place. After discussing the matter thoroughly, we soon found ourselves slipping into their state of dejection, although our arrival had helped to break the monotony for them. The Colonel began to pace the floor. The other two had spent the previous two days pacing up and down and were now content merely to lie down on the only camp bed.

I was too restless to sit down on either of the two chairs and it was impossible to join the Colonel in pacing the floor as it was too small, so I just stood by the tiny window and gazed out on to the courtyard below. German cavalry troops were being drilled in mounting and dismounting their chargers, whilst others were busy cleaning the stables and grooming the other mounts. There was no doubt that those animals were from good stock. "Probably some of those that we sold to Germany before the war," I thought. Italian soldiers as prisoners were few but they were mostly all employed as stable hands or in some cases employed as batmen to the German troops.

Through the thick stone corridors I heard heavy boots thudding along towards our door. As the noise stopped, it was replaced by a jingle of keys and a rattle of the lock. Then the door was heaved aside. *"Raukskommen!"* Without a word to each other we followed the guard. Tense though we were, each man bore himself calmly. I remember how lovely the fresh air smelt as we came down the stairs into the courtyard. Motioning to us to get on to a truck that was waiting under the arch was an officer, presumably the Commanding Officer. The guards jumped over the tail-board after us and yelled to the driver to go. We seemed to by-pass Parma by taking a road on the outskirts which headed north. For at least one hour we were subjected to choking dust which filled our eyes, ears and nostrils and we were dangerously threatened whenever we were tossed towards the tail-board by the menace of a bayonet.

Every bone was aching when we were made to get out of the vehicle. Our destination was an ex-Italian Artillery Depot and I subsequently guessed that we were at Mantova. Huge, sleek, black Alsatian guard dogs were tugging at their masters' short leads, showing their white fangs as though they were issuing a warning to anyone who might try to jump the brick wall. Strangely enough we were then left alone inside the compound. Seeing a few of our own fellow fugitives in the entrance to one of the sheds, we joined them and found them to be officers who had had similar experiences to ours whereupon we had great discussion comparing our mistakes.

After chatting for a little while, we listened to each other's stories and they were very interesting to hear such as those who had walked over the Alps into Switzerland where they were interned. We hunted around for a bed but as they had all been taken by the previous arrivals the concrete floor had to suffice. Some time later we were called by the German interpreter to get our food ration. As we went I was astounded to see hundreds of Italian prisoners pouring out of a large shed at the lower end of the compound. There were all types, from the Navy, the Army and even from the *Carabiniere.* To see the treatment being meted out to them by the Germans was appalling. For no apparent reason the guards would unleash their dogs, whereupon they would make a dash for the nearest helpless Italian and begin to tear him apart.

Several times we saw this occur. We lined up for our ration and I received a small mug of coffee, a piece of black bread and half a tin of some sort of Italian meat, similar to the type we had in the desert. I was very hungry so I took a large bite of the bread, but immediately spat out the lot. It was the first time I had seen or tasted the stuff and it was frightful. The meat went in one mouthful and the coffee in two gulps. I kept the bread and later on I gave it to an Italian who was begging for food.

Some American prisoners came in later that afternoon and we enjoyed chatting to them and were interested in their stories of how lucky they had been — or not been, as the case may be. Some of them had been air crews and were glad to be alive to tell of their adventures as some of their chums had been less fortunate. Their stories were buried with them.

I was happy to see the afternoon draw to a close and to welcome night fall. The past few days with so little food were beginning to tell on me, for I found I required more sleep. The cool breeze which stirred up the dust inside our shed made the night colder to bear. I buried myself in the one blanket that our hosts had issued and I began to sleep on the concrete floor. The Germans were shouting, "Lights out!" Those wretched dogs broke the silence of the still night air by barking. Their savage growls were followed by the terrifying scream of some poor victim.

No one dared to go out, not even to the latrines, for fear of those brutes. "Halt! Halt!" Those shouts would never cease, it seemed. Just as I was able to doze off, the steel doors clattered open and the guards came in with their dogs. "*Ein, zwei, drei, vier* etc." At the slightest move, the dogs would strain their leash in readiness to pounce. No sooner had I fallen off to sleep again, then I was awakened by the cold of the concrete penetrating through my blanket and making sleep impossible. The rest of the prisoners were up as early as I was, for they could not sleep either.

How grateful we were for a small mug of hot liquid. The Germans brought the ersatz coffee in a huge urn but seemed to pay more attention to the Italians, for which I was thankful. As long as those dogs were far away from me, I felt a little easier.

"*Achtung! Achtung! Achtung!*" This startling word was bawled out over the loudspeaker system. "All English and American prisoners are to line up in fives," to await the pleasure of the interpreter. Before we could realise what that was all about, a cocky little *Feldwebel* strutted up to the largest group of officers and, barking his commands, behaved like a bad tempered dachshund! The officers were ordered to line up in fives, with their belongings. By now we were used to this barking and we used to reply by causing as much delay to the orders as we could. Slowly we broke up and wandered into the shed to collect our precious bundles and with those we very clumsily formed up into a not-so-very-straight rank of 'fives'. Still barking, the interpreter yelled for more order and, pushing some officers into line, began to take the count. When he finished he wore the same worried look on his face as he had when he first began. I still don't think he knew how many prisoners he had to account for. It was at this point I realised that I had not seen the Colonel since entering the compound and wondered where he had been taken.

"Follow me," the *Feldwebel* said, as he continued to wade through a mass of conflicting figures on a dirty sheet of paper. Tripping over a stone, to the accompaniment of jeering laughter from us, he strutted off in the direction of a large shed at the far end of the compound. We followed slowly until we saw the dogs appear, then we gained momentum and followed the *Feldwebel* in a more orderly manner. We were halted outside the shed and only the first five were allowed in. The Commandant, the Assistant Commandant, the Orderly Officer and about twenty-five guards were awaiting our arrival.

I was one of the first five. The interpreter called us to post ourselves opposite a blanket, of which there were five stretched out flat on the floor. Each blanket was separated from the next by about two feet. The German officers stood in a group in front of the blankets and we were ordered to stand at the opposite end, facing them. The Commandant spoke to the *Feldwebel,* whereupon he turned around and ordered us to put all our belongings on to the blankets and strip completely. At this latest order we protested strongly, but one of the senior British officers told us to comply with the order, saying that he would make a protest later to the right source. We complied with the order and then there was a discussion between the German officers. Of course we were left standing stark naked and shivering. A guard came up to me and ordered me to put my hands on my head. He then ran his hands over my body and ordering me to bend over he searched my person in the most humiliating fashion. When he had satisfied himself that I had not concealed anything, he curtly ordered me to dress. While I was dressing he went through my few belongings. It was only when the guard had completely finished with me and had started to search the officer on my left that my temper started to cool down. Fortunately I was able to preserve the ownership of my penknife by forcing it into my anus and the fact that it had not been discovered pleased me greatly.

I could not help watching the expression of lewd gratification on the face of the Commandant each time his guards found something to confiscate. They were always such petty things like pocket mirrors, razors, metal toothpaste containers. In one case they wanted to confiscate a steel photo-frame, complete with the photograph of his wife and it was only after a very heated argument that the officer concerned was allowed to keep it. When the search was over we were ordered out of the shed and made to wait outside in a group, closely guarded. When everybody had been searched we were again formed up in fives and recounted. When this had been done we were ordered to follow the German Orderly Officer. We shuffled off, kicking up little puffs of dust across the compound, watched by crowds of haggard looking Italians. The Commandant stood at the gate and as we passed him a look of sadistic glee crossed his face that even Epstein could not model.

As our feet struck the cobble stones of the narrow lane outside the compound, they seemed to beat out a rhythm of defiance. My brain was working hard to devise a way to take my feet to freedom as soon as the chance offered itself. Mantova held no interest for me, nor did its inhabitants. I was only interested in escape. At the sight of the marshalling yard our hopes completely faded. Crossing one railway line and then another, we were halted alongside a long row of huge cattle trucks. Each one had its small windows closed with barbed wire. The sliding doors were open in readiness to receive the human cargo. *"Gehen in die reihe!"* was all we heard as we were pushed into line. The more they shouted and pushed us, the more we became obstinate. The Germans were usually methodical in their handling of prisoners, but this particular morning they seemed not to know what to do next.

The mist, still hanging low over the countryside, made the air damp and cold. The walk had warmed us up a little, but standing around cooled us down very quickly, so that our feet became numb. We tried slapping our chests, swinging our arms, stamping our feet, but we could not get warm. Some of us stamped up and down in the front of the trucks. It was when we did that, that we first noticed our guards had dwindled in number and those who were left were showing the embarrassment of our superiority of numbers by nervously fingering their rifles. On the other side of our line of cattle trucks, the Italians were shunting goods trucks from one line to another and pushing some wagons on to free sidings. Every now and then the view up and down the marshalling yard would be blurred by the fine mist, falling then slowly rising again to permit a little sun to penetrate. Terry, an acquaintance, standing just beside me, had apparently been watching me as I stared between two cattle trucks and out on to the rails beyond. He asked me if I was thinking of trying to escape. I told him to be quiet as I did not want anyone to know. He wanted to come with me but it was obvious from his appearance that this was impossible. He wore too many items of British uniform. A dirty bandage was peeping through his torn and blood-stained battledress pants. "Terry," I said, "your chance will come when you're ready, so don't worry too much." We gripped each other's arms and listened carefully. We heard a train coming, so I asked Terry to keep his eye on the guards and give me the O.K. as the train came alongside.

CHAPTER ELEVEN

My heart was beating fast. I was longing to know whether it was a freight or passenger train. Terry gave me the signal and I got myself between the wheels on the far side of the cattle trucks as quickly as possible. I laid low. It was then that I saw the train and with joy knew that it was a goods train. My heart thumped louder and louder. The train slowed down for the rail junctions and pulled abreast of me, just two tracks away. Looking rapidly up and down the line to see whether it was all clear, I ran for all I was worth across the lines and alongside the wagons until I came to the couplings between the cars. I grabbed hold of the buffer and swung my feet up on to the buffer of the following wagon. Then I worked my way over to the couplings and hung on to those for all I was worth, as the train ran onto another line, almost throwing me off balance. From there, I managed to swing my legs under the leading wagon and entwine them around the thick axle. Sliding my hands from one hold to another, I eventually gained a hold on the springs. Then I lowered myself down beneath the wagon, lying flat along the axle. This position afforded me very good cover, for the continental wagons have bogey wheels and are closely hung. If they had used the type we have in England, then such a means of escape would have been impossible. As soon as I had made myself secure I suddenly realised that the train might stop. It occurred to me that Mantova was not a large town and that this train could be a German supply train. With that thought another doubt assailed me, for if that were so, then it would be well guarded. Slowly, the train continued, crossing from one track to another until finally it came on to a straight line and began to pick up speed. I was shivering and wet from perspiration as I relaxed, knowing that the train had left the town and would have no reason to stop in that area.

As mile after mile passed, the train did not slow down. I was deaf from the noise of the wheels and my hands and feet had long since become numbed by the cold steel and the icy wind that was sweeping underneath the wagons with a vengeance. Often my feet would slip and many times I narrowly missed falling off the axle altogether.

Fear, fear, fear. The whole time I was in a state of fear, chiefly, fear from wondering if the train was going in the right direction and fear as to whether my escape had been noticed and the alarm given to all the stations along the line, ordering all trains to be stopped and searched. I tried to console myself with the thought that even had my escape been noticed they would not go to all that trouble for one man, so I tightened my grip and endured. I felt the train slowing down, and looking between the wheels, I could see we were about to cross a bridge over a wide river. Gripping the axle still more tightly and lying as flat as I could, I waited for the worst. Most of the bridges were guarded by German troops and I thought that surely this one, being so large, would not be an exception. Slowly the train ran on to the bridge and somehow I had missed seeing the sentry box. Perhaps it was on the other side and the Germans had seen me. No, so far everything was all right. There was still the other end to face. Still holding my breath, as if that helped, I peered between the wheels. Luck was still with me, for there was no sign of any sentries. Gradually the train picked up speed and once more I felt a little easier. That river was too wide and too deep to be anything other than the River Po. Everything was all right now for we were definitely going south. I tried to visualise the distance from the river to Bologna and estimated roughly that it would be another hour's journey. The country was greener here with plenty of vineyards and small wooded areas.

I began to work out a plan as to how I was to get free of the train, then I realised that the train was slowing down. Thinking that it was coming to a stop I lowered my legs but as they hit the track I was pulled off the axle and hit the ground with a bang. Shielding my head with my arms and hands and lying as close to the track as I could, I lay still. Overhead I could faintly hear the creaking of the springs and the clanging of the couplings, which told me that the train was continuing to pass over me.

I do not remember the moment the train had finally passed over me and left me exposed on the track. I can only remember when I awoke and felt the extreme pain in my legs. I turned, looked up and saw the brilliant sun set in a deep blue sky. All around me were woods and vineyards with a few small farmhouses dotted here and there across the countryside. I looked up and down the track, and to either side of the embankment, but no one was in sight. The only sign of life was the barking of a dog in the distance. I got up and started to run down the embankment, but the blood rushed to my head and I fell the rest of the way down. I found myself sitting in a ditch stuck full of thorns, so before going any further I had to pick these out of my flesh. With a little water from the ditch I cleaned the scratches on my legs and arms. I was grateful for that ditch water, it revived me a great deal.

Lingering no longer, I made for the woods and steered clear of the farms. After walking for what seemed ages, I finally came across a small country road junction and read from the hand-made signpost that Bologna was seven kilometres away. Still feeling like a battered pumpkin, I trudged on until I reached the main road from Bologna to Modena. As there were too many people about I retreated into the fields and rested there until nightfall. I scrounged from field to field and found some potatoes and a few bunches of withered grapes. It was not much, but it helped to stave off those wretched pangs of hunger.

As soon as it was dark I moved off and continued to make good progress. I crossed the railway, then the main road, without any difficulty and reached a farmhouse on the other side of the road. Keeping well in towards the wall, I passed the entrance to the courtyard without being noticed and faded into the shadows of the woods beyond. I tried to put as much distance as I could between myself and the more thickly populated area before taking a rest. How thankful I was when I finally sank down on the bank of a tiny rivulet.

I slept for a couple of hours and could have slept longer if only the night had been warmer. My legs were still too sore to rub in order to warm them up. The only thing to do was to press on and hope to find a haystack tucked in some corner of a field. I hadn't gone very far when I realised that I was beginning to climb. That was a wonderful feeling, to know that I was on the edge of the Apennines again. I looked upon that mountain chain as if it were a great friend — ready to hide me, ready to feed me, and ready to assist me in my endeavours to reach freedom. On and on I climbed deeper and deeper into the foothills, with feelings of happiness everytime I looked up and saw the silhouette of a mountain ridge against the moonlit sky. Then I could not proceed any further because of weariness and I just flopped down beneath a hedge to sleep.

On awakening the following morning I felt very much the worse for my previous day's experience. Every movement of my body was torture for I was so stiff and sore. Still, I was free and that in itself made me think of other things like home and how soon I could get there. Plodding on I came across a swiftly flowing brook, just what was needed at that moment. I had been longing for a wash ever since I landed in that filthy ditch at the side of the railway tracks. Stripping off my shirt, I ripped a big piece off. The water was refreshing, but how cold it was! When I had finished my ablutions, I used the rag to bind up some of the cuts that were still open. How well I remember wishing that I had the means to make a brew of tea.

Leaving the brook well behind me, I eventually gained the top of one of the highest summits around. Now I could see my whereabouts clearly. Away in the distance below, Bologna was sprawled out. Behind it, farther back, I could just make out the River Po. A little to my left lay Modena, but a ridge of hills hid Reggio, Emilia and Parma. From what I could remember of the small school map I had had before, I scratched out on the ground a rough outline of my position in relation to Mount Cisa, which must have been a good 100 kilometres away and, having studied it attentively, I covered it up again and set off.

All the berries had long since been finished and vegetables could not be found. Towards mid-day I felt I could not go on any further without having something to eat, but there was not one farmhouse to be seen, so I picked out the next leg of my journey and set off across a valley and up and over a fairly high ridge. I didn't sit down for fear that I should never get up again, but just kept on going. To this day I am sure that it must have taken me hours and hours to climb that comparatively low mountain, but it was worth it, for tucked away in a little copse on the far side of the valley was a lonely cottage. Practically all that could be seen was the smoke coming from an invisible chimney and the end wall showing a small window. There appeared to be no road leading to it and no electric cables or telephone wires. Casting caution aside, I hurried as fast as I could down the hill, then, almost out of breath, I began a steady climb. The house was definitely higher up the side of the mountain than I had thought and those last hundred yards nearly finished me. I heard a dog bark. I didn't care. I only thought of food, food, food.

I felt very comfortable and warm — and heard voices. How I

had got into that chair beside the fire, only those in the room would know. As soon as I awakened I was given a bowl of coffee, some bread and some cheese. I tried to hold the bowl, but it was useless, I was too weak. Then I got a good look at the kindly soul who was helping me. A grey-haired old woman with a deeply wrinkled face was standing in front of me. Sitting beside the fire in the other corner was a man whom I imagined was her husband. At a spinning wheel on the far side of the room was another woman, perhaps in her thirties. I drank the coffee and as if the old woman could read my thoughts, she filled the bowl again. I ate and ate bread and cheese until I could not swallow another mouthful. I asked them if I could stay the night, as I could not go on further that day. Their reply was better than I expected and they set to, making me as comfortable as they could in the big rocking-chair.

At about six o'clock the following day I was awakened by the old woman, who was called Amata, raking the embers of the previous night's fire and stoking it afresh with twigs and logs. She used a long hollow iron bar as her bellows, blowing down the tube and soon had the fire burning well. Then she hung a small cauldron on its hook and swung it over the flames. With a twig broom she began to sweep the floor. It was the first time that I had got up from the chair when I moved to allow her to brush around it and underneath. I felt very much better and I didn't hesitate to tell her so. She just replied that I still had to take it easy. I was wondering where the other two were. An ugly thought crept into my head that perhaps the young woman, her daughter I presumed, had probably gone off to bring the Fascists.

By the time the old lady had cleaned the room, the coffee was boiling, so, swinging it off the flames, she then went over to the door and yelled, "Amata!" Presently she appeared, carrying a huge water jug and a large bundle of twigs under her arm. I got up to help with the jug, but she was stronger than I. The old lady poured out the coffee into four bowls and then the old man came in through the front door, after first scraping his thickly mudded boots on an iron bar.

The peasants were very curious and asked me many questions. Was I an Englishman? Did I feel better or would I like to stay for a further day? They asked me my age and where I had come from and where I thought I was going. They wanted to know where I had lived in England — and if I was married? I answered as best as I could in my poor Italian. They seemed to be very interested to know where I had come from. Of course I only told them that I had come from a prisoner-of-war camp and was trying to escape from the Germans. They said that they would help me all they could. They then asked me if I could eat any more salami or cheese. My sign of rubbing my stomach was sufficient to tell them that I had had enough to eat. I told them that I wanted to leave because I wanted to get home to England before the cold weather started in properly. They understood quite well and immediately prepared a parcel of bread, cheese, salami and a bottle of milk.

I was feeling fit enough to tackle the trek again and so I tugged on my boots with the utmost difficulty, for my feet were still swollen. I picked up the parcel and thanked the folk for their kindness. I only wished that I had something to give them in return, but in this case I was the poor one.

The old man directed me over towards Mount Cisa. He discouraged me a little when I asked him how far away it was, for he replied that it was a good sixty kilometres. Thanking him again for his hospitality, I hobbled down a little path and then followed it up until it vanished in a wood on the side of the mountain.

When I got to the top there was a beautiful view of the surrounding country for miles and miles in almost all directions. Behind me the plain of Lombardy could no more be seen. Away over towards the west the mountains presented a picture no artist could convey. Cisa was still too far away to be seen. I tried to imagine what the sea looked like along the Riviera and thought of the distance I still had to cover before I got there. It was no use thinking about that, the distance had to be traversed.

I walked for two days, keeping to a strict diet, although I could have eaten my stock of food in one meal. I had discarded my boots, which had become unbearable, soon after leaving the cottage. I strung them around my neck by their laces, for I knew I would certainly use them when my feet became normal again. Surprisingly, it was not too bad having to walk in bare feet. By this time they were becoming accustomed to the sharp stones and twigs. I could always find a little cover in which to shelter for the night, although there was really no protection from the damp. When the cold prevented sleep I would talk to myself and recall all the happy events of my life. Abnormal thoughts, strange and imaginary incidents crossed my mind persistently, which under ordinary circumstances would never have occurred.

I had passed Pavullo, over to my extreme right. Five days had now passed since leaving the railway line and oddly I felt myself gaining strength every day. My bare feet were now completely conditioned to the hard ground but it was a thorough nuisance having to put up with the heavy boots around my neck.

Now and then I came across young herdsmen who were out in the countryside all day, moving their cattle and sheep from one grazing ground to another. Some of the cattle carried a Swiss type of cow-bell round their necks which acted as a warning of their approach. I tried not to let these people see me and I must have succeeded for I was never followed. In some of the woods there would be teams of peasants cutting wood for the winter. These people I avoided, not being sure whether they were working for the Germans or for themselves.

One little village I came to was so small and so elevated that it was almost impossible to avoid, being perched on a rugged peak in a break in the ridge of the mountains. As I passed through I felt eyes peering at me, but I was not stopped by anyone. Climbing down an almost precipitous slope which led to a well-cultivated valley a few hundred feet below, I crossed a narrow but very deep river by a little wooden bridge. I don't know what I would have done if that bridge had not been there. Still, I was glad to leave the village behind me, for I always had the feeling that someone might be suspicious and follow me to find out which way I was going.

I gained the top of the next summit and picked out a spot where I could study the next stage of my journey. I sat down on the rocks and ate a bit of bread and cheese. By this time the bread was really hard, but it was food. The cheese was still O.K., but the milk had almost turned to curd. Anyway, it was good stuff to eat. Once more refreshed, I slithered down the smooth and very short grass ending up on a ledge which circled the mountain. I followed this for a little way, then I went down into a little wood where I spotted some squirrels playing about. This was the first time that I had seen anything of wild animal life. I tried to coax them closer, but they were not prepared to be friendly. It was quite a relief to walk on the soft carpet that could be found beneath some of the trees. Coming out of the thickest part of the copse, I found that very thick undergrowth confronted me but pushing my way through, I continued to climb. The undergrowth consisted mainly of some sort of berry shrub together with wild blackberry bushes. Here and there were still some small half-dried blackberries, which I ate as soon as I saw them

I was just picking a long branch of a blackberry bush off my trousers when I was shocked to discover that I had been surrounded by a group of the toughest looking men I had seen since the desert days, who had appeared from behind the undergrowth in complete silence. Each had me covered with his rifle. My whole body shook and my heart thumped away. As soon as I had recovered from the initial shock I realised who they were. They were not Germans. They wore khaki uniforms of sorts and were bareheaded. The leather bandoliers and belts they carried were of the Italian Army issue. Then I noticed that their rifles were Italian too.

One sturdy looking individual, standing nearest to me, slung his rifle over his shoulder and came up to me. He motioned to me to raise my hands above my head. As I did so he searched me swiftly. Finding nothing he called to his men to lower their rifles. Not a word was spoken by the men and I was far too scared to say anything. I was still uncertain whether they were remnants of the Fascists and if so, what would be my fate?

The leader must have realised the situation and immediately indicated to me to follow him. He led me further down the thickets until we came out into a circular clearing just below a massive spit of rock which rose to a height of several hundred feet above our heads. The rest of the men sat down in a group around the leader and myself. Then the barrage of questions began.

I asked them who they were and the leader replied that they were now Partisans. They had been in the *Alpini* Regiment up in the Bergamo district. They had fought the Germans until they had to break away to evade capture. He went on to describe the furious battles his regiment had fought and the number of casualties they had suffered. He said that he was determined to fight the Germans and the Fascists to the bitter end. He showed me photographs of himself with some of his friends which convinced me that he had been in the *Alpini* Regiment. Some of the men in the photographs he pointed out to me were in the group beside us and they all smiled as he recalled the photographs being taken.

He then asked more questions about me. I told him that I was a lieutenant, an Englishman, and I told him about the camp from which I had escaped and what had happened since. With that gesture I was obviously accepted as one of them, for almost all of the lads came over and shook me by the hand. It was quite a relief to know that I had landed among friends instead of enemies. Gradually the tenseness disappeared. Some of the men busied themselves preparing a fire while others went out to guard the area. I remained with the leader, taking advantage of the opportunity to rest. He told me that he was a sergeant-major, apparently the equivalent of our Regimental Sergeant-Major, one of the men was a sergeant and three were corporals, the rest were privates. He had started off from Bergamo with fifty-three men, but owing to some breaking off to go to their homes, he was left with thirty-five.

He and the rest of the men lived in the area between Florence and Rome. He told me about seeing the Germans using the railway line from Parma to La Spezia and the road over the mountains from Parma to Spezia, Reggio to Spezia and Modena to Lucca. This area, he went on to say, was where he wanted to operate, for he thought that the Allies might try to make a landing between La Spezia and Livorno. He seemed to know that area well for he mentioned one or two small places where the Colonel and I had been such as Bardi, Corniglio, Solignano. He reached inside his shirt and drew out a wonderful map of the whole of the north of Italy, from Rome to the Swiss-Austrian border. The mountains were shown in relief and all the railway lines and roads were marked in. I was pleased to see that map, for it enabled me to study my position in relation to Cisa and the coast-line. I was still miles away from my destination.

He spread the map out in front of him on the ground and produced a well-chewed pencil from his trouser pocket. He drew a large circle around an area covering approximately 6000 square kilometres, saying this was the area he would operate in — Aulla, Castelnuova, San Marcello, Sasso Marconi, Vignola, Sassuola,

San Polo, Fornovo di Taro, Bardi, Mount Cisa, Pontremoli and back to Aulla. He had decided to fix his headquarters where we were for the time being, which was about twelve kilometres north of Fanano and Sestola. He told me that they had visited both those places and had been given all assistance possible from the villagers. I wondered where they had managed to obtain their food supplies. They had sacks of bread, a huge round cheese, tins of condensed milk, a whole salami and a bottle of wine. I thought I could do no harm by staying with them for a few days, for at least I could eat and rest well.

That evening we all lay around the fire after having eaten as much as we could. The men started a sing-song, accompanied by a mouth-organ. Some of them were chatting to their leader while others were picking a spot to bed down for the night. They all seemed to be very interested in how I had been able to walk so far with bare feet, some of the men even tried to copy my example, but they quickly put their boots on again. As twilight faded I chose a spot near the fire and went off to sleep. I only woke once, when in my dreams I was being hunted by the Germans and in order to escape them, I had to swim a wide, fast-flowing river. The current was too strong and it was carrying me closer and closer to the bank where the Germans were waiting to pick me up. On waking I was relieved to see the fire burning with a warm glow and a couple of the lads standing with their rifles slung over their shoulders, near the rim of the clearing. I was gazing at the starlit sky and the massive rock opposite loomed high above my head, when I saw something move. I looked carefully and could just make out a figure on a small ledge about a hundred feet up. The figure did not move, except to sit down now and again, so I took him to be one of the guards. I thought to myself that the Sergeant-Major was taking no chances and that he certainly knew what he was doing.

The following morning I was awakened by a shake from the Sergeant-Major. He asked me if I would like to go with him down to a small river for a wash. I complimented him on the way he had placed his guards overnight and he said that his men had now become used to this type of life and to keeping alert. Their military training clearly was an asset to them. I realised that this mountain camp life was ideally suited to these ex-*Alpini* troops.

The Sergeant and I went off with a few of the men round the crag along the foot of the mountain until we came to a very little brook. It was lovely clear water but very cold!

Feeling wonderfully refreshed and invigorated, we climbed back up through the thick undergrowth and along the side of the mountain until we came to a sharp drop down to the camp site. The Sergeant said he would demonstrate part of their training and, with his men, immediately descended the almost impossible drop. I didn't want to feel out of it so I tried too, but half-way down I almost lost my grip. In so doing I tore a gash in the sole of my left foot. I realised that to do any mountaineering one had to be well trained and better equipped and I certainly had never had the training. Those lads made their descent with the greatest of ease and I must have caused them some amusement as they watched me negotiating the sharp and dangerous footholds in bare feet. Anyway, they did me the kindness of bandaging my foot straight away. The rest of the men had brewed up a can of coffee whilst we were away, so we made our breakfast with that and some bread.

The men stayed around the camp that morning, cleaning their rifles and pistols and exchanging reminiscences of their past lives before the war. The Sergeant and I pored over the map, discussing the present situation and puzzling over what the Germans would do. At the same time he was trying to get me interested in his plan of action to fight the Germans. I had my reservations for I was reluctant to commit myself to any form of action other than getting myself back home. Inwardly however, his talk was stirring in me a longing to have a smack at the common enemy. I knew that the Sergeant would, sooner or later, ask me point blank to join him, so I waited for developments. I did not have to wait long, for while we were having some food in the late afternoon of the same day, the Sergeant asked me not only to join them, but to lead them! From the attitude of the men, I gathered that the request was made with their unanimous approval. There was little else for me to do but to accept the offer, and I told them it would be an honour for me to cast in my lot with them. They seemed such a grand crowd. My whole body tingled with the thought of the adventurous retaliation against the Germans.

We then celebrated with some red wine. The Sergeant gave me his Beretta automatic pistol and his map, but I told him to keep that as he knew the country better than I did — and that he would really be just as much leader of the party as I would be.

CHAPTER TWELVE

As the Sergeant-Major had already detailed his men for their individual tasks and had organised the group exceedingly well, we struck camp. By night-marches over mountainous terrain we reached a point about seventeen kilometres south, on the slopes of Mount Cusna and about ten kilometres from Bragile, due west. We completed the march in two nights. My feet were once again in a normal state after the period of rest, so I was able to wear my boots, with the aid of a pair of socks given to me by one of the lads. It would have been impossible to have kept up with the group without boots.

We found a grand spot for a temporary headquarters — a little valley about 2,000 metres up, with all the natural cover one could wish to have. It was from this point that we began to operate tactically, for our plans of action had been discussed and formulated with complete agreement. During the discussions I had been given tremendous help with the language problem by the Sergeant-Major. He no longer felt shy using his little knowledge of English and I battled away with my limited knowledge of Italian. Words that neither of us knew how to translate became drawings on a tiny pad. With his help, I continued to build up a fairly good vocabulary in Italian and whenever I could I learnt the words off by heart. The Sergeant-Major did the same in English.

The calibre of the men was excellent and they seemed to enjoy adventure. They were loyal to their leader and showed no difference to me although I was a foreigner. They maintained their respect to me as an officer and this I encouraged, in order to ensure that we had a well-run group. Each and every man had to study the position of the camp in relation to the future zone of operation. The Sergeant-Major would ask quick questions from one to another to test their knowledge. Whenever a lad could not remember a location, he would go over the point again and again until the lad could reach his destination blindfolded, or could repeat the message backwards.

The men knew the Sergeant-Major well and showed their deep admiration, almost a hero-worship, of him. Their response to his orders was extremely interesting to observe as there was no dissention — only jubilation.

With some of the sheets of paper from the little pad and the chewed-up pencil, I made a few maps of the whole area which the Sergeant had ringed on the large map. These I distributed to the junior leaders of each patrol who were placed in charge of nine men each. That number allowed us to have three patrols and left five men to remain with the Sergeant and myself. The other Sergeant who had always taken part in our discussions, was placed with the patrol which contained the youngest members. We gave a letter to each patrol — Z, Y, X, and our own patrol, which I suggested should have the letter H. All reference to headquarters was simply H.

About noon, the following day, we saw a very heartening sight. American heavy bombers flew over in a most perfect formation, flying north. Their roar made a cold shiver run down my spine. The men were very excited and this seemed to spur them on with renewed energy to do their bit at having a smack at the Germans. I must say that living in such lovely country one did tend to forget that there was a war going on. Little did I know what was to come.

That night Z patrol was sent out to survey the main road from Reggio to La Spezia at a point about half-way from Castelnove Ne'Monti and Busana, and between the road and the river Secchia. They were to remain there for one complete day and night. All traffic was to be recorded and German troop movements, if any, were to be carefully studied. Strict orders were given against the use of arms, unless seen and attacked by either German or Fascist elements. Y patrol was sent out to do the same on the Modena–Lucca road at a point between Lama Mocogno and Barigazzo. I went out with X Patrol south as far as Sala on the La Spezia–Castelnuova–Lucca railway line. The Sergeant remained with H patrol to go out scouting for food supplies. About ten o'clock two-and-a-half days later, we returned to camp to find the Sergeant-Major jubilant over his haul of food and drink which by good luck he found at Piandelagotti, only a few miles away. At Sala, there were no Germans and rail traffic had ceased since the armistice. We received some information about a Fascist who was giving some trouble in the area and living in Sala, but there was nothing to worry about as far as we were concerned.

Z Patrol arrived after one o'clock and later, at about dawn, Y Patrol came in feeling a bit worn out. They had had the most difficult route, for the mountains are high and rugged in that area. All were happy to have been out on an actual mission and related their stories excitedly to the Sergeant-Major. Z Patrol reported a considerable amount of German transport going in the direction of La Spezia. Mostly they were in convoy. The mountains commanded the road well where it snaked through a deep gorge making a good observation spot and being well wooded they were afforded good cover for sniping. One artist amongst them had drawn a sketch on the back of his fiancée's photograph, showing a precipitous bend in the road and a point where it would be appropriate for us to set up a road block. I wish I had kept that sketch, for he drew in the road block and the leading lorry crashing over the fence into the deep ravine. Y Patrol reported no movement at all and seemed jealous at Z Patrol's fortune. I was glad to see that even from the start there appeared to be a sense of patrol competition which later on I encouraged with great success.

I tried to transfer one or two members from one patrol to another just to test their spirit, but the lads were having none of that. They felt proud of their own patrols, and so each man stayed in the same patrol in which he had started. It was better that way, for many reasons — namely competitiveness, comradeship and knowledge of each other's capabilities which subsequently made our efforts so effective.

We ate well that day and rested before the next mission. That night we struck camp, and with each patrol carrying a fair share of the food, we set off for the Cisa district, in a direct line about 45 kilometres away. Five nights of hard marching over one range then another brought us to our destination. During the day-time we hid up and rested. We kept to the crests of the mountain to minimise the descents and ascents and so made better time than if we had gone lower into the densely wooded areas. We were all feeling in top form.

When we arrived at our destination in the early hours of the morning, the first thing we did was to chose a site for our camp. Finally we found a fairly good spot, but nothing like the one we had left, facing the village of Berceto. I showed the men how to build a 'lean-to' out of brush-wood and evergreens, and with a few of those we made a semi-permanent camp. The only limitation about this camp was that we were on such a steep slope! That day we 'dug in' and made ourselves as comfortable as we could. The men demonstrated a trick or two of camp life, that they had been taught during their army service. They dug out just enough earth from the slope to allow a person to sit straight in the excavation. Should there be any earth movement from above, the occupants head would be protected by the in-cut. The soldier's rain cape would act as cover. That night the patrols again went out: Y Patrol going to a spot where there was a break in the tunnel on the railway line from Borgo V. di Taro to Pontremoli, Z and X Patrols going to survey the railway and the main road from Parma, about fifteen miles south of Fornovo. The Sergeant-Major and I went with Z and X Patrols while the Sergeant stayed with H Patrol in camp. We reached our destination by dawn the following morning. We made a rendezvous mid-way between the railway track and the road for the following night at eight o'clock, which would be one hour after dark. The patrols then parted. I stayed with Z Patrol and the Sergeant-Major went with X. Z reached a point overlooking a small station and village. In the course of patrolling along the track for about two miles I found that the line ran between gorges almost the whole way. Supply trains were moving regularly from Spezia to Parma and the small station was commanded by a handful of German soldiers who were controlling the traffic. One train stood idle in a siding opposite the station.

When nightfall came, we moved down on to the track. Two of the men covered the station with their rifles, while the rest of us examined the train to find out which truck afforded the easiest entry. They were all heavily padlocked and barred. One of the lads in a group further up the line managed to prise open the lock of one car and was inside it like a shot. It was full of technical equipment of all sorts, including automobile parts, automatic rifles, pistols, army clothing and large drums of diesel oil. We loaded ourselves up with the Schmeissers and the pistols, soaked as many of the bales of clothing as we could with the oil and left the door closed with the lock placed in the locked position. We scrambled up the embankment and got away as fast as we could. Every man worked quickly and quietly which enabled us to carry out the whole exercise unobserved.

We retreated about a mile, where we hid the arms under bushes in a little ravine. Taking our bearings from the prominent trees we made our way carefully, in open formation, until we again reached the track. As soon as we arrived, I placed the men along the whole embankment, well under cover, so that they could survey the track on the following day. They would report any movements which showed that suspicions had been raised at the train having been raided.

We were bored stiff lying under cover throughout that day and were only too thankful when twilight came, when we retreated and made our way back in line to the ravine. There we held a brief discussion. Not one of the lads had anything to report, except that a train had passed right through in the direction of Parma. It was an Italian local train, carrying passengers only. We gathered up the loot and made off for our rendezvous with X Patrol. The patrol was already there when we arrived and without wasting time, we all hurried back to the camp.

While chewing huge chunks of bread and cheese around a warm fire, we discussed our various adventures and our newly acquired weapons created much excitement. The next matter we had to concentrate on was how to obtain the ammunition for them. The Sergeant-Major reported having seen substantial German traffic on that mountain road which was always heading in a southernly direction. No tanks had been observed. The men who were with me chatted away to those who had stayed behind, telling them about our experiences. I was tired out and could see that some of the others were too, so we told the men to bed down and to take it easy because we had planned a large-scale exercise for the following night.

All that day we slept and ate our fill. As soon as night came, the whole group was called together and the Sergeant-Major explained our plan to the men. Two patrols would accompany him to the spot visited by X Patrol the previous night and two would go with me to the little station. The Sergeant-Major explained to my two patrols what we had to do, giving his own men a similar explanation. Collecting up enough food to last for three days we set off after arranging a rendezvous back in the camp some three days later.

We arrived at the railway about the same time as on the previous occasion, to find the station full of German troops, with two trains, one occupying each track. The siding was occupied by a different freight train consisting of low-loaders, carrying Volkswagen scout cars, some half-tracks, tanks and the deadly 88 mm dual purpose artillery gun. Other vehicles were too well protected by tarpaulin sheets for us to see what type they were, but it was obvious that the whole train was part of an Armoured Division. The train nearest the station was a troop train. There were no guards on our side of the track, nor, as far as I could see, were there any guards anywhere. I attributed this fact to our exploit the other night being undiscovered.

As there was nothing for us to do and it was now becoming lighter and lighter, I moved the men away to our old spot in the ravine, where we laid low for the day, leaving three men behind to watch developments.

When night came, the three men returned and gave me their report. The troop train had moved off about a couple of hours after we left. The next one, an empty goods train, left at the same time but went to Parma. The vehicle train went off in the Spezia direction shortly after noon.

I took the men off to survey the activity at Fornovo. We marched parallel to the railway until we came in sight of the lights of Fornovo, then we crossed the track and the River Taro, and headed over the mountain, passing the spot that I had visited along with the Colonel, namely, Fosio. We then crossed over the River Ceno at the same place where the Colonel and I had crossed. We made for the mountain on the far side of the road which connected Bardi to Fornovo. Quite a few lads were soaked when they slipped on the stepping-stones while crossing the river, but such problems were merely part of the day's work. Their clothing must have become unbearable to them, but they stuck it out well. We worked our way round Fornovo until we came to the railway bridge which crosses the Taro just outside the town. I sent two lads down across the road and as far as the bridge to make a short reconnaissance. When they returned they reported that no-one had been sighted. I waited for a while to ensure that there was nobody about at the time, and then we moved down to the bridge.

Slowly, keeping well below the skyline, under cover of the stone walls and using both sides of the track, we crossed over. We found only one sentry on the other side. We froze where we were, whilst one leading lad went forward and dealt with him so that he would only wake up when we were far away. The trick was done neatly and we propped him up against the wall, relieving him of his rifle and ammunition and his Luger automatic.

Dodging through alleys we crossed over the main road to Parma and climbed the hill behind the town. Here we enjoyed a ten minute rest. We walked towards Parma a little way so that we could get a good view of trains crossing the bridge. No train passed through from the west, but four trains in one hour travelled south on the main line from Parma immediately below us. All the trains were freight trains.

We climbed the mountain a little further to enable us to get well away from any houses and then made our way back to the ravine. As we crossed the main road, we saw two lorries and a light car coming out of town, so we dashed down a lane and hid in the bushes with our eyes glued on to the road. They were Germans. In numbers, there must have been half as many more of them than there were of us but luckily they drove past up the hill. They were really tearing up the road!

We finally reached the ravine just as the sun was coming up. Flopping down deep into the bushes we took off our boots, washed our feet in the cool stream and left a couple of guards on duty while we went to sleep. I remained wide awake, calculating what our next course should be. Every two hours I relieved those who were on guard.

Next day was very cold and cloudy, threatening to rain at any time. Some of the lads could not sleep any more, so I sent them down to the line to watch rail traffic. As it was daylight I told them to remember to keep themselves well hidden. About four o'clock in the afternoon I sent a lad to bring them back. I asked them the name of the station and they told me it was Solignano. I knew it from the days when the Colonel and I had passed nearby. Troop trains and freight trains had been rolling by all day, all travelling in the direction of La Spezia. The Germans were certainly not losing time and were taking the utmost trouble to ensure that their supplies were directed to the south.

We waited until dark and then we set off — to meet our first bit of trouble — one of the lads sprained his ankle as he slipped jumping a ditch. It was our first casualty but, thanks to a measure of good luck, it was not too serious. We cut down two good-sized ash branches and made a stretcher with rifle slings. We took it easy that night, doing only half the trip back to the camp and lying up the following day. That night we reached camp where the Sergeant and his party had been waiting for us since five o'clock that morning.

Huge spots of rain began to fall until there was almost a cloud-burst. The bright fire was soon put out. Some of the lads unfortunately had not roofed over their 'lean-tos' with enough branches so they were soaked in no time. We heaped up the dead leaves from the ground and hurled them on top of some of the shelters and we then had to cram the lads into those which were driest. When we were quite organised, in spite of the cramped conditions, the Sergeant-Major told me of his adventure. They had ambushed a convoy of trucks heading south, about three miles from Berceto and as a result had a running battle with the German guards. They knocked out a few Germans who were forced to surrender. The patrol then ransacked the trucks, puncturing all the tyres, and then stripped the Germans of their boots, their weapons and ammunition. They had left them to their fate and by a wide circular route made back to camp. The amount of their loot was very creditable as I examined it, where it lay sprawled out in front of shelters. There were several tarpaulin sheets from the trucks and small canvas rolls containing lightweight tents which were a joy to see.

The rain, still pouring down, was really beginning to make life unpleasant. The Sergeant took me over to one of the driest shelters and showed me one of the lads who had received a rather bad bullet wound in the shoulder. I examined the wound. He was still losing blood so I grabbed the stretcher, and after covering it with leaves and a greatcoat belonging to one of the Germans, placed the lad upon it. The Sergeant and eight men went off with him to Corniglio, to seek out our old friend the padre, in the hope of enlisting his help to obtain urgent medical aid. Poor lads, having to make that journey in such filthy weather. The Sergeant-Major cleaned up those men who had a few scratches and attended to my laddie, who had sprained his ankle. The others made themselves as comfortable as possible with the available canvas and then slept.

The following morning, the rain was still coming down in torrents. Luckily, the shelters kept out rain adequately. I proceeded to examine the loot. There was a long narrow box of rifle ammunition, two Tellermine boxes, full, and a fairly large drum containing some kind of high-explosive. Lying beside this was all the paraphernalia for firing charges electrically. The convoy containing this loot was apparently part of a company's transport.

The remainder consisted of six pairs of binoculars, compasses, dry biscuits in large tins, maps and some parachute-type jackets made of rain-proof canvas, which we only discovered when we opened up the wooden crate. There were fifteen Schmeisser sub-machine guns, plus their full magazines, and a small wooden crate of Schmeisser ammunition. I asked the Sergeant how it was possible to find all that? He replied with a hearty laugh that he had 'persuaded' one of the Germans to show him where he could get hold of the materials required. The canvas was as great a prize as the arms.

We distributed the Schmeissers around and issued the ammunition to those who had sub-machine guns stolen at our little show at the station. I was particularly sorry not to have found those rain-proof jackets before the lads went off to Corniglio. The biscuits, made of rye were rather good. I went through the maps, one of which was of the Naples area, with blue markings around small villages between Naples and Benevento. I supposed those to be the area in which the trucks were to be deployed.

I suddenly remembered those trucks and the sight of the car dashing out of Fornovo in the early morning. So that was why they were in such a hurry! Perhaps the Germans had walked bare-foot into Berceto and had telephoned Fornovo for help. Anyway, I was thrilled with the success of the action. I examined the explosive equipment and with the help of the Sergeant-Major I was able to follow the German instructions as to how to operate the plunger. The Sergeant told me that the explosive material was the equivalent to our T.N.T. — I was as happy as a sand-boy now. I tested the binoculars and found them to be almost identical to those issued to us in the desert. Still, they were good enough, and were very useful. The lads prised open one box after another, just like children opening their Christmas parcels.

Meantime, I did not expect to see the Sergeant, nor the lads. It was about three o'clock the following morning before I heard one of the guards yell out a challenge. It was the Sergeant bringing back the wounded boy. They had contacted the padre and while he gave the men some food and drink, he had relighted his fire so that they could dry themselves. Then he went off to fetch the only doctor available. When the doctor arrived, he wanted the lad to go to hospital at Pontremoli at first, but the boy had no wish to go there. So the doctor extracted the bullet and cleaned up the wound there and then. The Sergeant had warned them that if any word was passed around to those who were opposed to our cause, there would be trouble. The padre told them not to worry as the villagers were wholehearted in their support of those who were fighting the Germans. He did warn them however, of two young lads who were inclined to favour the Fascists, and he gave the Sergeant their addresses.

I must say, the doctor did a nice job on our lad, but I was uneasy having him with us in that condition. The weather and our living conditions were far from contributing to his quick recovery. I sent him off again the following night with the Sergeant and the same party, back to the village. I gave instructions to the Sergeant to ask the padre if he would take care of the boy until he was better. Having the doctor right at hand would be far better for him. The lad did not want to go, but we finally persuaded him that he would be all right and that we would come and pay a visit now and then.

For a few days we went down to the railway and took up positions on either side of the track at the top of the cutting. We watched the movement of the trains and took a census of the types and of the troop movements. A great deal of stuff was going through. One afternoon a large troop train pulled into the station and remained until dusk. We covered the whole area of the cutting with our weapons and waited until the train pulled out. As soon as the train entered our cutting, we opened up and sprayed the train with bullets from the first coach to the last. When the last coach had reached the end of the cutting, we held our fire and retreated to a distance well into the mountains. After midnight the patrol which had been operating on the other side of the track, crossed the line where it passes under the mountain. They joined us at a point 20 kilometres south-west of Fornovo and mid-way between the line and the main road.

When we were all together, we moved down to the embankment opposite the station. There we found that the station personnel had been reinforced, and guards were patrolling the track and a freight train which included some tankers. We 'bumped off' two guards and sent the remainder running for cover. We then sent a burst into one of the fuel tanks on a low-loader and exploded it. This caused tremendous havoc to the rest of the train. The Germans inside the station were at a complete loss for they were unable to see us in order to prevent further escalation. The fire from the fuel burnt so brillantly that we were completely hidden in the darkness. The fury of the burning trucks became so intense that we could not see the station either, so I ordered the men to retire.

CHAPTER THIRTEEN

We force-marched back to camp and for the following two days and nights we laid low. We did not even light any fires for on no account did I want to give our positions away, in case the Germans sent out a strong patrol to search for us. I placed men on all available heights and in the event of their seeing troops of any kind in the area, they were to send up smoke. If they found that to be impossible, they were to fire three successive shots. Nothing happened, except that one of the men in the course of relieving one of the guards came across a peasant wandering around. He was trailed for a while then finally held up and brought to the camp. The Sergeant and his party were once more back in camp, so we handed the peasant over to him for interrogation.

He was a man in his thirties and a native of Fornovo. He had heard the Germans talking about the hold-up on the Berceto road in a bar. Then he had watched the glare in the sky over Solignano perhaps resulting from our recent exercise. He assumed these actions were caused by partisans and surmised we were operating in the Cisa area. He begged to be allowed to join us and provided us with some valuable information. The Sergeant threatened him that if he were ever to do anything against us, to leave without warning, give information which could be used against us by the enemy, do any injustice to any one member of our group, or bring in false information which could risk the capture or life of one single man — the penalty would be death. The Sergeant then made the man swear on oath his allegiance to the group and the partisan operation as a whole. When the brief ceremony was over, the Sergeant-Major brought the man over to me and told him who I was.

The lads reacted favourably to his arrival, for they felt that the more there were of us, the better it would be. The man told us of many young lads in Fornovo who were eager to do a spot of work against the Germans. The whole countryside was talking about the activities of our group apparently. Now we had kindled a spark of resistance to the German occupation, everywhere the Germans, being thin on the ground, were becoming very embarrassed. I gave orders to the group that, if at any time any man should see or should contact one of their own nationality who behaved suspiciously, they should bring that person in, without fail. If resistance were met, it must be overcome by any appropriate means. The Sergeant-Major placed the newcomer with the Sergeant and the lads immediately made him feel 'one of the family'.

Late that night, I took the Sergeant-Major and a bunch of the lads with me to the padre's house at Corniglio. We managed to get into his yard behind the church and seeing a light burning we quietly crept up to the window. Lying asleep on a couch in what appeared to be the lounge was the wounded lad we had left in the padre's care. I tapped on the window until I awakened him, which nearly scared him out of his wits. Then, realising who we were, he opened the window for us. We climbed into the room, one by one, helping each other.

The Sergeant-Major left a couple of the lads in the yard and two more within the shadow of the outside door leading to it. The wounded boy told the Sergeant-Major how he had been treated and it was obvious that the care shown to him was of the highest standard. The doctor came to see him every night and the padre changed his dressing during the day.

He was asked by the Sergeant-Major what he had heard from any of the villagers and he said that everyone in that village knew of the incidents caused by us. The boy told us that the padre kept him well informed and each time the padre returned with fresh news to report, the boy felt more and more envious that he was not in the 'show' with us. I reassured him that that day would soon come, and that he would be able to join us when he felt able to handle a gun without difficulty. We told him we would return in another couple of days to see him again. We gave him a message for the padre, then we left in the same way as we had entered. The guards had seen nothing whilst we were in the padre's house, so we closed the yard gate quietly behind us and made our way in the shadows along the little streets until we were able to come out safely into the open.

On our way back to the camp, I could not stop thinking about the newcomer in our midst. I guessed that the other lads in Fornovo who were anxious to join us might repeat his manner of approach to us. There was always the possibility that their actions could bring disaster to us and cause suspicion. I could not help feeling a little worried by this prospect. It was almost day-break when we arrived back at the camp, and at this point I called the new man over to the Sergeant-Major and myself.

I told the Sergeant-Major to send the man back to Fornovo to contact all those who wished to join us, and to follow my instructions very carefully. He was able to mix in with the normal life of the place as if he had never been out of the town. He was never to meet his contacts to obtain their addresses except when he was alone. He was to attend at a pre-arranged rendezvous on the third night. This rendezvous point would be the railway bridge, down a lane from the road junction, one kilometre south of the town, and the time fixed was 04.30 hours. The Sergeant-Major gave the man my instructions and he departed.

I spent that day looking over the camp and repairing the holes which appeared in some of the roofs of the shelters. The previous couple of days' rain had made a bit of mess, but we soon had everything back to normal. In the afternoon we organised a boxing match between the boys. We had some fun, for very few of them had any idea how to use their fists properly. Some of them got a real pasting and whenever someone tried to use wrestling tactics I broke up the match and showed them the better way of real boxing. They liked the sport immensely and later it became very popular. It was one way of keeping them happy when we had to stay in the camp for the whole day. I enjoyed hearing the lads laughing and joking between themselves, although I was at a great disadvantage, not having sufficient command of the language. Their actions however enabled me to understand the verbal exchanges.

Only once did we have trouble amongst ourselves. Two fellows started to fight over a cigarette, but they were soon stopped by the Sergeant-Major and after a short while they were friends again. On the whole, considering the conditions under which we were living, the lads showed a fine example of comradeship.

That evening we went off to study the possibilities of blocking the railway at the entrance to the tunnel near Borgo di Taro. We marched over the mountain as far as the exit, about five kilometres from Pontremoli, where we found that neither the entrance nor the exit to the tunnel was a sound proposition for 'blowing'. The Germans, using Italian labour, could easily clear away the rubble and therefore it would not be an effective block.

We took the route back to the camp via the road from Borgo until we were nearly level with the camp; there we found that the railway twisted itself over the road twice and then the road went over the railway once. The River Taro runs very close to the road and the railway passes over the river at almost the same spot. This location proved itself to be a more vulnerable target for our activities and as it was free from guards of any description, we were able to study the construction of the various bridges.

The railway was built high up on a masonry bridge spanning

the gap from the mountain side, over the river and almost to the level of the road. The road then dipped to allow the railway to cross the road in the shape of a complete 'S', passing over three bridges and finally the road turned again to go over the railway. All the bridges were of concrete with masonry abutments, with the exception of one railway bridge which had been made of rolled steel joists resting on masonry abutments. This pleased me as I visualised the three rail bridges 'blown', causing the whole line to be completely useless.

I drew sketches of the bridges whilst the lads kept watch and when I had satisfied myself that I had all the data, we climbed the steep side of the mountain and returned to the camp. Our guards who had remained behind had nothing to report.

The Sergeant and I decided that although those bridges were a wonderful target, there was nothing that we could do to them as our equipment was not sufficient to ensure a good demolition. In the early hours of the following morning I sent out a patrol to take up positions on the mountain side overlooking the bridges and to snipe any German transport or troop trains that passed. I sent another out to the main road between Berceto and Pontremoli to do the same. At the same time I accompanied the Sergeant-Major and a third patrol down to the railway cutting south of Solignano. A few peasants were taking their cattle and sheep out into the lower regions of the valley, but as we kept low until they were well out of our range, we managed to reach the embankment without being seen. There we hid up until nightfall. At times like this I was always afraid that we would suddenly be found by a squad of newly formed Fascists and that in any ensuing fight perhaps we would not be lucky enough to escape. Now and then I would send out scouts to look around and I always felt a sense of relief when they declared "nothing to report."

Seven trains passed through that day, of which three were troop trains. The Germans were pouring their troops into Italy. I shuddered to think of the rail traffic that was passing via the other routes. However, when it became dark I left the men to cover the area of the track I wanted to survey, while I took the Sergeant-Major with me. We walked along the line for about a mile.

On either side at this point the mountain rises sheer from the track, with the river on the far side. The cutting begins where the river sweeps round the mountain and runs under a sturdy bridge, for there the line takes a sharp turn from the far side of the river onto our side.

We had nearly reached the end of the cutting, when we heard machine-gun fire. We ran as fast as we could, keeping close to the face of the cutting until we saw a tree which appeared to grow from a ledge of solid rock about twelve feet from the ground. Finding some foot-holds, we struggled until we gained the ledge. After scaling the rocks, we eventually reached the top.

The firing continued without any breaks and during this time the Sergeant-Major, who had climbed the cliff-face in much less time than I had, kept shouting to me to hurry up! I was panting hard by the time I had climbed up, so that when I finally reached the men I could not give orders at all! I could only just manage to see what they were firing on. With grunts, I told the men to hold their fire. Apparently, a German patrol had been ordered to 'recce' the line and they were using a very peculiar type of vehicle. It was really a small armoured car, but with steel wheels to run on the rails, with a Spandau machine-gun mounted in the back. The lads had seen this coming down the track and, knowing that we were in the cutting, had opened up. We were unable to see whether we had hit any of the crew or not, but judging by the tailing-off in the numbers replying with their fire it sounded as if we had scored a hit or two.

The car's lights were extinguished and our fire had kept the crew hemmed in but as soon as we ceased fire, the car reversed as fast as it could out of our range. I collected the lads together and found we were one man short. We searched the shrubs and the long grass around the area along the embankment, but could find no trace of him. One of the lads remembered that during the firing, one of the sub-machine guns near to him had suddenly been silenced. We went over the area where he had been positioned and searched. Then we saw his Schmeisser lying on the edge of the embankment. We soon found his body on the track below us. The Sergeant, with two of the men, slid down the embankment and we then hauled the body up to the top. The lad had obviously been killed instantly by a shot through the head. We carried him back to camp over our shoulders, taking it in turn, until we arrived at camp.

The men were furious and vowed to kill three Germans to avenge his death. Up till now, the men had thought it was almost an impossibility actually to be killed. That showed how much trust they placed in their invincibility, but the probability of meeting death on such an adventure was always a real worry for me. I thought a great deal of those men and when one of them received a wound, I felt as though it had actually happened to me.

We gave the boy a decent burial, marking the place with a small cross. I looked over his documents and wrote out how his death occurred. I gave the report to the Sergeant-Major, for he would be remaining in Italy and I would not.

On the following day the group was fairly silent. Italians are perhaps more emotional than we British, but it was as painful an experience for me as for them. I felt this death as a deep personal loss.

That night the other patrols returned from their ventures and those who went to the track outside Borgo thoroughly enjoyed 'warming-up' each train we had seen passing the previous day.

It gave us some satisfaction just listening to their recitals. No fire had been returned by anybody on the trains. This was very interesting to me and, I thought, worthy of note. I thought to myself that the Germans were using their heads here for if they had opened up, it would only have caused us to change our tactics and shoot them up somewhere else. By holding their fire, they were trying to draw our fire as much as possible. After a few nights' attack from the same spot the Germans would have located our position very well and would perhaps have sent out a patrol to hit our lads from the rear. From this time my actions were based on this reasoning. For two successive nights I sent half a patrol down at the same spot. They had orders to shoot at all the trains that passed, except locomotives, for they were manned by civilians. The Sergeant-Major took up his position with the other half and one other patrol almost on top of the cutting about 500 yards away. I took a patrol up on top of the peak of the mountain which governed the approach to the bridges. From that position I could see along slopes of the mountain where I expected the Germans to make their appearance.

The first night nothing happened until about 3.30 a.m. Then the leading scout scrambled back from his position to tell me that he had seen enemy figures approaching along the path which led up from the road to a point behind the mountain we were patrolling. I waited until they had all reached the path from the road and then I opened up with my Schmeisser. The Sergeant-Major and his men kept silent. I forced the party back on to the road to take cover under the embankment, but there they became visible to the Sergeant-Major. He opened up and flattened the leading members of the party straightaway. The return fire was wild, for they could not see our positions and we had taken them completely by surprise. The remainder of the party left very smartly, with a few rounds of ammunition from us to help them on their way!

We left our position and joined the Sergeant-Major and the patrol which was covering the track and then we made our way back to the camp. We remained in the camp the next night and then, during the following evening, we went down to the rendezvous at Fornovo. As we crept along the little lane towards 'Bridge Two', we could hear a faint chattering coming from under the little bridge. We climbed over the other side of the hedge to find out first of all whether the chatter was coming from the men we were supposed to meet. When we manoeuvred so that we could see them all outlined under the arch, we saw that none of them was armed, so we approached carefully and found them to be recruits.

The man who had joined us previously came up to us immediately and told the Sergeant-Major that he had managed to find eighteen men. He then took the Sergeant around the abutment of the bridge to the far side, showing him a neat pile of German arms that the lads had stolen from a truck that had been parked outside a cafe near the main road bridge in Fornovo. They told the Sergeant that there had been a guard in the truck at the time, but they had managed to avoid attracting his attention. Italians are past masters at this, due to having to use sabotage against a superior enemy. It was helpful to me at that time. "God, they had guts!" I said to myself.

I ordered the new group to place themselves between the two patrols who had already 'slung' the newly acquired arms. Leaving the Sergeant to look after them, the Sergeant-Major and I led the way back to the camp. We found freshly-made coffee waiting for us on arrival, prepared by the lads we had left behind so, after a warm-up by the fire, we all soon felt better.

Our own men were studying the newcomers very closely and they remained on edge until the Sergeant-Major called the recruits up on their feet in front of the fire and began to talk to them. He gave them the routine address, inviting anyone who did not want to continue with the venture to say so. No one answered and so the Sergeant-Major proceeded with the enrolment ceremony. I shall never forget these ceremonies. The tense look on each of their faces was lit up by the glare of the fire while they answered the Sergeant's questions and repeated the vows of allegiance. The rest of the men were silent as the ceremony was performed, watching closely for any one who failed to utter his individual, personal commitment.

When the Sergeant-Major had completed the ceremony, our own lads then handed each man a rifle and in some cases, a sub-machine gun as well. When I saw the boys doing this, I felt secure in the knowledge that the new recruits had passed the test. Our own lads immediately introduced themselves and soon all the uneasiness had gone. They were shown how to make their own shelters from pieces of tarpaulin and canvas bags and were helped to dig trenches to drain the water away from their so-called 'new homes'. Judging from the conversations they were all enjoying themselves. I told the Sergeant to prepare a record of each man's name and address in the morning. In the event of any more casualties this would enable us to give the man's particulars to the padre at Corniglio.

It was about mid-day when the lads had completely finished their shelters and in the meantime I had been able to make a closer study of our new intake. Without exception, these were a completely different set from the others, and not so soldierly. Anyway, I thought, I would soon be able to see what mettle they possessed on our next mission.

I had not long to wait to find out, for one of the new men came up along with the Sergeant, and the Sergeant-Major asked him to explain thoroughly what his intentions were and what methods he would engage to carry them out. He said he would mix as normal with his family and friends and would carry on helping his aunt who had a vegetable stall on the market. There he would be able to listen to all gossip about the Germans and the collaboration of any local Fascists. We discussed this among ourselves, having to trust him and finally gave him the O.K. to go ahead with his plans. We arranged how he would communicate the information he obtained and where he should go if he got into trouble.

In the evening the lad went off with only a small Beretta pistol in his pocket. The Sergeant wanted to take two patrols off to the Bologna – Florence main road and railway to see what was going on there. We stacked them up with food and ammunition and provided the Sergeant and his own patrol leaders with maps. They were to use the old camp at Sestola as their H.Q.

Leaving a skeleton section in the camp to guard our supplies, the Sergeant-Major and I took the remainder of the lads on an extensive tour. We went down as far as Fivizzano and over the heights of Mount Cusna to a very small village called La Torre. Here we were welcomed by the villagers and given fresh supplies, and we also picked up more recruits. The whole area was rapidly becoming used to hearing about us. Whenever we met a peasant in the fields, he would always volunteer some kind of information as to the whereabouts of any Fascists, or the places where the Germans obtained their wood. The Germans never left their vehicles to go on foot, they sent the Italians into the woods to hack down trees for them. Whenever we encountered peasants doing this for the Germans, we always approached them and persuaded them to tell us where the Germans had their headquarters. We discovered that they were too scared to tell the Germans they had encountered us, for they knew that they would die if they did. All this information was plotted on the maps.

After a week's absence we returned to camp and all recruits were immediately sworn in. Our contacts with Fornovo proved to be a great success. Now we were in a far better position to rid our area completely of any Fascist or German elements. We were much stronger than the Germans, for if they chose to send up a company, we could rely upon the co-operation of the peasants to warn us of their coming. Their lack of knowledge of the mountain areas would prove a distinct disadvantage to the Germans. Here we could rely on our superiority. Maps are always useful, but cannot be compared to the cunning we were able to employ after our practical experience gained in exploring the little crevices, woods and hide-outs that exist in those mountains.

One of the sentries had taken up his position in a tree above the camp, and he gave the warning that a large party was approaching from the direction of the main road. We quickly took up our positions and I went up and climbed the tree to see who they were. It was our Sergeant and his men, bringing in a whole bunch of new fellows. There were some strange looking individuals amongst them. In their midst I could spot, with my binoculars, five German prisoners; who were being led with eyes blindfolded. When they were brought into camp, I gave orders that they must be blindfolded until nightfall and that they must be kept tied up. On no account did I want them to see our camp, nor its surroundings, as I would have to let them go later.

The Sergeant-Major interrogated them and found that they were going to La Spezia with a load of explosives. I asked the Sergeant what he had done with the explosives and he reported that he had hidden them near the road. After the interrogation, I told the Germans that they had nothing to fear, but that it was necessary to keep them blindfolded until dark. The Sergeant-Major made the translation for me and added that if they gave any trouble during the day, they would not see daylight again. The men guarded them closely, now and then checking that their hands were well tied behind their backs and that their blind-folds were secure. The only occasions they were unbound was to urinate. They were hand-fed by the men and supplied with a smoke when requested. Meanwhile I sent two patrols off with some new boys to find the explosives. The lorry had been pushed down the embankment far into the valley below, minus its tarpaulin cover.

The latest bunch of men were from the Pistoia district and had fled up into the mountains to avoid being taken by the Germans for slave labour in Germany.

Our original party had now grown somewhat in size to become almost a full company with this new arrival of twenty-eight men. The Sergeant-Major took them well away from the prisoners and proceeded with the usual ceremony. Unfortunately, they were very badly equipped for partisan warfare, especially as the weather was becoming worse but they did have heavy overcoats and waterproof capes. The nights were cold almost beyond endurance and the clouds were beginning to hang low on the tops of the mountains. Not one of the newly arrived youngsters had much idea about warfare and I left the training to the Sergeant and Sergeant-Major. Now and then I showed them some of the better methods of drill and how to use camouflage. With the aid of the Sergeant-Major they were told a thing or two about using the element of surprise. They showed great keenness, and of course made the 'old sweats' laugh on many occasions.

When night came the Sergeant-Major and I took two patrols along with our prisoners to the main road, but to the far side of Berceto, towards Parma. Here we took off their blindfolds and untied their hands. I was not at all sorry for them for, on the whole, we had treated them as best we could under the circumstances. The Sergeant-Major told them how far it was to Parma and told them to get moving and never to show themselves around this area again if they wanted to live. They seemed to be completely baffled by our treatment and even thanked the Sergeant-Major for letting them go free. We watched them stumbling off down the road, as their eyes were still unused to being without the blindfolds, although it was in fact rather dark.

When they were almost out of sight, we took ourselves off to the valley where their vehicle had been dumped. We proceeded to cover it up with bushes — then we made our way to the padre's house at Corniglio. We were pleased to find the young lad still making a good recovery and doing well. The padre gave us some of his best wine and we were allowed to listen in to his radio for a while. We heard that the Germans, who were still counter-attacking south of Naples, were bringing more reinforcements over to the western sector from the eastern sector. Later on that evening, the doctor came in and he told us about a German officer who had been killed in Fornovo. We kept quiet about the lad who volunteered to work on his own down there, but I did think to myself that he might well be the one who had done this. The doctor went on to say that the Germans were taking hostages in retaliation. I was very worried about that fellow, but we behaved as if it was of no concern to us. As it was nearly time for us to be returning to camp, we thanked the doctor and the padre for doing their best for all of us and especially for caring for the boy. Then we set off, with the poor boy doing his utmost to persuade us to allow him to rejoin the group. As he was still not able to use his arm properly, that was out of the question. He came with us as far as the gate in the yard, then turned back as we departed.

We reached camp to find that the young lad we had sent to Fornovo had returned. He told us about the new German officer who had been sent from Bologna to enquire about the partisan activities. His methods, were so ruthless that the population did everything possible to hinder his work. In retaliation he had arrested some young girls and tried to obtain information from them. He had threatened them saying that if they did not help him, they would be transported to Germany to be used as prostitutes, A local padre, on hearing what the Germans were doing, had tried to help some of the young girls, and for doing so he was arrested and shot in the square in front of the villagers. Our young lad, whose sister was in jail, had waited for the opportunity to meet up with the officer. When he did, he had emptied his magazine into this brute and had run away until he could run no more. He had laid low the following day and when night came had made straight for our camp. The poor lad was almost out of his mind with worry when we saw him. He was terrified that the Germans would find out who was responsible for the killing and that his parents and his sister would be killed in revenge. We assured him that we would do our utmost to protect him and that he must have courage. We gave him food and hot coffee and made him feel a great deal better.

That day I tried to work out a plan along with the Sergeant and the Sergeant-Major as to how we could best deal with those fiends. The sergeant thought we should go in at night and blow up their headquarters. The Sergeant-Major thought of one party blowing the road bridge across the Taro and one party blocking the southern exit from Fornovo. Meanwhile the third party could weave round to the northern entrance to the town and block off all access. The fourth, and strongest group would come down from the eastern angle and deal with the Germans when they were asleep.

I certainly wanted to blow that bridge, for the Germans were using it a great deal. I wanted to liquidate the German garrison, yet at the same time I did not want to become involved in a running fight. We thought over the whole exercise and eventually we agreed on a plan.

We loaded ourselves to capacity with ammunition. I took two groups with me. The Sergeant would block the northern entrance with one group and the Sergeant-Major would take two groups with him to go into the town from the east.

Precise instructions were given to all men and in case one should get separated from the others they were told what to do. Towards evening we gathered up our explosives and other equipment and all the groups gathered together to set off towards the ravine. We had judged the time nicely, for when we arrived the dawn was just breaking.

We stayed there all day until evening, when we marched over the railway, across the River Taro and up over the mountain overlooking Fornovo before crossing the River Ceno and arriving above the road bridge about 2.30 a.m., feeling like nothing on earth. We had been soaked crossing the Ceno, as it was fairly full owing to the rains, which meant we had had to wade across the parts where the water had risen over the stepping-stones. The night was damnably cold. Our clothing stuck to our bodies so any movement was almost unbearable.

Up till now, nothing had been heard from the town, for which I felt relieved for our journey had taken longer than planned and we had to place our charges and set out lines before the Sergeant-Major could start the operations.

We crept down on to the bridge and were half-way along it when the first shot was heard. Some of the lads came forward in front of me to provide cover, whilst the boys and I hurried to lay the charges. The rattling of sub-machine guns could be heard getting louder and louder, until all of a sudden the town became alive. People were dashing here and there out of side alleys, and amongst them were the Germans trying to get their lorries through the crowd and down the hill to the north road.

The Sergeant must have brought his men up a little for I could hear him open up at the transport. Then something happened which I did not count on. The Germans tried to get across the bridge. I threw all the explosives into the river and took up a position behind one of the abutment walls.

I gave the order to fire — and we gave them all we had. The

leading trucks were stopped and we caught many Germans as they tried to get away at the back. Some of them remained and tried to fight it out from behind the wrecked vehicle. Then a Spandau heavy machine gun opened up, and as we failed to silence it our position became too warm, and we were forced to retreat.

The firing stopped as soon as we managed to get away from the bridge, but as we were going round the houses we were fired upon from one of the windows. We darted into the shadows, and along a ditch, holding our fire. I had the impression that whoever was firing might suppose that we were Germans. We watched the window in question, but there was no-one to be seen. Then the door opened and quite brazenly, out stepped a man. He scanned his surroundings in an agitated fashion. The lad who was nearest to me whispered to me to watch what would happen next.

Before I could prevent him, the lad jumped out on to the road, yelling out that he was a partisan. The man turned round immediately and drew up his rifle, but he was too late! One of our fellows in the ditch had him covered and shot him before he could take aim. That was the first Fascist we killed.

We could still hear the firing going on in the town and I was longing to get over there. However there was nothing else for us to do but to return as fast as we could, getting ourselves into a fine mess in the river as we made our way back to camp.

Just below Fosio we flopped down on the side of the hill. We rested there for a while and then tried to get across the Taro. We waited, overlooking the railway and still on the wrong side of the river. One of the lads had lost his sub-machine gun in the Ceno as he was trying to cross a deep section of the river. Another man had nearly drowned. By a stroke of luck we had managed to pull him up as we saw him go under. In his excitement he had forgotten my orders to hold on to each man behind and in front of him, so forming a chain.

Heavy clouds came over and blocked out the sun that might have dried us a little, and towards mid-day it began to rain. We were nowhere near trees or shelter of any kind so we had only rocks to hide behind. It rained the whole day and was still raining when night came. Aching all over, we got up and gladly left that area. We crossed the river and the railway — how relieved I was to see the Sergeant-Major waiting for us in the ravine. With the rain still pouring down, we got back to camp as fast as we could.

The Sergeant-Major arrived back by another route before we did and had organised the camp for food and drink. Although the drink was cold it was good for it was wine, and seemed to warm us up. It was impossible to light a fire for the rain was still coming down in torrents. We tried to stop the water which was swirling down the mountainside and as the new lads had not dug themselves in properly, the water was beginning to wash their 'lean-to' shelters away. Finally we had to abandon the camp. We gathered together as much as we could of our equipment, burying the remainder of the stuff which we could not carry in a nearby ravine.

We set off for Corniglio and had not gone far before some of the men's boots became waterlogged. The continued marching had made their feet sore. All the way over one mountain, and then another, I could hear the men cursing away in their best Italian. I shall never forget that night. I thought we might have some deserters.

How thankful we were to stumble into the little village! We got into the courtyard behind the church, where the men made straight for the out-houses. The Sergeant-Major left the Sergeant in charge, checking on the numbers we had, whilst he and I went over to the padre's house and wakened him. The young lad, still with his arm in bandages and supported by a sling, was so happy to see us.

The lad helped the padre to light a huge fire and prepare some coffee. I told the padre that we had brought the whole bunch with us, at which news he was very pleased. He had been having difficulty with two local Fascists. They had been enquiring about the stranger who was staying with him. The padre told them that there was no one except his staff and himself in the house. One night they even searched the place, but fortunately one of his parishioners informed him beforehand. This had given him time to hide the lad and the dressings left by the doctor for his wound. He was anxious that something should be done about these two Fascists who had become nuisances.

The padre was of the opinion that as we were all there, those two Fascists might go and report us to the Germans. I asked him where he thought the Germans might be and he said they had come up to Ranzano for wood. I left it to the Sergeant-Major to deal with the question of the two Fascists.

When the coffee was ready, the padre produced another big coffee pot, poured some into the fresh pot and took it outside to the men. He then gave them a huge salami and a sack full of small rolls of bread, which he said was the villagers' bread for the next day. However he knew that the people would be willing to bake some more. He gathered together as many towels as he had to spare and gave them out to the men so that they could dry off. Most of them were standing there just in their trousers, as they had discarded their upper clothing, to feel more comfortable. I was too happy to worry about wet clothes now that I had a roof over my head. Still, when I saw the Sergeant-Major remove his shirt, it reminded me to do the same. Those who had remained back in the camp were wearing the German waterproof parachute jackets, so only their lower halves were wet.

The padre showed the men over to a large barn standing near the front of his house. It did not take long for the lads to make themselves comfortable there. The padre said he would try to get their clothes dried in the morning. When we were nearly ready to go out to our 'lodgings', the Sergeant-Major said that he would have a word with the men about guard duties. I left him to continue the good work and to get rid of the two Fascists quickly. I did not hear him return as I had slept well into the following day. When I finally wakened, the Sergeant was already up shaving from a trough in the yard. I had to ask the padre to cut my beard before I could use the razor, which had been well used! They seem to use only the cut-throat type in mountain areas!

The weather had cleared a little, but the rain still came down. Some of the padre's parishioners hesitatingly came into the court-yard with all kinds of food and articles of clothing. They gathered around the padre when they saw him, jabbering away fifty to the dozen! The Sergeant-Major joined them and listened carefully to all that was said. Apparently they were tremendously excited by something the Germans had done during the night. I went over to listen, but could not understand one word. I asked the Sergeant what was going on. He told me that two men who had been called outside by a Fascist had told their parents that they would later be going off with some Germans, to join the newly re-formed Fascist squads in Bologna. The women were not worried about those two going away, for they were the two young Fascists who had given a great deal of trouble to the villagers. They were more anxious about the reported appearance of the Germans, and now they had come to warn the padre and the doctor, in case they returned with the two youths to arrest our friends for their anti-German and anti-Fascist activities.

I noticed one of the German parachute jackets hanging on a door in one of the outhouses. Whilst the women were talking to the padre, I removed the offending article and hid it under some sacks of maize flour. The Sergeant-Major realised what I was doing and quickly went over to the other lads and warned them to hide the rest of the jackets.

The padre told the women not to worry, as we had come in to the village to stay for a few days, so, if anything should happen, we would see that they would be well protected. When the women looked round the yard and saw just how many of us there were, they felt more secure and went off to their domestic work. The padre then called the Sergeant-Major and myself inside his house and asked us what had happened last night. I left it to the Sergeant-Major to explain.

After the majority of the lads were settled in the outhouses, he and the Sergeant had taken a few men, all wearing the German parachute jackets, and went off to the house where the two young Fascists lived. He got them up and told them a yarn about a recruiting drive for the Germans who, they said, were outside waiting to take them to their new commanding officer down in Bologna. He told them that he was head of the Fascist squads in that area and that he felt proud of the past actions of the two men in reporting all information about partisan activity. Apparently the two were taken in and were very happy to hear that their work had been recognised and hurried to dress. They left their home without any suspicion and followed the Sergeant to where the 'Germans' were waiting. The Sergeant described how they saluted the decoys who kept silent the whole time and how he had told those two that he had orders to remain silent until they distanced themselves from the village. I watched the padre's face during this time and when the Sergeant-Major had finished his story, I was relieved to see similar relief in his expression as many 'crosses' and *Ave Marias* were being performed. There was a brief, silent spell and then the padre told the Sergeant-Major that what had to be done, was done. He asked the Sergeant-Major whether the peasants would be likely to find the bodies. The reply came that only the worms would find them!

For three days we were entertained by the padre and the villagers, with the men chatting over bottles of wine in the 'local'. Others, taking their turn to have their clothes dried by the peasants, had to remain in the barn. As more and more of them cleaned themselves up and donned dry clothes, morale was gradually revived, reaching the level we had previously shared. The padre's radio was a great joy. I had of course lost count of the number of weeks since I had last been able to hear good music.

The padre, the Sergeant and the Sergeant-Major played the strangest card game I had ever seen. They called it *Tre-sette* — and when they tired of playing that, they went on to play *Briscola*. I tried to learn, but after a short while was forced to give it up as a bad job. I couldn't understand the cards, for they were totally different from the cards most of us are accustomed to, even the number was different — forty cards to a pack — and the suits were not our spades, hearts, diamonds and clubs. Still, it was interesting to watch.

The men had finally got their clothes dried and felt very much better after the time of relaxation. Now they were restless, for they wanted to start back again to the old camp, to continue the fighting. We arranged with the padre that we would leave when the first fine day arrived. The lad who had been in his care was now almost well, so we would take him along with us, to be included again among our activists. Needless to say, he was like a dog with two tails on hearing this piece of news.

That evening the doctor was called in by the padre to confirm this decision. When he came, he brought rumours that the Germans were coming up to the village. The doctor examined the lad's arm and was very satisfied with the improvement, so much so that he gave his sanction that we could take the fellow with us. The lad was thrilled and gathered up the bandages, cotton wool etc., for his arm dressings, stuffing them into a small haversack given to him by the padre. The doctor told the Sergeant how to change the dressings and instructed him to see that the lad was careful and that he must not use his arm for heavy work for at least another week. The Sergeant went out to round up the men, whilst we thanked the doctor for his skill in caring for the lad.

We removed all traces of our stay and set off, humping the sacks of fresh supplies given to us by the kindly peasants. Having arrived at a spot overlooking the village and the road, we stopped to watch for any signs of the Germans. We must have waited a full hour but nothing happened, so we called the men together again and set off once more. A bitterly cold wind was blowing, making our hands feel frozen. I carried the sack in front of me, to shield my chest from the cold wind. The others copied the idea, finding it a great advantage, until their feet slipped on the rough stones and they went sprawling. With these sacks, the equipment and the wind against us, we very soon lost all the benefit of the energy we had stored up over the last few days. Struggling like a lot of labouring ants, we staggered on until we were forced to rest.

Eventually, in the early hours of the following morning, we reached the camp. Some of the lean-to shelters had collapsed under the rain and the wind, while others were just skeleton structures, with only their posts left standing. I organised the men to stack the sacks together, advising them to take a well deserved rest, after first calling for volunteers for guard duty. The volunteers went off right away, to the surrounding posts. We located the equipment that we had buried and spent the day organising the camp in a better way. We piled the food up neatly and arranged for one of the corporals to be in charge of the 'kitchen'. We could hardly call it a cookhouse, for there was nothing to cook — unless we cooked the coffee! The lads were whistling and singing now that they were back in camp. They were obviously happier and of course I felt the same way. By the time twilight came, we had everything well organised, the lean-to shelters had been repaired with canvas and the number of support poles were increased. We covered the roof of the stores shelter with large squares of turf.

That night and during the following day and evening, I sent patrols out in all directions to survey the countryside for any German or pro-Fascist movement. The Sergeant-Major and I went with one section down to the railway line. Troop trains and supply trains were coming and going fairly regularly and the cutting seemed to me to be the best place for us to cause a little bit of trouble for the Germans. We decided on our line of action and returned to camp without further delay in order to complete our plans.

Using the Sergeant-Major's scribbling pad, I made a little sketch map of the cutting and the escape routes from it, while the Sergeant busied himself in preparing charges for explosives and made himself familiar with the propellant. After finishing the map, I studied the fuses of the Tellermines and rearranged the German rolls of instantaneous detonating fuse. It was very peculiar stuff and there was no way of finding out its precise burning rate.

That night the weather was bitterly cold. We huddled together near the fire and slept whenever we thawed a little. I had already developed a cold from the night when we returned from the village. The Sergeant-Major was also feeling unwell, but of course we just had to ignore these signs.

I was not surprised to see little patches of snow on the tops of the higher peaks surrounding us, when we got up on the following morning.

The patrols began to trickle back earlier than normal, for they were almost frozen after walking throughout the night. We gave them hot coffee and lit another fire so that everyone could warm themselves up. When the last patrol reported back, we outlined our plan while everyone warmed themselves by the fires.

For a couple of nights and days, a party was to go to the positions commanding the road and rail bridges outside Borgo di Taro.

There they would snipe all trains and vehicles which approached. Other parties would go to the Berceto road and snipe all German vehicles. The rest of the group were delegated to go over to the Spezia–Reggio road and harass enemy transport there.

The men were very keen and wanted to know all about the plan. It was a great incentive to them when any scheme was afoot, for they did not mind what they were asked to do, even though it might only help the cause indirectly. They never grumbled and, wishing to maintain that spirit, I changed the patrols around so that each would have the chance to see some active service.

The wind was very fresh and cold. The clouds travelled swiftly, high in the sky, but now and again the very welcome sun penetrated through.

Some of the men were looking over the arms supplies and replenishing their ammunition from the crates. Those who had the job of sitting tight in their positions overlooking the bridges, were sorting out the parachute jackets to see which ones fitted them best.

We were alerted by one of the guards who had spotted some smoke wreathing high up in the sky towards the coast. As we watched carefully it approached with incredible speed. The smoke turned out to be vapour trails caused by big, four-engined American Super-Fortresses. It was wonderful to see them flying tightly together and looking just like a huge shoal of tiny, silver fish. The roar of their engines quickly became louder and louder until it was deafening, extremely frightening. When they were almost overhead, we could see the American markings and other details on each aircraft. I shuddered to think of the havoc their bombs would cause. The men gave them a cheer as they flew majestically and unmolested on their mission.

CHAPTER FOURTEEN

The boys who had been keeping the bridges under observation had given the Germans enough trouble, which set the time for our big job. Now we sent the patrols out in different directions to raid any German convoy or settlement and to keep up the sniping at the bridges and the station at Solignano. The Sergeant-Major and myself, with a handful of men, took all the demolition equipment we could carry, and made our way to the cutting. We placed our charges along the whole stretch of line without much difficulty, but when it came to connecting them up, it was not as easy as we had thought. However, we did finally manage it and then took up a position overlooking the cutting. There we awaited our opportunity.

Very early next morning, when the mist was still lying close to the higher points of the countryside, two trains stopped in the cutting. The one headed for Spezia I could just make out to be a troop train. I had heard this train cross the bridge from the far side of the valley. It seemed as though a transfer of troops from one train to another was proceeding, but without waiting further, I thrust down the plunger. Up went the whole lot in huge masses of dirty smoke! The tremendous roar of the explosion seemed to rock the whole countryside like an earthquake. Between the clouds of smoke I could see, with the binoculars, little red patches of light reflected against the walls of the cutting. We quickly left the area and joined up with the lads from the bridges and made for camp as fast as we could.

When the rest of the men came in that evening, they reported that they had seen fresh German troops coming down from the north and going towards the south. There were Armoured Divisions, Artillery and plenty of mechanised Infantry.

We struck camp that night and made off for our first camp at Sestola. During that march we encountered many young men, all trying to contact some kind of unit, who were fighting against the Germans. They joined us and gradually our outfit grew, until we were about four hundred and fifty men.

It must have been about the end of October and the weather was now turning very cold. There was always frost and light snow on the high parts of the mountains and it was impossible for us to use the low ground, for we were now closer to the areas where the Germans were more numerous. I was really feeling the cold, for I was still dressed in thin clothing which I had put on when I left Fontanellata. The only extra garment I had found was a German jacket.

We fixed up the camp to house all the members of the unit fairly comfortably. We contacted the village of Sestola for supplies and the village folk did everything they could to help us. But the weather continued to worsen and this made me decide to return to my original plan of making my way to the coast and trying to get over to Corsica. I did not know how to break the news to the Sergeant-Major, so I waited until we had gathered around the large fire for the evening meal. The men were talking about the job which we did down at the cutting and telling the new arrivals all about our previous exploits. The Sergeant-Major and the other N.C.O.'s were talking about the same subject, saying what a pity it was that we could not have waited to see how much damage we had caused.

At this point I broke into the conversation and told them I felt it was useless my staying on, for I was not equipped to stay throughout the winter, apart from which it was my duty to reach my own lines as soon as possible. There were immediate appeals from the N.C.O.'s and the lads for me to remain, but the Sergeant-

Major carefully explained my reasons to them. I felt sorry to be leaving them, for they were such a grand bunch of men. I tried to strengthen their morale by saying that our troops would not be long in arriving in this area and that they would then receive plenty of support. I made them promise that they would do only such operations as could be passed as partisan activity. They all swore that they would do their utmost to fight the enemy with all their strength and that they would persevere to the end. I gave the Sergeant-Major instructions to make sure that their activities were directed only against the Germans and the Fascists, and that on no account should civilians be allowed to fight with them. Care was also to be taken to ensure that civilians should not be punished by them for alleged collaboration with the enemy, unless the crime had been sufficiently proved.

The lads packed up a small haversack for me and one of the new boys gave me his civilian jacket in place of my German jacket. With my haversack well stocked up with food and one of the maps in my pocket, I set off at daybreak. I felt quite strange on leaving the group, for I had become so well accustomed to being with them and sharing their rough life. I could not help wondering what it would be like to be back in the normal routine of army life. The Sergeant-Major accompanied me for a little way until we parted, exchanging mutual wishes for good luck. As our lives followed a separate course I never heard from them again.

I walked south as far as the Pass of Abetone and arrived just north of Castelnuova. From there I crossed the railway and made my way over to the Mountain of Pisanino, walking along the ridge until I reached a point between La Spezia and Aulla, where I hid up for the night. Each time I glimpsed a peasant I hid myself until he moved away. This became a tiring business, for there seemed to be so many peasants in this region.

On the following morning I passed through the more densely

populated area behind La Spezia, all the time keeping to the higher slopes of the mountains. I was obliged to penetrate further inland however, when I came towards Sesto Godano, to avoid the main coast road which leaves the coast at that point. Until now, I had not felt the cold so much, for I travelled parallel to the coast-line and kept approximately twenty to twenty-five kilometres from the sea. But here I had to slow up my progress because there were far too many peasants around and the risk of my being seen was becoming greater. However I had such a long distance to travel that I could not afford too much time, otherwise I would be caught up in the snows and then I might be completely isolated. So, making cautious progress in the day-time I made better distance at night, trying to cover as much ground as I could in darkness.

I had eaten all the food that the lads had given me so I was compelled to rely on peasants. I called only at the loneliest cottages and found that everyone did their utmost to assist me. One peasant and his family fairly 'stuffed' me with chicken and fried potatoes — I had very nearly forgotten what such food looked like! Other peasants allowed me to stay long enough to get my wet clothes dried. Periodically the weather would break and when the rain came down, it didn't just come down in trickles!

After travelling for five days and nights, excluding two nights when I rested, I saw in the distance the mountain of Mongioie, with clouds resting on its white peak. I fought against my fatigue and fortified myself with the thought that by the end of the day I would be in Oneglia, on the outskirts of Imperia. Consulting the map which I carried, I chose a route which should have brought me to the town by nightfall. I slipped past Ormea, but just as I was trying to get across the road outside Pieve di Teco, I was stopped by some children who wanted to know who I was. I didn't dare to open my mouth for I would have given myself away immediately. I couldn't blame them for being curious, for I must have looked a strange sight. One little beggar ran off down the road as fast as his legs could carry him — and I did the same in the other direction, heading for a little brook which was well covered by thick undergrowth. Here I hid for a while whilst I got my breath back!

Then I heard the shouts of the children returning. I saw some *Carabinieri*, along with a few civilians, all of whom were carrying rifles. I tried to get up the steep bank of the river but I missed my footing. I grabbed hold of a branch in order to pull myself up but it snapped and I fell down, hurting my foot on the stones below. That was when they spotted me. If the *Carabinieri* had not been there I would have been shot on the spot. The men argued between themselves whilst they helped me across the brook. My foot was hurting badly. I told them who I was immediately and the *Carabinieri* stepped in, saying that they had to take me to their headquarters.

When I reached the village I was kept outside the Police Station where I was stared at by the local population. I was glad when they brought a truck around and I was told to climb in. I was taken to the German Headquarters at Imperia. After a wait of about half-an-hour, I was then taken for another ride by the Germans to Genova.

I was very glad to get away from those civilians who had arrested me for they looked hostile. The Germans were normal army personnel and so far I was glad of that. We only stopped once on the way to Genova, at a German supply depot at Savona. The Germans there were very curious to see their latest 'haul' and kept peering in over the tailboard of the truck. One of the guards brought me a cup of coffee and a hunk of black bread. In Genova they transferred me, with an escort, on to a train. The soldiers were also curious, badgering the guard for information about me. I felt extremely dirty and had long since given up hope of any rest. The exchange of conversation between the troops kept me awake.

By the following evening just before twilight, we arrived at Piacenza. I thought then that I was going to have to endure the same procedure at the hands of the Germans as I had previously when I was with the Colonel. I spent the night at the same German Police Headquarters.

Early next morning I was taken by truck back to Parma. It was the same place as before, only now the *Gestapo* used it as a concentration camp. The menacing black uniforms made me feel dispirited. All the time I spent in the interrogation room I could hear people in the buildings on the far side of the compound cry out in pain and terror. The raucous voices of the guards could be heard above the shouts. There were guards everywhere. A *Feldwebel* called those in the room to attention as a smartly dressed, but very surly looking German officer in a black uniform walked in. He asked me my name, in English, and where I had been caught. He then tried to interrogate me further as to what I had been doing in the mountains. I did not reply, except to say that I would not tell him anything more than my name, where I first escaped from and my army number. They had suspicions that I was responsible for the partisan activity in the mountains but I refused to give them any help in the search for the truth. I was then taken out into the courtyard and led up to the old, familiar block of cells. I was pushed in with no chance to make any requests before the door was slammed against me. I was left to speculate on my fate.

There was nothing at all in the room — no chair, table, bed, not even hay to lie on, and the floor was filthy beyond words. I sank down in the middle of the room and just howled my head off. The strain of the last few days suddenly crept over my whole body, taking away all my remaining strength. I could not get up, so I stayed where I had slumped, and just buried my face between my arms.

I looked for any scratch marks on the walls left by our officers on previous internments for a form of comfort. Sleep was impossible. I experienced one nightmare after another. That explosion in the cutting haunted me time after time, and I began to worry whether in my sleep I had perhaps yelled out some information about the incident.

From early in the morning the courtyard echoed with the bullying shouts of the guards, accompanied by the screams of those prisoners who, being slow to respond to orders, were beaten with whips. Some of the prisoners were being forced to build an air-raid shelter on the far side of the courtyard, towards the men's barracks. Whenever one of the prisoners stopped to ease his back, he would receive a lash from the whips which would send him down on to his knees. One poor Italian cut his bare foot on his shovel as he was digging out the hard soil. He asked his guard if he could go and have it attended to, whereupon the guard sent him flying with a heavy blow from his whip. When the poor fellow could not get up he was repeatedly beaten, until he lay motionless, dead. The guard ordered the prisoners to carry the body over to a corner near the stables, where it was dumped on top of a manure heap.

That day I had no food or drink of any description. I was obliged to use a corner of my cell as a latrine, as my repeated calls to the guards met no response.

It was impossible to tell who the occupants of the other cells were. I was kept awake during the whole of that night, for the brutes had found something suspicious in one of the prisoners' huts and were obviously taking reprisals. The resulting noise made the night a hideous experience, and nearly drove me crazy.

Later on, when the screaming had ceased, the guards who were on duty celebrated by drinking themselves silly. One of them went over to a hut near the guard-room and dragged out a rather scruffy-looking girl. What must have followed I leave to the imagination. The following day more prisoners arrived and I watched as they were counted in the courtyard below my window. There were men of many nationalities, including French, Yugoslavs and Poles. The great majority of the prisoners were Italians, and these included women and children. When I saw the children come in with their mothers I found it unbearable to watch.

The night air was usually shattered by the harsh voices of the guards — rarely was there a quiet spell. Only on a few nights was it possible to sleep from about midnight until around five the following morning. Three days and nights had passed, and still I had nothing to eat or drink. I had become accustomed to lying on the hard floor, with only the dirty ceiling to stare at. I remembered the Colonel and wondered where he would be now. Meanwhile I still had to contend with the foul smell from the corner of my cell.

Working parties were always coming and going about the camp. They were escorted by guards, who delighted in showing off their disgusting, sadistic tendencies in front of their comrades. The children were all kept in one hut on the far side of the stable. This was quite visible to me and, when the guards permitted them to visit their parents, they would trickle out of the hut in a timid fashion, before scampering across the yard to the hut where their parents were prisoners.

Towards the end of the fourth morning, I could hear the thud of heavy boots approaching my cell. I was then ordered out and escorted between two guards across the courtyard to the interrogation room. There I was told to sit down in front of a desk. Soon afterwards the smartly dressed surly German SS Officer appeared in front of me. He began to question me about what I had engaged in, during my time in the mountains. I told him that I had been attempting to reach the coast in order to rejoin the British forces.

The more I kept to my version of presenting answers to his questions, the angrier he became. He told me I would get nothing to eat until I told him the truth — and then he ordered the guards to take me back to my cell. As I passed among the poor prisoners in the courtyard, many of the faces looked up from their work to stare at me. I found myself hoping their numbers did not contain one who might perhaps have seen me during my stay in the mountains.

I left the fresh air of the courtyard, climbed the staircase and then entered my cell again. I was almost sick at the sight of the dirt and retched as I breathed that foul air. There was nothing else to do but to stay near to the window and try to take in all the fresh air that I possibly could. Despite feeling quite groggy I was aware that the hunger pangs were becoming worse.

During that afternoon another poor Italian prisoner caused anoyance to his guards. He was then brought to the centre of the yard where there was a small circular plot of grass. They stripped him of his upper garments and placed two heavy machine-guns under his armpits. He was then made to trot around the circle. After some time of this, he was made to stretch out his arms, whereupon they placed two more heavy machine guns across them, with the first two still placed under his armpits. Then they made the poor fellow run round the plot once more, until he began to sag at the knees. At this point they lashed him with whips and forced him to run faster. Every time one of the guns looked as if it might fall, the guards gave the man a heavy blow with a rifle butt. Finally, the man could not endure the treatment any further and just collapsed. He was already bleeding from the weals of the lashes but that did not satisfy those brutes. They all joined in the frenzy, until they had another death. A fair-sized revolt by the prisoners erupted when the poor fellow died. It was reminiscent of bizarre medieval occasions, which until now I had only read about, but from then until I was able to leave that camp nearly sixty people a day lost their lives in that courtyard. It did not matter to the Germans who the victims were. When they decided to kill, someone was promptly killed. If the deaths had been caused by bullets alone the victims would not have suffered so dreadfully, but many deaths occurred after cruel tortures that no reasonable, civilised human being could imagine. After listening for days on end to the horrifying cries of pain, I had resigned myself to whatever my fate would be. When some children received the same treatment, I tried my best to cover my ears.

One evening my door was suddenly swung open. Four of the guards literally threw an Italian prisoner into my cell. After the door had been locked again I went over to the still body. As I turned the man over on to his back I noticed that he had no eyes — they had apparently been removed by burning. The smell was dreadful. I could no longer control my emotions for the realisation of this prisoner's suffering was more than I could take. I simply could not stop crying like a child. I tried to help him, but he was beyond help. I could not even bear to look at his poor disfigured face.

Throughout the night he kept murmuring for his *Mamma*, until his spirit failed and left him without further pain. In a way, I was really glad to see him set free of his misery. The following morning the guards must have known the victim could not have survived for they unlocked the door and dragged the body out, just like hauling a heavy sack. I was unable to understand the remarks made to me by the guards, as they once again closed the door and left me with the aftermath of another long night of horror and revulsion.

I tried to hang on to my reason by forcing myself to think of home and all its peaceful surroundings. My mind endeavoured to recall those happy days spent with my elder brother, my younger brother and my sister, but it was to no avail. I was utterly depressed and hungry, and my head was full of the continual ringing screams of my fellow prisoners.

I walked over to the window to catch some fresh air. As I looked out I noticed a party of soldiers escorting an Italian who had his hands bound behind his back. Behind this group was the German SS Officer, whom I heard the guards call *Hauptmann*. The Italian prisoner was made to stand up against the wall to my left facing the firing squad of five men who had their rifles at the ready. The Captain stood between them and the wall, just below my window, with his pistol in his hand. The pistol was raised, which was the signal for the squad to do the same. Then, in German the officer yelled out — "Fire!" I could not help myself, I just stared at them in a state of near-hypnosis. The crack of the rifles drowned the thud of the falling body.

I was startled out of this condition by the sound of heavy jack-boots approaching, and to my horror coming towards my cell. I slid and shrank away from my position at the window, landing on the floor. I dreaded to think what would happen next. Surely they were not coming for me?

Of course I was wrong to suppose anything. The door of my cell opened and all at once I felt myself being picked up by two guards, who made me walk between them. I shook myself free of them defiantly and walked down the stairs as steadily as possible. As I shook myself clear of their grasp I began to sense a strangeness which I could not explain. There seemed to be a Supernatural Presence, powerful, sustaining my personal strength of mind and body. I knew I no longer felt afraid; my legs no longer ached carrying the weight of my body. Even though I was unable to see clearly, through blurred surroundings my mind was clear and sharp.

I continued to make my way downstairs. When I came out into the courtyard, I could see the same firing squad lined up, facing the same wall where the lifeless body of the Italian prisoner remained where it had fallen. I glanced at the officer and the soldiers and at the dead Italian slumped at the base of the wall. I was propelled over to the same section of the wall where the previous execution had occurred. As the guard led me over I had to step over the dead body, so that I was standing on the exact spot required by the officer. The officer raised his pistol and then for a brief moment I was engulfed by fear. As I stared in horror at the rifles pointing at me, I silently asked God for strength to overcome my immense terror. I could see fields beyond and felt myself running over towards a scenic river, feeling free and happy. It was as though some Person or Power supported me. The scene changed back again just as quickly, so that all I could now see were the menacing rifles and the ugly faces of the guards. The Captain was clearly becoming annoyed, as if his little plan was not going to work.

I began to tire of the sight of those rifles being raised to the 'aim' position, then being lowered again. This exercise went on for what seemed an age. I considered the reality of my present situation and decided that if I was going to die, it would be best for the bullets to find their mark accurately and quickly, putting an end to this torture. I could not stand the delay, so I yelled with temper to the officer to shoot me — adding that if he killed me, it would be quite impossible for him to obtain the information he wanted from me.

Without realising it at that second, my statement appeared logical to the German. There was no further delay, the officer gave the orders for the guard to hustle me to the interrogation room, while at the same time he dismissed the firing squad.

I told myself, as I was being led to the room, that if I could keep my reason a little longer, I might still get away with my life. I fought with all my remaining strength to withhold any display of fear, although inwardly it was nearly driving me crazy.

When I entered the interrogation room however, and saw the officer and some of his henchmen standing around a chair, I was unable to keep up my pretence any longer. I had tried very hard to resist but my strength was already weakened by the many days of starvation. Therefore I was an easy target for these brutes who held me in their power. I was forced into the chair. They strapped me down tightly with strong leather straps around my feet, and my hands were bound with rope behind the back of the chair. My head was pulled back by a pair of rough hands belonging to one of the guards. The officer held a strong pair of pliers in his hand. Oh no, I thought, not my good teeth. I broke the strap on my foot, so they waited until one of the guards brought a pair of steel hand-cuffs and fastened my feet with those. Several pairs of hands fell upon my shoulders and they went to work with the pliers. I felt the cold steel in my mouth, then on my teeth. I began to scream and the screaming continued until I could scream no more.

CHAPTER FIFTEEN

I could still hear the reverberations of my own screams. While I attempted to regain my bearings, I discovered I was wet from head to foot, but I was back in my cell, and alive.

I do not know how long I had lain there with my face resting in a pool of my own blood. I tried to turn over onto my side, then I knew that the last possible remnants of my strength had disintegrated. Whenever I moved my face, I felt the most excruciating pain penetrating my entire head. I had difficulty in managing to understand what had happened to me to make me feel like this. Then I recalled the pliers and their coldness on my teeth. Gradually I began to connect my present experiences with the memory of the events in that room. I was shocked to discover that my mouth was completely twisted as I carefully traced the outlines of my face with my fingers. I found I could not use my voice, either to speak or to cry out. I was stunned to find I could make no sound and felt powerless.

The blood from my mouth had congealed into black jelly-like substances which had formed while I lay there on the floor. I was nauseated by this sight, so sickened that I crawled over to one of the corners of the cell, unable to find comfort anywhere. The pain was total so I stayed where I was, hoping that someone would soon come with at least some water to drink. I tried to calculate how long I must have spent in this condition since I was returned to the cell, but this was impossible to estimate. I propped myself up against the wall and then caught sight of my hands. I could not recognise them as being mine. Where the ropes had bound them so tightly, my arms and hands were black and the flesh was raw from chafing. My arms and legs were unbearably painful, yet not as agonising as the pain in my face. I could not move my legs, they seemed to be semi-paralysed. I suffered repeated dizzy spells, weaving in and out of consciousness. I made the only choice open to me and laid my head on the floor.

When I awakened, I found a bowl of water and some black bread placed near my head. Oh! that water! Never, never, never, had water tasted so lovely, yet in drinking it I was nearly demented. The pain was excruciating as I tried to move my mouth in any way. I tried to soften the bread but it seemed to use up too much of the precious water. I could not eat the bread. I think I had been given the hardest loaf they could find.

There was so much blood on the floor I reckoned I must by now be fairly short of it. My clothes were starting to feel very hard and sticky, and I was aware of dreadful smells. I wondered when I would get some medical treatment. The sores on my wrists were beginning to take on a very ugly colour. I could only support my body by putting the weight on my knees, for my ankles were still too tender from the steel handcuffs to take any weight. Where the teeth had been extracted, the gums were still too tender to touch. It was difficult to direct my fingers into my mouth for it was no longer in its usual place. Instead it seemed to be twisted up towards my right eye.

I considered a new approach. I decided that it was a case of mind over matter, and in order to come to terms with this pain I would have to use my mental resources. This resolution was a considerable support and it strengthened my will. I hoped it would be forceful enough to enable me to overcome any further developments of likely inflammation or infection from my various sores. I was also anxious to find fresh courage to combat all the difficulties I would be likely to encounter before I would see my own family once more.

One of the guards came into my cell during the afternoon. He gave me fresh water, and a bowl containing some kind of soup. This had strange objects floating on top, but it didn't seem to be too bad. I sipped it very slowly, at least it was warm and it did me the world of good. I used a little of the water to wash out my mouth, and tried to move it back into place, so that I could experiment with speech. However my jaw-bone was apparently out of place for I couldn't move it. The slightest touch would almost send me sky-high with pain.

Towards evening, my thoughts were interrupted by the key turning in the lock. Two guards and a German doctor came in. The doctor gave me a hurried glance and examined my mouth and my wrists. He made some comment to the guards and then they left me. After a little while the guards came back. They took hold of me by the arms and helped me down the stairs. There I was given a wash by the doctor and then he bandaged up my wrists. He called the guards over to him and said something to them in German.

The next thing I knew I was on a bed back in my cell. I thought that I was dreaming, but it was true. The guards had given me a bed, and on a little table near me there was a jug of water and some tablets in a little bottle. I could not make out what they were, for the details on the label were in German. I was pleased to find that I could speak again, though with difficulty. I rejoiced in the knowledge that I was able to utter some audible words, even if only to myself.

So that was what the doctor had done. Why, I asked myself, did they go to all this trouble after nearly killing me? I decided not to ask myself any more questions. I was more than grateful for the bed and my mouth was now in a less painful position. I felt my gums and realised that I still had some teeth left if only the molars.

The doctor returned and made me take some pills. He changed

my dressings and took another look at my mouth. It was noticeable that he made no attempt to talk to me, but just attended to what he had to do and then left. Later on that night he came back and gave me something fairly hot to drink. This nearly sent me mad again, for my gums were so tender, I could hardly bear to touch them with my tongue.

I was beginning to feel very much better by the early hours of the morning. I was able to walk around the cell for a little while. I was feeling very much warmer, for whatever medicine he had given me had obviously restored some energy.

Later in the morning I was allowed out of my cell for a brief walk in the courtyard under heavy guard. It was really no pleasure for me, seeing the dirty condition of the yard which was splashed with blood in many places. I was still very weak and feeling quite sick. On the far side of the yard, next to the dung heap, there was a huge mound surrounding a large square which had been dug out to provide a communal grave. Patches of lime could be seen mixed in with the top soil. I paused for a second as I passed near this ghastly sight. I wondered how many victims it had claimed. How many innocent people had died before being thrown into this awful pit? Down at the bottom of the compound, I could see the huts where the poor prisoners were kept, and again I reflected on the misery there.

On the way back to my cell I passed the buildings which had formerly been stables. No horses were there now, instead they were used for the admission of newly-arrived foreign prisoners. Here they would await their fate, which, once inside a camp like this, would be on a very delicate balance. The longer the time I spent with the *Gestapo*, the more I became convinced that they were like wild beasts rather than humans.

When I finally returned to my cell after being in the open air, the reeking stink of the atmosphere met me. I rested for a while on the bed and could not help wondering what tricks these Germans would next play on me. I was suspicious of the sudden and unexpected humanitarian treatment, and soon my mind was filled with considerations of possible further torture. I did my best to turn my thoughts to other matters, but the combination of recent experiences, added to the unremitting pain in my jaws and gums, prevented me from being able to control my thinking.

At midday the doctor called again, still accompanied by two guards. He gave me a mouth-wash, more pills and fresh dressings for my wrists. As soon as the doctor had left, the guard brought me some cognac in coffee and some foul smelling soup. I managed to drink the coffee, but the sight and smell of the soup nauseated me so much that I could not eat it.

Half-an-hour later the guards yelled to me to get up and follow them. I walked as far as the end of the corridor outside the cells, where there was a little wash-house. Judging from the smell I guessed that the guards used it as a latrine. I couldn't face it and I backed away, but the guards only pushed me in. There was no alternative but to obey as I was not in a condition to resist. After cleaning out the wash-basin as best I could, I gave myself a wash under the slow running tap, using only my hands. As I took off my shirt I noticed that my skin had changed colour to a light yellow. I thought the cold and lack of proper feeding accounted for that. The guards gave me a very torn shirt to use as a towel. I noticed that it was an Italian shirt and could only guess at where it had been before. My own shirt was becoming like a piece of paper, and as I put it on I knew it was lousy. I suppose I could not say I felt cleaner, but I did at least feel more refreshed.

I was back in my cell, just dozing off on my bed, when I was called out again by the guards. I began to feel very nervous, for I thought I was about to be interrogated once more. We went downstairs and at the foot of the stairs I saw four guards clubbing an Italian to death. I wanted to go back to my cell and bury my head in the straw mattress, but the guards grabbed me by the arms and led me past this demonstration of slaughter and towards the archway. Here we met the German Captain, standing on a step outside the room where I had been interrogated, and partly against the back of a truck.

Lengthy orders were issued by him to the guards and then I was ordered on to the truck. The top and sides of the truck were made of steel, and instead of the usual canvas drop at the rear there were doors, with three visors in each to allow a little light to enter. There were fixed benches on either side, and beside each space for passengers, handcuffs were fixed to the walls. As my wrists were in bandages I was not handcuffed, luckily, instead I was placed between two guards, with two more sitting opposite.

Of course I was not sorry to be unable to take a last look at the camp as we drew away. Even as the vehicle moved off, the screaming sounds whizzed around inside my head unceasingly. I was quite resigned and prepared to accept any destination they had in mind for me, for no place could be worse than that camp.

As we travelled on it seemed like hours since we set off, and I became more and more fearful as to what my fate would be. Eventually we made our final stop. The door was opened and I was surprised to discover that I was once more back in the old Artillery Barracks at Mantova.

There were changes in the camp since I had been there. More Germans were in evidence, and there were heavier security measures, with barbed wire stretched the whole length of the Barracks, on top of the walls. The compound was sub-divided by barbed wire enclosures. The only prisoners who caught my eye were Americans, who stood around in large groups outside a huge shed.

I was led, by my new guard into a big wooden hut, just beside the main gate. The lorry backed out and moved away. I was escorted through one room, occupied by German clerks, into another small room, where I was required to wait.

Presently I was ordered into another office, preceded by one of the *Feldwebels* carrying an envelope. Here, behind a huge desk, sat a stout, stocky, high-ranking officer, well decorated with medals. He wore an immaculate black uniform, with the name 'Herman Goering' showing between two gold-threaded lines on his left sleeve. The officer stretched himself backwards in his chair and studied a piece of paper which was lying on the desk in front of him. In broken English, he asked me for my name and then asked me where I was caught. After each reply of mine he would grunt, "*Ach so!*"

It was near nightfall and I knew that prisoners only ate one meal in the day. As I had therefore missed my only meal, I asked him if I could have something to eat. He spat on the floor immediately and told me that we "*Englischer Schweinhund*" didn't need food. I replied that as one of his prisoners-of-war he was obliged to treat me according to the Geneva convention. He became very annoyed at that and yelled a loud, "Bah" into my face. I persisted however, telling him that I had not eaten a reasonable meal for weeks. He called an orderly in and shouted something in German, while I waited nervously for fear that I had said too much. My anger was making my head ache again.

The door opened and the orderly came in with what resembled one of our Christmas pudding basins in his hand. He brought it over to the Commandant, whereupon he gave orders for him to give it to me. I took it from him and looked at the stuff in the bowl. It was three-quarters full of the most foul-smelling ditch water, with a sediment of dirty black mud lying at the bottom. Of course I couldn't tell what it was. Without knowing exactly what I was doing, I threw it at the Commandant, striking him well in the face and spoiling his uniform. Before I could do any more I was grabbed by the orderly and thrown out of the office with the Commandant yelling orders. Very soon I had more than one pair of hands upon me and I was quickly dragged across the compound, to what had once been a cookhouse. There I was thrown down some stairs. I was roughly handled along a dark corridor towards a door. I was stripped naked, including my boots, and flung into a tiny cellar. Then the door was hurriedly closed behind me.

A little of the remaining daylight could be seen through a tiny slit high up in the wall. The floor was flooded with what must have been coal-dust blackened water. I was soon quite filthy, having splashed myself in my efforts to find the window. The water was very cold, and I was becoming blacker than ever as I searched around the place. Now I had given up all hope. This time I really had asked for punishment and of course under the Germans one could not forecast what that punishment might be.

By ten o'clock that night I was very, very hungry. I felt myself doubling up with the sheer agony of hunger. Now I was unable to support myself and I began to slide down into the water where I was obliged to remain. I kept trying to struggle back up on my feet, but it was useless. Finally I propped myself up against the wall, then I fell asleep.

I woke up a little later as the water was really very cold. I decided to try to walk about, but all efforts were impossible as I was too weak. Time and again I collapsed, the strain was overwhelming.

When the sun came up the following day I had a better view of my surroundings. Yes, the cellar had once been a coal-cellar. I had no idea how it became flooded, of course. No one came near me that day, or the following day. By the third night I had difficulty seeing — and I began to wonder if I would ever see again. I was so weak I could not stand. My head felt empty, yet at the same time I could hear people whispering! I did not bother where

I urinated but got a shock to see that the colour was a deep rusty brown. I crawled to the door and banged on it, but there was no one there to answer. I thought I had been left there to die, and no-one would ever know about it. I tried to scream, but I could make no noise. My jaw and gums throbbed mercilessly.

Very early on the following morning I was aware of a slow tightening around my waist. Half-awake I groped around. Then I realised the water I was lying in had actually turned to ice. It was not thick ice, there was just a thin film on top, but oh, how cold it was! I tried to move my feet but there was no feeling there. I sensed some kind of response but there was no real sensation. My whole body began to ache whenever I moved, until I reached a pitch where I was one entire mass of pain. My side hurt most, just above the hip. No amount of feeble rubbing seemed to do any good and I lacked sufficient energy to rub properly. My wrists were very sore, still not strong enough to do much rubbing.

I could not reach the door for nothing would function so I remained lying where I was. Again no one came anywhere near me that day. I knew the weather outside was appalling. As the rain trickled down from the 'window' I made an effort to crawl near to drink the drops filtering into the cellar.

At last, when through sheer desperation, I managed to get on my feet I realised, with tremendous joy, that I still had some strength left in me. I banged on the door with all the power I could summon, but there was no reply. I began to scream for all I was worth. I kept it up until I thought I might completely exhaust any remaining strength and pass out. Despite the precariousness of these successive, cruel situations, one's capacity to find even the smallest grain of resilience of spirit is very surprising. I felt sure that someone would come, and this encouraged me to continue banging on the door. My wrist scars began to open up again as blood seeped through my bandages. My cries had been heard, for all at once one of the guards opened the door and came wading into the cellar. My feelings of relief were indescribable. He took me out and gave me a rub down with a towel and handed me back my clothes, which had been dumped in the corridor.

I told him I wanted to see the Commandant so that I could apologise to him. I could not tell whether he understood English or not, nevertheless, he gave the impression that he understood. He even helped me on with my boots and when I was dressed and ready to leave, he led me up the stairs and out into the compound.

How lovely it was to realise I could see the daylight properly and to get away from that horrible cellar! I was led into the Commandant's office, where he was sitting, with his back up, like a cat. I begged him to forgive me for what I had done in a fit of temper. I explained that my behaviour was the result of my past experiences, but that now I could not care less what happened next. He gave me the impression that he accepted my explanation, but nevertheless he barked and yelled at me — half in English and half in German.

I submitted to all his abuse, as I was anxious to avoid doing or saying anything likely to warrant more punishment. When the tirade was over, an orderly appeared carrying a loaf of bread which he handed to me. I looked at it and offered my thanks to the Commandant. His response was to inform me that I would be going to Germany the next morning.

I left the room with the guard, who led me over to the washhouse. He told me to get myself cleaned up. The bread, so precious to me, was carefully placed under my damp clothes as I stripped off. Then I went under the shower, which seemed the best place to stay for as long as possible as the water was so lovely and warm. The guard, meanwhile, watched me the whole time. I was sorry to be told to get dressed, but I was now willing to obey all orders.

I noticed the loaf was missing but ignored the matter. I was allowed to join the rest of the prisoners, and even with the persistent pain in my side, I felt a hundred times better. I was grateful to see some Englishmen among the crowd, and Americans. Later I watched as they played a game of football which was a mixture of English and American styles. It was fun to watch them and to hear their laughter, although we had little cause to laugh. I was thankful for even this limited sense of 'freedom'.

I must have looked like some weird creature from the bush, judging by the looks the men directed at me as they passed. I wore a long beard and my hair must have been a sight, but I thought there must be something else wrong with my appearance to attract this attention. An American came over to have a word with me. He told me could spare his bed for my use as he had his flying jacket to sleep on. He would not allow me to argue, so I was pleased to accept. No sooner did I get onto the bed than I went right off to sleep.

On the following morning, the same American came up to me and ask how I was feeling. He was honest enough to tell me that I looked like death warmed up — and that my colour had changed from yellow to a peculiar green. I told him that perhaps he was right for I could well imagine it.

When the Germans brought in the coffee and the soup ration later on, I realised that there must be something drastically wrong with me, for I vomited at the sight of food and I had the feeling that my insides had been ripped open. I went to the latrines and collapsed there. The colour of my urine was getting darker and darker.

I came round to find myself on the American's bed with faces peering at me from all sides. One of our field officers suggested that a doctor should be called. Some said that would be impossible, Italians had been allowed to die before anything was done about calling a doctor. That was cheerful news for me but I didn't feel that I needed a doctor. I just longed for rest. One Englishman tried to give me some of his meat ration, but I couldn't look at the stuff.

During the afternoon, the Germans came in to the shed to tell us that they were taking us to Germany. I tried to imagine what our permanent camps would be like. Perhaps the famous Red Cross had swung into action, with the various camps having their hospitals well set up. I longed to get into a good bed and feel fit once again.

We waited anxiously for the Germans to move us but it was not until early the following morning we were moved out of the shed. After numerous counts, they marched us to the station. Not the same station as the one from which I had escaped. This one seemed to be much further up the line. As soon as we arrived, we were counted again and made to stand beside the cattle trucks reserved for us. It was a bitterly cold morning. I could hardly stand up, but with the help of two Americans I managed to rest on their shoulders until we had permission to get aboard. When the door of our truck opened, we noticed that there was nothing at all inside, either to sit on or to sleep on. We complained to the N.C.O. of the guard, but it did not seem to make any difference to him.

Outside on the ground there had been a light frost and here and there it lay in large white patches. The Orderly Officer and his N.C.O.'s came along the line of trucks with the guards. They ordered us to remove our belts, braces, shoes or boots, and socks. We had no option but to obey, so for a while we were left standing in bare feet. The guards took away all our discarded kit. I asked the *Feldwebel* if we could have some straw to sleep on during the journey. He walked on without replying. Presently he returned, walking in front of a cart heavily laden with straw, followed by the local fire engine. He ordered the firemen to connect up their hoses to the water mains and to spray the straw. When this was done, the guards pitched the straw into the trucks. This was their response to my simple request. The prisoners were ordered to mount the cattle truck and then the sliding door was slammed tight, locked up from the outside and all the tiny windows covered with barbed wire. My fellow prisoners and I speculated at length on how long we would be cooped up in that truck before being allowed in the open again. We spent another few hours waiting before we finally moved off. I was really happy to hear the movement of the wheels, especially as I thought that it might be possible for me to receive some medical treatment before long.

CHAPTER SIXTEEN

There were about twenty of us in the truck, made up of Englishmen and Americans. Some of the more adventurous ones began planning to escape as soon as the vehicle began to move. They tried to open the sliding doors of the truck, but the doors did not give way. The walls were of thick heavy wood but in one corner the wooden floor had become a little rotted. Immediately they busied themselves trying to enlarge the hole. Unfortunately the lads had no tools for cutting the wood; they only had their hands.

They worked hard to open up the hole. At mid-day we were stopped when the guards came along the line to inspect the trucks. They came into our truck and looked around, but one of the our fellows pretended to be asleep in the corner of operations — so the guard failed to see what we were doing.

On and on we travelled until it was getting dark. Again the train stopped and this time we found ourselves at Trento. Here the guards reappeared along the track, accompanied by some railway personnel who carried lamps. Each truck was inspected very carefully. When we heard them coming nearer to our truck we all held our breath for fear they would discover the hole. And when at last they did, chaos reigned.

The doors were opened up and with their bayonet points they got us all up on our feet. Those who really had been asleep were slow to appreciate the orders delivered with a jab of cold steel. The officer in charge of the train was furious and came in brandishing his Luger, threatening us all with death. They searched for the implement used to enlarge the hole, but in their rage, they looked in all the wrong places. As soon as they left us, we had to decide on another place from where to attempt to escape. The remaining corners had been used as latrines.

Our next stopping place must have been Bolazano, a strategically vital rail junction which our Air Forces kept hammering. We heard the air-raids alarm as soon as we arrived, but we had to remain locked up in trucks, whilst our guards no doubt took cover.

Presently, we heard the drone of the aircraft overhead and then down came the bombs. The trucks shook as each stick found its mark. I decided to put myself as close as possible to one corner of the truck where I buried my head in my arms. If the truck was damaged, we were ready to make a get-away. Luckily for us, the raid was directed against the bridge which we had just crossed. Although some of the bombs fell very close, none of them actually hit the train.

As soon as the raid was over, the Germans moved us on. The escapers busied themselves cutting a hole in the roof just above one of the doors, finally suceeding in cutting a nice square just big enough for one man to squeeze through. From where did they get the short bayonet I asked myself. One of the fellows, just about to leave by this route, asked me if I would like to join him, but I was too weak. Four chaps were going but before the first man prepared himself they rigged a dummy, in case the Germans had machine guns trained along the roofs. The dummy was poked up and down through the hole, but nothing happened. Wonders never ceased with escapees.

The train was still travelling at a good speed when the first man departed, assisted by the remaining three, keeping low on top of the roof to await the others. It was disappointing for me to watch them escape so easily when I could not join them, for soon we would all be on German soil. The other three men escaped from the truck and joined the first man on the roof. We heard them 'leopard crawl' along the roof of the truck, followed by silence. We covered up the hole with the canvas as best we could and slept for the rest of that night.

The following day we arrived at Moosburg, near Munich. I was feeling so ill that I could neither see properly nor control my arms or legs. Some of the chaps from the train helped me to walk the little distance into the vast camp. We were shown into a hut for the purpose of recording our personal details and for our clothing to be completely changed. I was given a French, light blue great-coat, a pair of Yugoslav breeches and an Italian shirt, and allowed to keep my boots, which had been given back to us when we arrived at the siding.

Then we were made to go over to the French compound where we had a very hot shower in the bathhouse. I borrowed a razor from one of my friends and with considerable pain, scraped off my lengthy beard. Soon we were taken to another hut where we were given our first letter-card to write home. They were so small, we could only write a few words. Still, it was enough to let our dear folks back home know that we were safe and alive.

I was sent straight into hospital in the French compound. As I was being led away under escort, I saw that the officers were being made to line-up for a roll-call. I wondered then if the Germans would discover there were a few missing since their earlier count.

A closely guarded gate was opened and I was taken over to a dismal looking wooden hut, one of many in a neat row, marked with a big red cross on a white circle. I was surprised to see that an American doctor was in charge of the ward and that the hut was full of men of all nationalities. As soon as I was given a pair of Red Cross pyjamas, I was happy to get undressed and slide into bed.

Later the doctor gave me a thorough examination and told me that I had jaundice. My treatment commenced immediately. A large bottle of glucose liquid was suspended from a broom handle, tied to the end of my bed. A huge syringe drained the liquid into my legs which was designed to arrest the illness, although as far as I could assess my general physical condition, I did not feel that I was getting much better.

All the events of the past weeks haunted my mind, and, coupled with the noise of the various languages being spoken in the ward, gradually affected my nerves. I could not bear to listen to those Indians bemoaning their lot and the French always spoke too fast and too loudly. Our own chaps were usually cracking jokes and that made me feel annoyed too, because I didn't have enough spirit to laugh with them. Russian soldiers of all types crept around the ward trying to make friends. It was difficult for them as no one understood their language, nor was anyone familiar with their style or presence. In my weak condition the whole atmosphere depressed me beyond endurance.

In the connecting ward the majority were French and beyond that, in another connecting ward, were the Russians. The French were well treated by the Germans, for they were being used for labour, so of course they were interested in their welfare. At that time the poor Russians were treated worst. The Germans paid no attention to them whatsoever and seemed happy to see them die, which they frequently did. Under those circumstances the Russians were not entirely to blame for their miserable state. They received no comfort parcels, nor any news from their homes, unlike the French and ourselves. Whenever clothing was given out, they were given the rags which were left. Although the Frenchmen had been prisoners for a longer time, they were without doubt known as the 'wealthy' crowd out of the 30,000 prisoners. They had their connections well established with very corruptible *Wehrmacht* soldiers, so together with the private parcels they were allowed to receive from their families in France, they lived what seemed to the others to be a life of comparative luxury. They showed great reluctance to part with any portion of their 'wealth'. The rest of us who had any bread to spare — that is to say — those who through illness were unable to eat their ration, gave it to the starving Russians.

It is only under circumstances such as these, when one is mixed in with many other nationalities, that one is able to measure what each man is made of ... the Russians, stupidly so dogmatic, but extremely brave; the Indians, so tenacious in battle, yet spiritually so weak in captivity; the Yugoslavs, who were so very hard to understand and the French demonstrating that their selfish attitude was "I'm in the lifeboat, Jack, you can push off!"

I heard that the Germans were taking the British officers to another camp somewhere in Czechoslovakia and that it was reputed to be the best German camp. I pleaded with the doctor to let me go, because if I was kept in that hospital any longer, I would probably lose my reason. The doctor accepted that it was the atmosphere which was preventing me from getting well again, so he authorised me to return to the British compound.

Next day we were off on a journey which was never to be forgotten by me. I realised that I had sacrificed the treatment of my jaundice for the sake of keeping the balance of my mind. The jaundice gradually became worse and worse until my colour of olive green had changed to a dirty brown. I did not have the strength of a fly, nor did I care what was going on around me. I was helped onto the train after being counted with the rest and put down in one corner of the infamous cattletruck. I was told that in our group was a Welsh doctor.

From time to time the lads kept me up-to-date with the stages of our journey while they kept their noses pressed to the extremely small window, protected only by many strands of barbed wire.

We passed Regensburg and for a brief moment I managed to haul myself up in the order to see the Danube. When we were well into the heart of Germany, the fellows at the window yelled excitedly to the rest of us to see some extraordinary sight. The train had slowed up quite considerably, and we were alone without guards. We were able to see what the Germans certainly did not wish us to see. As I was taller than the few in front of me, I had a good view. The lads pointed to a dirty, grey stone building with small windows, which looked as if it had once been a factory. The place was surrounded by a very high barbed wire fence, double spaced, and at the corners of the little compound were the usual tower-like sentry boxes. By all appearances and every impression received by us, this was the location of a notorious concentration camp. Instead of men and women however, these inmates appeared to be hundreds of little children, none looking to be any older than twelve years, both boys and girls. Each one had their hands tied behind their backs, as far as we could see. All had to suffer the humiliation of wearing the regular concentration camp striped uniform. We were relieved that the train did not stop there for it really was a ghastly sight.

Just as we pulled away, I glanced at the main gate and saw another cart-load of children arriving. Hitler Youth boys, who were the same age as the child prisoners, seemed to be in charge of them, although older 'braves' were also in evidence. We all agreed that if we had not seen this, we would not have believed that this level of inhumanity existed. But that was only one of many sights to remind us of this depravity, despite this being the twentieth century.

We arrived at a small country village called Moravska Trebova late at night, and after a few counts and re-counts, we were taken off to the camp. It was all I could do to last out until we got there, and this was only possible thanks to the help of the doctor and my companions. We submitted ourselves to the routine German documentation procedure and then crossed inside the wire. Our own camp officials required details of our records for our own orderly room. Thereafter we were led by various group commanders to our new quarters in different parts of the camp.

I had spent only half-an-hour in the room allocated to me when the camp doctor came along and whipped me straight into hospital. Owing to my condition, I cannot clearly remember the events that took place after my admittance. However I do recall the Christmas Eve celebrations happening about the second night after we arrived. I celebrated my Christmas Day by being unable to see anyone, or eat anything at all except one biscuit out of the Canadian Red Cross parcel, and even that biscuit had to be softened down to a mash for me.

The following event I do remember, when I was taken by stretcher from the camp to the train, on the back of a sled-cart. The snow was thick everywhere. I was taken to hospital at Lansdorf, about twenty-five miles west of Breslau. This was the base British hospital for prisoners-of-war for the whole of the south-eastern part of Germany. The train journey nearly finished me, and if it had not been for a tin full of sugar, that good old Doc Jones had poured down my throat, I am sure that I would have died. The weather was exceedingly bitter and I was far from being equipped for the snowy conditions.

They certainly did a wonderful job at the hospital with my jaws and gums. They completely restored my physique too, bringing my weight back to normal. In return, when I was well into recuperation, I helped to look after the surgical cases when the doctors were short staffed. Seven weeks after admittance I returned to Mahres-Trubau a fit man.

During my time in hospital, the officers at *Oflag* 8F had turned the camp into one of the best we had ever been in. We were lucky in having a very good supply of Red Cross parcels. Clothing supplies had been coming in well and the morale of each officer was as high as could be expected. Rugby matches were in full swing and the 'muscle factory' was very popular. The theatre group was running up to almost repertory standard, and the 'Cloak and Dagger' boys were very hush-hush. Unfortunately, shortly after I got back, the Germans were alerted to a reported mass Polish underground move to release us. Within twenty-four hours the complete camp had been re-organised for a long train journey to Brunswick.

Before embarking on the cattle trucks, the Germans read out a proclamation stating that as our troops had found it necessary to handcuff German prisoners taken at Dieppe, so the Germans would reciprocate. We had to give up our boots, belts or braces and have crude German manacles on our wrists. We were then ordered into the trucks, whereupon the guards placed a double barbed wire fence across the width of the truck, hemming us into the smallest area. There were approximately twenty-three officers to each truck. We were given no blankets and the only seats were benches placed on either side, which of course allowed only a few of us to sit. The remainder laid down on the floor of the truck, which was very unpleasant.

After the first day, I found a key from a bully-beef tin in my pocket and managed to use this to get my handcuffs undone. I then passed it round to the others, who did the same. It was a very welcome relief to get those iron bracelets off our wrists. I soon became tired of playing around with the manacles and waited for the opportunity of disposing of them. The only place to lose them was in the latrine bucket at my side — when I asked the guard to empty the bucket next morning, the wretched manacles disappeared! Arriving at our destination, we found that the off-duty guards in the following truck had received the full force of the contents of the emptied bucket. The train halted in a small siding just outside Brunswick and we were made to dismount and to form up in fives to be counted.

We were instructed to raise our hands so that the guards could unlock the shackles. We raised our hands well above our heads and then we had fun! The Germans were at a complete loss to know how we got out of the shackles and where they were now.

When the furore was over, we marched to our new camp called *Oflag* 79. We had experienced a fairly tough journey and were only too grateful to see the new camp come into view. As we approached the entrance we could see that our bombers had been very active in this area. Heavy concrete air-raid shelters spanned each side of the main entrance and the main guard room at the gate looked a very formidable affair.

We then marched up a cobble-stone road between an avenue of tall pines and came upon the actual compound. The buildings appeared to be quite modern and large, but the camp was situated in a pine forest, creating a heavy surrounding atmosphere. The first building, just outside the compound, had been hit by a bomb and another one, we were told, had been partly destroyed by a crashed aircraft. We never found out whether it was one of ours or a German.

Once inside, we were shown where to go by our own staff, and as soon as we had each claimed a bed, we went on a tour of inspection of our new quarters. We were told by our own official interpreter that the camp had formerly been a *Luftwaffe* Training School. He said that directly ahead of the main entrance was a large underground aircraft factory, and over to the north side was one of the largest aerodromes in Germany. Those details were very interesting of course, but far from causing any amusement. We realised that there was every likelihood of our Air Force paying more visits in future.

Moving from one camp to another, no great amount of time was needed to settle down. Usually by the end of the first day, one knew the camp fairly well. A long motor transport shed had received a pasting and some buildings outside our compound had been gutted by incendiaries. The Sapper Section in camp had replaced a few tiles on the roofs, and inside, the buildings had first-class shower baths. In some of the alcoves, murals had been painted by the Germans, depicting actions and heroic deeds performed by their famous *Luftwaffe*. One mural showed Junkers bombing London and another, which was extremely good, was a picture of a typical Austrian mountain scene.

Our first raid took place on the afternoon of 5th August, 1944. We watched from the compound. The 'planes came over very quickly and at high altitude to begin with — we only spotted them after the German anti-aircraft guns went into action. In a matter of seconds, the Germans guards hurried to their shelters before the bombs rained down. The 'planes circled over the aircraft shadow factory and wave after wave of them unloaded their cargo. The air soon became filled with dust, blocking out the sun with a brownish-yellow vapour. It was a grand sight to see the bombs dropping from the bomb-bays and to watch them fall on to their target. As fast as the planes had come, so they went.

Later, news came into the camp that the nearest bomb fell about seven hundred yards from the main gate. The raid did not frighten us, it merely strengthened our courage as we realised this war would not last much longer.

The energetic ones amongst us organised study groups; Bible study, architecture, law, mathematics, philosophy, art, music, architecture and accountancy. Those few who had never had the chance to take their Matriculation at school, managed to obtain the forms through the Red Cross and to sit the examination. One of our groups entertained the sun-bathers with their gymnastic displays and acrobatics. Often I would sneak around the corner of a building and try to do some of those intricate balancing feats, but without much success.

The sporting types, under Bill Bowes, the well known Yorkshire cricketer and Freddie Brown, who was later to captain M.C.C. and England, erected a volley ball net and organised many good games. The Indians played most of the time on two deck-tennis courts. One day, the Germans told us we had to move one of the courts as it was in the way of the refuse cart on its rounds. We could not find a decent alternative spot, for there were too many pine trees. Eventually we made a site along the front of one of the buildings on the outside of the camp, but within the wire fence. As we were very restricted for space, the edge of the court came very near to the trip wire, which the Germans had placed about eight feet from the main wire fence. Between the trip wire and the main fence was an area known as the danger-zone or 'no man's land'. This particular day, there were many matches being played between the Indian officers and the rest of the in-mates and often during play the quoit was flung out of play into the danger zone. We obtained permission from the sentry in the tower to retrieve the ring and each time we managed to recover it without many difficulties. Later, when four Indians were playing, the ring went out, and one of them asked for permission to retrieve it and received the O.K. from the sentry. As he returned to the court, the sentry shot him in the back. We could not believe the news that the officer had in fact been shot dead. Rumours spread later that the sentry responsible for this death had been sent to the Russian front line.

One of the greatest events in the camp was to be the planned celebration of the King's birthday. The Senior British Officer had spoken to the German Commandant, saying he wanted to hold a parade in the King's honour. The Commandant warned the S.B.O. that any demonstration would be banned, as he had orders from his High Command that prisoners were not allowed to hold any patriotic demonstrations at all. The S.B.O. explained that we were only wanting to parade in honour of our King. Still the Commandant refused our request and warned that the guards had orders to shoot anyone carrying out any demonstration of any kind.

The S.B.O. told us all what we would have to do, and so that night we cleaned up our uniforms and went scrounging around the camp for black boot polish, which some of the more fortunate prisoners had received in their next-of-kin parcels. Our extremely worn battledress pants were put under the palliasses throughout that night. The following day all company commanders formed up their own officers and led them round to the 'parade ground'. There Tommy Sampson and his band played two appropriate numbers whilst waiting for the S.B.O. to appear on the parade ground. As we stood 'at ease' we saw that the Germans had reinforced their guards with Spandau machine-gun crews spaced opposite to us and that the machine-gun posts on the towers had orders to stand 'at the ready'. Tension was rather high, as more guards appeared round the outside of the wire fence with their rifles positioned, waiting for our parade to begin.

The S.B.O. came on to the parade ground and the band struck up our National Anthem, with the officers in chorus. The S.B.O. made a short speech, wishing the King excellent health and a happy long life, then asked us to pay tribute to the King by giving three hearty cheers. I am sure that the people in Brunswick must have heard us cheering. Then the S.B.O. dismissed us. Not one shot was fired and we had the satisfaction of celebrating the King's birthday as we wished — I would have given a great deal to have seen the look on the Commandant's face when he realised we were defying him. He really could not shoot the lot of us and he knew it.

Aircraft activity had been slackened off quite considerably in our area, although in other areas it had been stepped up. As soon as the 'yellow' warning went, we would go out into the compound, or the top floors of the buildings to spot the 'planes. Mostly they came from the north-west, flying wide of us, high up, heading towards Berlin. On many occasions one could hear the distant rumblings of the bombs being dropped, then some time later, see the 'planes coming back again.

One day, a returning flight flew rather low in tight formation and kept that formation, although meeting a rather nasty ack-ack barrage over Brunswick. No 'plane was shot down but shortly after they had flown over, one single Lancaster was limping home on three engines, with perhaps more damage than we could see. We all cheered it on as loudly as we could, as it was trying to escape the murderous anti-aircraft fire. The 'plane was travelling slowly, weaving in and out of the air bursts very pluckily. With our hearts in our mouths by this time, we watched it fly beyond the range of the ack-ack. We hoped it made its base safely.

Shortly after this incident, the raids were intensified close to our area. The 'planes were picking out oil refineries and as many as seven hundred and fifty bombers were taking part in each raid. They looked wonderful, high up, with the sun shining on them, causing vapour trails in the atmosphere.

On August 24th 1944, the camp was full of activity. The Drama Group was preparing for its next production, various classes were in progress and as it was a hot day, many of us were sun-bathing. The 'yellow' warning sounded, but as always, not many of us took any notice as we carried on with our work. Then someone spotted our 'planes and gave a shout. There were five groups with at least two hundred bombers in each group, flying at a great height eastwards. Everybody promptly abandoned what they were doing to watch their flight. They seemed to be flying in the direction of Berlin and as they were almost out of sight, we assumed that Berlin was about to get another pasting. Then the roof spotter shouted that they had turned and were heading straight for the camp. This time we were taking no chances and we all started towards the entrances of the shelters, in the basements of the buildings.

In no time, the 'planes were on top of us. They were American Super Fortress Bombers. I looked up as if hypnotised by their great size, fascinated by their crews indominable spirit. Next, I saw the bomb doors of the first flight open. That was when I ran for cover. The shriek of the big bombs as they came down scared the life out of me. As I ran towards one of the buildings, it suddenly seemed to jump several feet in the air. I darted away from that building, only to run into another building which had just been hit. The whole time the air was filled with the shrieking of bombs and the tremendous explosions as they burst; choking dust and the smell of burning was everywhere. Buildings at the far end of the camp had been hit and were burning quite furiously. The huge pall of smoke started to spread over the whole area of the camp, blocking out the main target, so the remaining bombers found their objective masked. The Americans always bombed into the area set out by their marker bombs, dropped by the leading aircraft. Down came more and more bombs. The earth shook all around. I did not know where to run for safety. Then I heard someone yell that our hut at the lower end of the camp had been hit. That meant some of the Indians must have been trapped. Accompanied by many others, I ran down to the building, but just as we got half-way another shower of bombs could be heard falling, so we darted towards the nearest building. I had stopped beside a Colonel on the roadway, who was watching the falling cluster of bombs when two chaps flung themselves through a basement window. Unfortunately, the bombs were falling more quickly than we thought. I just managed to get in, landing on top of the chaps already there, when the bombs seemed to lift us all into the air.

We thought that the building really had been blasted. When that particular shower was over, I crawled out back on to the roadway. As the dust cleared, I noticed that someone was lying on the road near the orderly room. The raid continued and we sensed that there were more 'planes on the way. I went over to the body lying on the road. Someone else turned the body over and we were shocked to see this was the Colonel beside whom I had been standing some minutes earlier.

The officers dashed over from one building to another, in search of the wounded, including Germans who had been trapped in their quarters. The Germans suffered more casualties than we did, but ours were bad enough.

Many of the buildings around the outside of the camp were burning furiously and some were completely demolished. In the camp area, one bomb had exploded alongside the building where our other ranks lived and were sheltering. Fortunately the only damage it had caused was to blow out all the windows, take off nearly all the roof tiles and generally shake everyone up. Another big bomb fell plumb on to our water mains and another landed on the kitchen, completely demolishing it. Another one smashed the electricity junction box. The whole camp was a complete shambles. Many buildings were without glass in the windows or tiles on the roofs. We all tried to help in recovering the wounded, and retrieving the dead, of which there were three including the Colonel. We placed warning notices around shrapnel bombs which had failed to explode.

There was not one single wall of any building which had not been completely peppered by shrapnel. That raid brought to an end the general practice of watching 'planes approach. As soon as the 'Red' warning went, all the officers, except the foolhardy, took shelter.

CHAPTER SEVENTEEN

As the Allies advanced, the succeeding winter was bad. We had no fuel to cook with and our Red Cross parcels had long since stopped. We existed on the German rations, such as they were. Now and again we supplemented these with the equivalent of a quarter portion of what a Red Cross parcel would contain — this would be all we received for a week, sometimes for two weeks.

The entertainment section of the camp built an extremely good 'Night Club' down in one of the basements which we called the '*Rum Pot*'. Tommy Sampson supplied the music with all his splendid musicians. Some of the characters who participated in the 'theatre' provided a cabaret which worked wonders for our morale. We reckoned tnat if we were going to be hit by bombs on another occasion, perhaps we could die laughing at some of the cabaret turns!

Snow had fallen fairly thickly. There was no fuel and no water. The latrines became unusable so we had to make arrangements to dig one outside. German rations became less and less. Red Cross parcels became a mere dream of the past. Mail from home practically ceased and only a few letters came trickling in to us. The raids were incessant, by day and night, and our tempers were becoming more and more difficult. We tried by all methods to show the Germans that they could not get the better of us — and that the day would come when they would regret the treatment they were giving us. Throughout this time the theatre was marvellous, going full blast with one good show after another. The S.B.O. gave us a talk one day. He reminded us that more severe days could be expected before this war was over as the German supplies were diminished. The cold weather made us shiver day and night. We wore all our clothing, using the only blanket we each had to cover our legs like a skirt, but it made little difference.

Those who had been fortunate enough to receive cigarette parcels whilst the mail service was good, had a hold on the food market. They bartered their cigarettes for food offered by officers desperately in need of a smoke to quell their nerves. The food situation was now critical. We had come down to queueing outside the newly erected cook-house for potato peelings. Fuel and water were so scarce that we had to eat these raw, still covered with soil, just as they had been handed in from the German Mess. Any little herb was regarded as a prize find. The price of food and cigarettes rose enormously. Officers would give I.O.U. chits in sterling, drawn on their bank balances at home. One man paid fifteen pounds for a tin of condensed milk. Another man paid twenty pounds for a cigarette. On one occasion I was reduced to paying seventeen pounds for half a loaf of black bread. Empty stomachs, frayed the nerves. To see a cigarette being smoked would send one nearly crazy. The German mint tea ration was always smoked in odd bits of paper. Some preferred to smoke rather than eat, as their nerves were so bad.

The hospital filled and one poor chap lost his reason as a result of the strain. The rest of the fellows began to abandon their various occupations, doing nothing apart from resting in bed to conserve their energy. I was one of them.

The arrival of spring saw matters go from bad to worse. Mail had completely stopped. Many times the Germans would arrive in the camp to tell us that a train load of Red Cross parcels had arrived at the station. As a result some of the boys would rashly consume their tiny reserves of food, in anticipation of further supplies. When the party detailed to help unload the parcels returned empty-handed every time, they would make begging rounds of the various quarters.

Perhaps twenty letters would reach us after a period of several weeks or even months. On one occasion I saw an officer faint as a result of over-excitement at the prospect of receiving a letter!

The Germans did manage to get a little water running in the shower baths — a drip at a time, but it was always cold. In the showers we became aware of our skinniness. Some fellows didn't have the strength to get to the showers, so they remained on their beds. Others who managed to reach the showers looked a very pathetic sight when stripped.

From the German papers we learned that their forces were falling back on all fronts. Then came the brief respite when their forces broke through in the Ardennes. They declared openly that the war was lost for us and they would chase our troops back to where they came from. However, that little effort was their last. For soon afterwards our troops crossed the Rhine, while at the same time the Russians on the eastern front advanced nearer and nearer to Berlin.

Our bombers seemed to fill the air the whole time. No sooner did one raid finish than the next would start. We heard through the grape-vine that some other camps had been moved back towards Berlin and there was every likelihood that we would also be moved. That fear made the Germans uneasy as well as ourselves, for the Germans knew that if they had to move approximately two thousand officers they would encounter trouble on the way despite the weak state we were in. We did not want to be taken back towards the much discussed Berlin for several reasons. The principal one was that we were in no condition to walk long distances. Another was that Berlin would be turned into an inferno. Finally, if we were eventually overtaken by the Russians we did not know when we would be sent home. These ideas were running through each man's mind. The fact that we were unfit for a long march was all too true. The general notice-board, and the map above my bed, very quickly became dirty from hundreds of finger marks following the progress of the Allies. Some of the men ran a sweepstake on which of the Western Allies would reach us first. Others preferred to say a little prayer that they might be saved from the bombing raids, and eventually see the liberation forces and find freedom.

No one knew exactly where our Forces were but we guessed they must be very close. For several nights we were kept awake by the movement of heavy transport along the autobahn to our north in the general direction of Berlin. Tremendous rumblings could be heard towards Hanover and around to the south-west. Of course, they could be bombs, or then again, they could be shells. After only a few nights we knew that they were shells, for some of the big stuff came flying overhead, landing beyond the pine forest behind the camp. The Germans had brought up some of their artillery to cover their retreat. Throughout the night the shell-fire kept us awake. Most of the prisoners spent the night in the shelters in case the camp would be a target for allied gunners. For all we knew, the Germans might have had an observation post situated on the corner of the *Luftwaffe* sheds on the western outskirts of the camp.

When morning came, many hearts were relieved to hear the shell-fire from both sides quieten down. There was just an occasional round going off from a fanatical German 88 mm dual-purpose gun crew, somewhere in the pine forest to the east. It was the eeriest silence that greeted me and the rest of my room-mates, so we wandered out into the compound, to see what would happen next.

Just as we were passing one of the huge bomb craters, we saw some fellows running out of the hospital building. Like bees swarming out of a hive, men appeared from windows, doors and indeed some seemed to arrive from nowhere. Men ran with sheer desperation, some of them ran before dropping with fatigue, others crawled, but their spirit gave them the strength to get up on their feet and make the effort to catch up with the rest. They were yelling and screaming as they ran towards the main gate. I arrived just as the gate was being forced open — and amidst the crying mob I glimpsed an American soldier's helmet. It was impossible to get anywhere near the jeep and its heavy machine gun crew. The Americans were completely bewildered by the chaotic reception. Perhaps they thought the Englishmen would just say, "Thanks very much, old boy!"

Tears rolled down many faces, including mine, as we gaped at the reality of being liberated. The word 'liberated' now has a very special significance for me and I shall always respect it. The only previous occasion when I experienced this feeling of total helplessness was when I was first captured. Along with many, many more I could only stand there, trying to recover my senses again.

It was a 'recce' crew from the Second U.S. Cavalry Regiment that actually liberated us, and the Sergeant in charge quickly arranged for the surrender of the German garrison. There were some candidates for voluntary surrender. by war-weary German soldiers, who started to line-up, ready to be marched into captivity under the eyes of the alert American Sergeant and his crew. Those of us who had long since given up counting the days asked one another what the day was — in order to jot it down for a life-long memory. It was April 12th 1945 ... what a day!

We had taken the radio set out of the German officers' mess and had it erected over the hospital block. In the evening of 14th April 1945, we collected in the evening under the speaker. Absolute silence then fell upon the whole camp. Big Ben rang out a note of cheer and then as the familiar sound faded, we heard the voice of the announcer reading the evening news. "... the Allies have captured Brunswick. Five miles from the town a prisoner-of-war camp of over 2000 officers and 400 other ranks has been overrun. No names have yet been received. The next of kin are being informed as soon as possible. The name of the camp is *Oflag* 79".

Again and again the air echoed the tremendous cheers from the lads. We cried openly, we talked of reunions, and parties, and how we would get home — but no one could talk sensibly, the excitement was too great.

We were all allowed out to wander within a certain distance of the camp in order to get food. We heard that one man died through eating too much after he had scavenged the countryside. Some fellows managed to pick up abandoned cars in Brunswick and found no difficulty in obtaining petrol either.

My friends and I went over to the airport and had a look around. It was a huge aerodrome. The workshops had been well stocked with the best tools which were now lying around in complete disorder. The officers' mess there had been a very elegant affair, but now, after the poor Russian slave workers had done their looting, it looked as if a hurricane had blown right through it. In the entrance to the dining-room was a marble pedestal, broken at the top. Lying at its base was a bust of Hitler.

That afternoon, we saw two 'Mosquito' 'planes which had landed on the 'drome. What grand looking machines they were. It seemed incredible that such a comparatively small, light aircraft could carry such heavy bomb loads. We recalled how, night after night, those 'planes had kept us awake in a state of nervous tension with their accurate bombing.

We went over to a village on the far side of the aerodrome, seeking food. We stopped at one farmhouse, but the farmer's wife said she had nothing to give us. However, just as we were about to move away, an American light tank from the same Cavalry Regiment came wheeling into the yard and stopped just in front of the door. They asked for something too, and the woman gave the same reply. Without arguing, the crew put a round from their cannon straight through the front door. They got what they were after, and so did we!

Unfortunately, we had to wait for the settlement between the Americans and the British, as to who would be responsible for taking us out and back down the line. We were told to have patience, but the waiting caused as much stress as participating in a major battle. The camp looked so depressing and brought back so many unpleasant memories for us. It was difficult to feel happy whilst we waited for transport.

Finally, on 26th April 1945, just after mid-day, the Americans and the R.A.F. flew into the aerodrome — 'plane after 'plane. The excitement was tremendous when the first Dakota was spotted and our Commanders ordered us to move over to the air field by companies. As soon as one 'plane filled up it took off and this continued until the whole camp had been evacuated.

We flew straight to Brussels, where the Red Cross awaited us. In one of the hangars the Red Cross personnel had arranged for us to be fed and supplied with cigarettes. From there we were transferred to another aerodrome, where we were put onto R.A.F. Stirling bombers and flown home — the last leg of our journey from the continent.

No words can adequately describe my feelings when I saw the coast of 'Old Blighty' once more from the glass nose of the bomber. As we landed in the country at Blackbush, near London, the evening was drawing to a close and everything seemed so peaceful.

We were taken to a transit camp nearby, where we were able to bathe and were given a change of clothes with all the various items so special to an officer's uniform. There was a sumptuous meal to enjoy, and afterwards we were truly able to say we felt like a million dollars. We were then shown to our sleeping quarters, furnished with comfortable beds, and real, clean sheets.

The following morning we were issued with ration cards, railway warrants and money. To handle real money again was an incredible feeling. We received instructions as to where to report on completion of our leave. Then sensing an air of instability we succumbed to the kindly directions of our Army personnel, to board the awaiting transport to take us to the local railway station.

In the little country villages along the route to the station, the villagers had hung up huge banners reading, "WELCOME HOME LADS" and red, white and blue bunting decorated the hedgerows and front doors. The station was decorated with rosettes and bunting and even along the route to London, villagers and townfolk had put out "Welcome Home" signs to give us feelings of happiness and comfort.

That homecoming was tremendously exciting yet bewildering for me, but perhaps for some the homecoming might not be so welcome. I thought of those who had lost loved ones, whether on the home front or abroad, and those who would meet someone who had taken their place in the home during their absence.

On arriving in London I had to change stations and immediately I was scared by the multitude, dashing to their destinations. I was very weak and only weighed six stones. I knew that my appearance was drawing embarrassed looks from the military and civilian travellers who showed their kindness by hailing a taxi for me.

The nearer I came to my home, the more nervous I felt, and the fidgeting led to involuntary visits to the toilet. The pleasure was almost becoming an ordeal. I had dreamed of this happening many, many times whilst in captivity. Each and every returning liberated prisoner had his own homecoming story to tell and that special moment of family reunion will be kept most sacred. Mine will be treasured, never to be forgotten.

But my abiding memory will be that of seeing an English girl, for the first time in years, at the entrance to the Red Cross hangar at Brussels where she was distributing the cigarettes. I felt so grateful to be alive and as we approached her she had such a smile on her face. Stretching out her arms in happy greeting she said simply, "Welcome home, boys!"